Dialogues

By the same author

Women
Singular Encounters
Of a Certain Age
More of a Certain Age
Speaking for The Oldie
Asking Questions
A Timeless Passion
Tara & Claire
A Woman a Week
In Conversation with Naim Attallah
Insights

NAIM ATTALLAH

Dialogues

To
Ros
my muse
of time past..!!
with much Love
Naim xx
FEBRUARY 2001

QUARTET BOOKS

Published in Great Britain by Quartet Books Limited in 2000
A member of the Namara Group
27 Goodge Street
London W1P 2LD

A catalogue record for this book is available from the
British Library

ISBN 0 7043 7115 4

Phototypeset by FiSH Books, London
Printed and bound in Great Britain by CPD (Wales) Ltd, Ebbw Vale

for Joanna Hewitt

CONTENTS

LORD ASHLEY

LORD ASHLEY

Jack Ashley was born in 1922 in Widnes, Lancashire. He left school at fourteen to work as an unskilled factory labourer. In 1946 he was awarded a scholarship to Ruskin College, Oxford, and later to Gonville and Caius College, Cambridge, where he became President of the Union. He spent fifteen years as a BBC radio and television producer before entering Parliament as the Labour member for Stoke-on-Trent South in 1966 where he remained until 1992 when he was made a life peer. He is president of the Royal National Institute for the Deaf and he has published two volumes of autobiography: *Journey into Silence* (1973) and *Acts of Defiance* (1992).

You grew up in considerable poverty in the town of Widnes, but as you say in your autobiography this all seemed 'part of the natural order of things'. When did it strike you that it was not part of the natural order, that poverty could be alleviated, that people's lives could be improved?

It was in my teens when I began to kick against living and working conditions very strongly indeed, though this was something that was not done at that time in Widnes. I'm not saying I was a splendid fellow doing that, just that it seemed natural to act in this way. I started by complaining about the conditions in my own home and when the landlord reacted angrily, I began a campaign to try to improve conditions in other houses he owned. And as a trade unionist at the factory I did exactly the same.

There is still poverty in Britain today. How does it differ from the poverty you experienced, would you say?

From what I read about some inner cities, it's much the same as it was then – poor housing, inadequate income, bad health and in some cases bad health provision. All of these things seem to go hand in hand. After all this time there is absolutely no reason why anyone should be suffering the kind of gross poverty that is still prevalent in Britain today, but the basic issues are just not being tackled. Every government, including this Labour government, fears that there may be a reaction if they go too far too fast. In trying to eliminate poverty this government has done something very commendable in terms of income support and special payments. But if they go as far as to raise taxes to deal with poverty, they fear that there may be a backlash from what, for shorthand, I would call middle-class people. They are afraid they will not remain in power, and that, I think, is deplorable. This is why I have reservations about commending the government wholeheartedly. I do support the Labour government, and I think they are doing a very good job, but they should go much further, and if it requires increased taxation, so be it.

Your father died when you were only five, and you lived in fear that your mother might also die and that you and your two sisters would be sent to an orphanage. Do you think that these early experiences strengthened your character, or did the sense of insecurity remain with you into adulthood?

The sense of insecurity did remain, perhaps not into mature adulthood, but certainly for many years. My father's death strengthened my character in the sense that I became the man of the house and I took on responsibilities, not just material but also psychological.

Reading your autobiography, I was struck by the fact that you were lifted up to look at the face of your dead father. Do you remember that clearly? In the years to come were you pleased to have seen your father after he died?

I think so. It was something that struck me very forcibly at the time. I can remember it even now, not as vividly as when I was a child, but it was something I was rather glad I saw, full of regret though I was at the time.

Death seemed to be very much part of life in those days and it was quite normal for children to go and pray for the souls of the departed. Do you think this was preferable to what we do now, which is to hide death away from our children?

I have to say it is preferable. There was a certain rawness about it and it brought the community together in a very strange and remarkable way. You empathized with people – you couldn't walk into a house and see the body of a man or a woman or a child and then walk out unaffected by what you had seen. To that extent I think it was a good thing, but I cannot see people reverting to that kind of openness with death.

Would you say you were actually politicized by the experience of your childhood?

You can't go through the experience of being as poor as I was and working in such conditions without being politicized to some extent. The question then becomes: how do you react? In my own case I took on the landlord, got on to the council, became a shop steward and organized a trade union which then became a cohesive force seeking to improve conditions and wages. Not that we succeeded in all of these things, but at least we tried.

You left school aged fourteen to work as a factory labourer. Did that also seem part of the natural order of things at the time?

It was certainly part of the natural order of things in Widnes because everybody left school at fourteen. I vividly remember going on the bus with my tea-can to the factory, feeling quite at home really, enjoying the banter and the friendliness and the all-in-it-together kind of feeling. Had it not seemed part of the natural order, one would have felt very apprehensive. I didn't.

Didn't you feel at the age of fourteen that you were missing out on childhood years?

Not in the least. What could one miss out on in Widnes? If you didn't have a job, you stood on a street corner. But as a young man with a job I was earning money and I could take home part of my wages and have a little pocket money. That was something positive and constructive.

Application to the local grammar school was out of the question because it was non-Catholic. Were you aware of being disadvantaged as a Catholic in this way?

No, because I was never outstanding at school. I was always about tenth, maybe a bit higher or a bit lower, but I didn't feel the grammar school applied to me. I was content to go with the gang.

You write in your autobiography of the power and authority of the priest, something which you seem to have resented from an early age. You describe, for example, the way in which the priest would call each week to collect money from your widowed mother. Why do you think you were unwilling to accept the authority of the priest like everyone else? Do you remember your feelings about that?

Yes I do, very vividly. My mother was dreadfully poor, and we scrimped and scraped all the time. The priest lived in quite a posh house – I can see it now – a fine high building with highly polished brasses and smelling of furniture polish. To see a well-fleshed man living there in those conditions and taking money from my mother who didn't have two pennies to rub together – that stuck in my throat and I resented it.

You first became interested in trade unionism when you stoked furnaces at the copper factory. After an operation for appendicitis you asked for lighter work and were refused. I imagine you had a sense of terrible injustice...

Yes, and what I found when I tried to organize a union was that practically everybody else had a sense of injustice. But it was a far more deferential society then than it is now, and people just did obey the authority figure, whether it was the priest, the policeman or the factory boss. The men were passive and submissive, and when I organized a union it was fertile ground for people wanting to object who hadn't ever objected before. It became a kind of catharsis for people.

At the age of only twenty you were elected chairman of the shop stewards' committee. Was it not a daunting responsibility for a young man without much formal education at the time?

Indeed it was, and I remember being taken aback at the readiness of people to accept my leadership. I found it rather gratifying, but I was also anxious for a sense of responsibility to prevail, to make our objections disciplined. The easiest thing was to incite the men to violence. I remember when the secretary of the union in London addressed our meetings, he had a fine rhetorical line. He used to say: 'We won't have these employers dictate to us, we will tear this factory down brick by brick if they try to diminish us.' And of course the workers loved the idea of tearing a factory down brick by brick, but it was the last thing I wanted.

To what extent would you say that the struggle you were engaged in on behalf of your fellow workers was a class struggle?

I think it was finally a class struggle. We were the working class and the people we were opposed to were management who on the whole were middle class. There were one or two foremen who had been workers and they had just gone up a notch or two, but in the main they were middle-class people. Even though it was a class struggle, however, we didn't see it as that then. We saw it as a battle between us in our kind of job and them in their well-paid, cushy, collar-and-tie job. We had the tough jobs, loading furnaces, emptying wagons; we had the dirty clothes, the clogs, the scarves, the overalls. We saw it in black and white, not in political terms, more in material terms.

Do you think it will ever be possible to remove class from British society?

I'm always suspicious of the term 'classless society'. Early on at Ruskin College I decided that I was against the Communist Party because I didn't like their idea of a classless society. To try and impose uniformity on people is silly and obnoxious. The objective should be to try to reduce the inequalities; I don't think I would go further than that.

Your time as a shop steward was very much characterized by 'them and us' attitudes, the workers versus the management. Did you thrive on confrontation, or was it alien to your character really?

This is slightly tricky. I think of myself as a mild man and yet the truth is I did thrive on confrontation. I wanted to please people, wanted them to be happy, but I recognized the need to press the case strongly and pinpoint weaknesses in the opponent's case. And so I was forever confronting authority because my ultimate judgement is that if you don't persist you don't win. But it is a paradox in me.

You were completely dependent on your mother throughout your childhood. Were you acutely aware of the absence of a father figure, or do you think your mother did the work of two parents, so to speak?

There's no doubt that she did the work of two parents, and she was fantastically courageous in the way she brought up three children on her own in those days, because the poverty was absolutely devastating. Having said that, I was very aware of the lack of a father, though I didn't talk about it very often with my sisters. Of course, the love for our mother was the most important thing, and it was a wonderfully intimate, close, warm relationship, but underlying it was the fear that if anything happened to her, we would be off to the orphanage.

You were seventeen when war broke out, but after joining the army you were discharged after less than a year on health grounds, because of your increasing deafness. How much of a disappointment was it for you not to be able to fight for your country?

In a sense you are diminished by being categorized as unfit, and no one likes to be sent home. It was a great thing to be in the army with its wonderful sense of comradeship and *esprit de corps*, but you can't argue with the medical men.

In 1946 you were awarded a scholarship to Ruskin College, Oxford, a so-called 'working man's scholarship'. Was there a particular pride attached to going to Oxford as a 'working man' as opposed to, say, a public schoolboy?

I suppose I would have felt that more if I had gone to a normal Oxford college; as it was, Ruskin catered for people like me, so it didn't really arise. I was much more conscious of being a working man rather than a public schoolboy when I went to Cambridge. In fact – though I don't say this in a hostile way – my room was shared with a pompous public schoolboy who was very cruel for the first few months. We gradually did become friends, but I was very much aware of that kind of snobbish attitude, though I did feel a certain pride in having got there on my own as it were, without the privilege of a public school.

You must have had mixed feelings going up to Oxford, leaving your beloved family behind, giving up your wage which was important for the family budget, and the contrast between Oxford and your home town must have been huge. Did you have any doubts about leaving all that was familiar behind?

I had many doubts, but the main thing was the wage. I was so poor in Oxford that I went working part time for an old couple who had advertised for a girl to clean the house. They were astonished when I turned up but they gave me the job anyway. Another basic problem was having no educational background. Many of the students at Ruskin had been to night school or grammar school, and many of them were extraordinarily well read. I felt my lack of any formal education keenly. Happily, Ruskin was established in order to meet that kind of problem, and so it didn't become a great drama, but I was not wholly comfortable.

Did you feel when you went to Cambridge that you were competing on a more equal basis with your fellow students?

Yes, I think the two years at Ruskin really did make a difference to me. I learned how to read properly, how to handle books, how to listen to university lectures, and so on. I can't define why exactly, but somehow going to Cambridge felt quite different. I felt happier, more confident, more at home.

In what ways did university change you? Did it distance you from the idea of the working man at all?

No. One of the things I like to lay claim to, if I may, is having changed very little. This may not be a good thing, but it's true. When I became the MP for Stoke-on-Trent I was as much at home meeting working men as I always had been. And going back to Widnes is like slipping into an old overcoat. My approach to people in high positions and to working-class people is exactly the same as it always was. I'm less deferential now to toffs, so to speak, than I would have been in my younger days, but apart from that I see no significant difference.

At about the same time, according to your autobiography, you were questioning your religious beliefs 'to the point of rejection', and you refer in passing to your 'loss of faith'. Loss of faith, particularly perhaps for a cradle Catholic, is usually traumatic. What happened in your case?

What happened, I regret to say, was not traumatic – it would make a better story if it had been. I simply began to question the idea of a God and all the accompaniments, like the Resurrection, for example, or the idea that prayer could get you anything that you did not get if you didn't pray. I began to reject, not only the whole concept of Catholicism, but religion generally.

What about heaven and hell?

That's a bit of nonsense to me. It's just ludicrous that anyone should go to hell for eternity for committing one mortal sin. In my day a mortal sin was missing mass on a Sunday, and though I was devout as a child, I cannot believe as a responsible adult that you could be condemned to hell for missing mass on a Sunday, for maybe sleeping in for an hour. It's preposterous. There are other matters too. The Catholic Church says you can't have contraception, which in this age of AIDS is beyond belief to me. I also cannot accept the infallibility of the Pope. Of course, I'm well aware that there are millions of distinguished minds who are believers in Catholicism, and I respect that. I would never ever criticize anyone for religious beliefs; I say only that it's not for me.

Has your religious faith ever been restored in any shape or form since?

Not at all. In fact the older I get the stronger my lack of faith becomes.

At Cambridge you met Pauline, a Girton girl who became your wife and your steadfast and loyal companion through good times and bad. To what do you attribute the success of your long and happy marriage? Is it something that can be defined?

It can be defined easily. Quite simply, Pauline is understanding and tolerant of my foibles. We have had an intellectual and physical marriage which has lasted forty-nine years now, and whenever there has been a difference of opinion or a misunderstanding she has always been able to say, let's sort it out. I tend to stand on my dignity, which she thinks is silly, and she's right, and she's not as silly as I am. It is her rationality that is the key to the whole thing. I wish I were like that – it would make me get on better with other people – but I don't have her capacity for tolerance and understanding.

There is a notoriously high rate of marriage breakdown among politicians, often attributed to the stress of the job and other related factors. You had the extra stress of disability to cope with. How did you manage to succeed where others failed?

I don't know. It's a good question, because the stresses of total deafness were unbelievable, not only on me but on Pauline just as much. The burden on her was phenomenal. But somehow it brought us even closer together. She accompanied me to the constituency all the time and shared the work of all the campaigns. I couldn't have continued to be an MP without Pauline – it was a fifty-fifty partnership. When I won the Campaigner of the Year Award I said it was half for Pauline, because she did as much campaigning as I did. It has been a fantastically successful duo.

When you became MP in 1966 you describe entering the House of Commons as 'the stuff of dreams'. Was that your proudest moment?

It certainly was a proud moment, but oddly enough, and this will sound bizarre, my actual proudest moment was becoming a councillor in Widnes. I remember very vividly when the town clerk read out my name in front of hundreds of people from my home. I thought, gosh, I'm on the council, now I can battle. That moment beat the House of Commons by a short head.

After the onset of total deafness you seriously considered resigning. Looking back, how much do you think that was an emotional reaction to the devastating change in your life, and how much was it a rational thought process?

Very much the latter, because it seemed an impossibility to sit in the House of Commons, the greatest talking shop in the land, with no sound. Time and again I tried to talk to my colleagues; they would answer politely, but there was no way in. No, there was a certain emotion about my decision, but basically it was a rational one given the bloody good reason that I couldn't do the job.

You write, with great candour, that your own attitude to disability for many years had been 'casual indifference tinged with pity', an attitude which you say characterized your generation. Is there any evidence, would you say, of a radical shift in attitude today?

There is no doubt that there has been a definite shift in attitudes towards disability; there is more tolerance, more understanding. And there's going to be another tremendous change now because of the law. The Disability Discrimination Act has now been passed and it is about to be fully implemented. This will mean that no service providers will be allowed to discriminate against disabled people, a radical piece of legislation which will make huge improvements in the provision for disabled people.

You write that failure to tackle disability is 'a failure of democracy'. Can you elaborate on that?

In so far as you leave people to their own devices, they do not on the whole help disabled people; indifference and neglect prevail. Admittedly when there is a blind person trying to cross the road some people will help and feel they've done their boy-scout thing for the day, but if you get someone in a wheelchair, someone who is deaf or someone who is mentally handicapped or has epilepsy – all the unfashionable disabilities, and they constitute the majority – people simply don't want to know. When they manifest this indifference through the ballot box, governments react to their indifference and don't do very much. Happily, as a result of our campaigning to amend the legislation, we are changing, not the public mind, but the government's mind in order to lead the public. And that's no bad thing in a democracy. When the Conservative government was in power and we demanded legislation, they killed the bill which I moved in 1982, saying what you need is education and persuasion, not legislation. But that has been tried for years and it has not worked. What you need is the full rigour of the law.

With your background in the unions and in working-class Lancashire, you can probably be described as Old Labour. Would you be happy with that designation?

Yes. I think there is a lot to be proud of in Old Labour, though that does not mean opposition to New Labour. The two can go hand in hand, but there is a very clear difference of emphasis. I would go much further than Tony Blair and his colleagues do, but, having said that, I'm happy with the general direction the government is taking.

You say that you lost none of your friends when you became deaf, but that it was not until you were deaf that you knew who your friends were. It was obviously a severe test of real friendship. Were you surprised by those who passed the test and those who failed?

I was not surprised by those who passed the test, I was surprised by those who failed. When you are an up-and-coming, successful MP on very good terms with many people, you can be naïve enough to assume that these people are real friends. So it was a great shock to find that no matter how regretful they were, they nevertheless didn't want to continue the relationship because it might mean speaking a bit more clearly. It was a stunning experience, almost a disorientating one. But I very quickly and realistically came to terms with it. Gradually, some of the old friends tried to come back a little bit, no more than a little bit, but as far as I was concerned the relationship was at an end.

You describe how some of your fellow MPs would refer to you in the Commons rather as Victorian men did to ladies, or would treat you a bit like 'a courageous invalid'. This must have dismayed you, but did you never think that it was perhaps a question of ignorance – in other words, they simply did not know how else to behave?

It was very definitely a question of ignorance, and although at first I was irritated by it, I gradually came to recognize that some people didn't know how to handle it, and that they were in fact trying to be helpful and friendly. And so I would make a joke of it, and once it became a matter of humour and goodwill then the problem vanished.

One of the most telling passages in your book, it seems to me, is where you write, 'I came to realize that the loss of some relationships can be as useful to a man as shedding fat is to an athlete.' Was this a painful lesson to learn, or was it perhaps invigorating?

It was both really, though I wouldn't like to exaggerate the extent to which it was invigorating. The fact that I had lost some of my friends meant that I paid more attention to those I had, and in that respect it was invigorating. Perhaps the word 'invigorating' is slightly overegging the pudding ... I think I could say it was stimulating.

You seem to have spent quite a lot of your life being angry, mostly on behalf of others, I should say. Or perhaps you don't see it like that...

It's a fair point really. But to be a successful advocate you have to really feel things. You're right, I do often get very upset and very angry with injustice, particularly where disabled people are concerned, but I think it's no bad thing to articulate it. In the early days I used to try to be polite all the time, but now I believe there's nothing wrong with expressing your anger, especially if a minister is prevaricating or refusing to help people who can be helped. If you don't, you will be brushed aside, and by being brushed aside you're letting down the very people who are looking to you to champion their cause.

You say that you never became reconciled to your deafness. How best would you describe your attitude to it?

To me deafness is appalling, dreadful, a truly wretched thing. And I also had tinnitus, a screeching roaring in the head, so I couldn't even have silence when I wanted it. Fortunately, there are now cochlear implants which can help people who have been afflicted by total deafness in later life, and also children up to the age of ten who have been born deaf. Sadly, there is conflict in the deaf community about these implants. Some people, mainly those who have been born deaf and who say they are proud to be deaf, oppose them. They want to keep their deaf culture and their sign language. I support them in wanting to use sign language and to have more interpreters – I've even fought for this in Parliament – but I find the opposition to cochlear implants bizarre. To me it's a miracle to be rescued from the appalling world of total silence, a real miracle. I bless it every day. I myself can now walk in the park and listen to the birds. And I sing with them.

INTERVIEW CONDUCTED JANUARY 2000

RABBI LIONEL BLUE

RABBI LIONEL BLUE

Lionel Blue was born in the East End of London in 1930. He read History at Balliol College, Oxford, before taking a degree in Semitics at University College, London. He was ordained a rabbi in 1960 and has been a lecturer at Leo Baeck College since 1967. He is a writer and broadcaster and a regular contributor to *Thought for the Day* on Radio 4. He is the author of many books, including *A Backdoor to Heaven* (1979), *Bright Blue* (1985), *Tales of Body and Soul* (1994) and an autobiography, *My Affair with Christianity* (1998).

According to one interviewer you have turned Jewish neurosis into an art form, which puts you up there with Woody Allen and other gifted neurotics. Would you agree with that analysis, and if so, are you happy with the company you share?

Oh, yes. There's a quality about Jewish neurosis which is optimistic. Somehow you manage to come to the surface, even after something like the Holocaust. I watch this bobbing-up quality in Jewish life and I have seen how, despite all the neuroses, people create little sane communities on the ruins of the old. I think Woody Allen is extraordinarily funny, and he's got that survival quality. When he asks the girl out on Saturday night and she says, 'Saturday night I'm going to commit suicide,' he then says, 'OK, what about Friday night then?'

During your childhood you were left with your grandmother while your father looked for work and your mother was either ill in hospital or working late. Do you think that a troubled childhood was a prerequisite for the rather angst-ridden adult life you have led?

I suppose it was. But I did have an awful lot of love, and although some of it was very manipulative, there was a lot of it around, and it gave me a lot of strength. However, since I was the only grandchild in my family, I was also expected to be the messiah. And there were some tough bits, especially after my grandmother died, like wandering the streets after I came from school and watching all the other children go and have tea with their parents.

As you said, you had love in abundance, being the adored only son, doted on by your grandparents. Why then do you think, long before the trauma of wartime evacuation, you saw yourself as an outsider, the class oddity, the monster of ugliness, which clearly you were not?

For one thing I was destabilized by the amount of anti-Semitism there was even in the East End of London before the war. There were the Mosley marches going on, the refugees were coming in, and some streets were too dangerous to walk on. I honestly thought at that time that Hitler was unstoppable. The other thing was that I was a sort of displaced person because my mother desperately wanted to get out of the ghetto and out of the poverty trap, so the one thing I was required to be was clever. She dressed me in little silk suits which made me a kind of oddity in the playground, but sometimes when I had had enough I used to kick them off and go roistering with the gang.

You have written at length about your mother who lived with you until she was ninety. But what about your father who is mentioned only rarely?

I think he was too good a man for me. You see, my mother and father weren't happy for many years of their lives – it had been a sort of arranged marriage which didn't really work out – and I knew in order to survive I had to go with one or the other. My mother was the stronger character so I went with her. My father died over thirty years ago, at a time when I was still reacting against both my parents, and so there was an awful lot unsaid between us. He was a very good man, but he wasn't a successful man. I always remember one incident on Whitechapel Road. It was a Saturday evening when we were supposed to be a nice family going out in our best clothes to the West End. My father saw a coloured man being thrown out of a pub, and he went in all fists flying, and there was an absolute riot, and my father was knocked out. When he came to, the owner of the pub said, 'Herschel' (that was my father's Yiddish name), 'do you know why I threw that man out of the pub? I kicked him out for making anti-Semitic remarks.' My mother was heartbroken, not least because the Saturday night was ruined. Again, both my parents had such different ideals from me. My mother wanted me to be a solicitor, a sleek businessman, while my father, who was a referee in the boxing ring as well as a tailor, wanted me to be an athlete. The two just didn't combine, and in the end I did the dirty on both of them by becoming a rabbi.

At the age of sixteen you talked to your mother about your sexuality, and you know she told your father, yet he never mentioned it. Have you held this against him?

No. He was always courteous to anybody I brought back home or was in love with. He was a very traditional man, and yet he somehow seemed to absorb it all, because the only thing he was interested in was my happiness.

And both my parents felt a lot of guilt about me. Like most parents, they thought it was all their fault, which it wasn't. But my father never made things difficult or protested at all – he wasn't like that.

How did your father's death affect you?

At the time I never grasped it. I only absorb things after a very long time. It was a good day, and I just thought my father would have liked it because it was a fine day for gardening. It's only in the last ten years that I have really mourned my father. It's taken me a long time.

As an evacuee during the war you were moved sixteen times, which seems appalling by any standards. Why was it necessary to move you so often? And why did your parents allow it?

Well, my parents wanted to do the best for me, and they overdid it as they always did, and I ended up getting the worst of all possible worlds. First of all, my mother's boss said as a favour to my mother that I should go to Canada and be with his children, and so I was sent from place to place waiting for a ship, but every ship that I was supposed to go on got sunk. And so I got shifted around from place to place with no time to make friends or put down roots, just waiting for this blasted ship. After Dunkirk it looked very much as though we were going to be invaded, so my parents then said I'd better come back to London. The happiest time of my life was when I was with both of them in London during the Blitz.

Were you always sent to Gentile families?

Yes, because not many Jewish people live in the country. I saw Christianity in all its brands. I was quite interested in all these variations, and I insisted on going along to Christian assembly at school, and also religious instruction. I read *The Pilgrim's Progress*, and that book has remained with me for the rest of my life. It taught me that life is a journey and that we are not just bodies travelling the world but also souls going towards eternal life. The one Jewish family I remember were Rechabites, who were against the demon drink. We used to go in processions singing, 'My drink is water bright, water bright,' and I remember singing this when I went back to see my grandfather. He was furious because he himself was a great believer in whisky.

You were fourteen when you became fully aware of your homosexuality, and were horrified. How did you explain it to yourself?

I remember my father was reading a Sunday paper and he remarked to my mother about these awful perverts, men who liked other men, and I just went white and rigid because I realized that was what I was. At least it indicated that there were other people besides me like that in the world, but I didn't know where to find them, because not having brothers or sisters or even the time to build up a relationship in which you could ask such things, the only evidence of these other people was the graffiti in public loos. Very depressing. So I was aware that I was a part of an underworld but I didn't know how you got in touch with it or what you did there.

Did you see your homosexuality as innate or did you feel that your life experience had somehow caused it?

I saw it as innate. Before I was evacuated I was interested in little girls – like most children we used to play doctors and nurses, and I think I have always been bisexual, but I am mainly homosexual.

Were you later attracted to girls?

I wasn't actually attracted to girls at all, but I did fall in love with some girls, although not physically. Later on there was a girl in my life I was able to talk to, and she loved me, and we were thinking of getting married, but there were so many problems that I eventually said I thought we had better not. It's one of the greatest might-have-beens in my life.

Was the relationship purely platonic?

We had sexual intercourse about twice, which gave me awful feelings of tremendous panic. But there were bits of it I enjoyed. For example, the actual orgasm was much deeper than anything I have encountered in homosexuality, but it was overlaid by so many layers of complex feelings. Putting it simply, if I was sitting in a café and a beautiful girl passed by, and then a beautiful chap passed by, well, the girl was beautiful intellectually, but I would be physically attracted to the chap straightaway. Girls went against the grain, but there was definitely something there, which is why I think of myself as bisexual. I don't know what would have happened if we'd got married, but I think the poor girl would have had a hell of a time.

Sexuality apart, do you enjoy the company of women?

As a matter of fact, I prefer women's company and I've always had women as my closest friends. Put it this way: homosexuality was natural for me, whereas heterosexuality was difficult and awkward, though there were some things in it which I enjoyed and which – who knows – I might have enjoyed more and more if I'd stayed with it. But I don't think it really was possible, because the first attraction was always to a man.

You say you considered marriage... yet you were fully aware that you were gay and presumably she knew...

Yes, of course, I told her.

She was also an Anglican, which meant a difference in basic religious outlook... I hope you will forgive me if I say it sounds to have been quite a mad idea. How could it possibly have worked?

Because she loved me, and because I was beginning to love her, and that made all the difference. I think in the end she would have become Jewish and done anything for my sake. We didn't get married because I didn't think it was right to put all this on somebody, but I'm very muddled about it still.

Did you hope to have children?

She wanted children. I just didn't know what I wanted. I also didn't know what sort of father I would make. An awful lot would have depended on her. It was something that was out of my reckoning. It was her I wanted, not children.

Do you regret that you are childless, that the family line ends with you?

Sometimes. That is why I was very happy when I looked after my mother and aunt when they were in their nineties, because they were my children, and I liked it. Yes, I'm sorry that the whole line ends with me, it seems a bit of a waste, but in a way, in doing *Thought for the Day* you end up with a lot of children. It's the same with teaching in the seminary. That's the only way I can deal with it. How I would have behaved with a real child, I just do not know. There are many homosexuals who want children and many of them have become wonderful parents, but I find with myself and my partner, that our relationship is more than enough for me to cope with.

Your saving grace as a lonely, friendless schoolboy was that you were clever, but instead of its boosting your self-esteem you felt the increased pressure of family expectations. Why didn't you feel you could meet those expectations?

I think because I felt they didn't do justice to me, in the sense that my family's idea of worldly success somehow seemed very cramped, and in the last resort I wasn't that interested in money. Just when I thought I would be a real drop out, two things happened: one, I caught religion, and two, I met an analyst at a party. The two together were my salvation, and I was born again, so to speak.

Why was the analyst your salvation?

He was the first person I was able to be honest with. I had tried before to be honest, first to a rabbi, then to a teacher, and they both were horrified and sort of threw me out. The analyst was the first person who seemed to like me as I was. I met him shortly after I caught religion and

I asked him in a rather prissy way if my sexuality would destroy my religion and he replied that in so far as my religion was neurotic, it would, but in so far as it wasn't neurotic it wouldn't. He also became interested in spiritual matters and went to an ashram in India, so that was something else that connected us.

How were the two things – sex and religion – connected in your mind?

To begin with I thought I had to sublimate all the sex to religion, and in trying to sublimate sex I found myself back in my childhood again being neurotic, and I thought, no, no, no, it can't be like that. Then through the Quakers I developed a kind of inner voice which told me to break out. At that point I felt I had had enough so I decided to say yes to everything, and I went to Amsterdam, which was the sort of Greenwich Village of Europe at the time. And there I found religion again, because I discovered that people are very vulnerable, especially with no clothes on. I found out a lot of other things as well. For example, I went to a kind of gay sauna in Amsterdam and after experiencing the two or three seconds of relief, I began to think it was the biggest con trick ever. I thought, is this the thing I've been mad about all these years? And the inner voice said to me, 'Lionel, you don't get much from it because you don't give much.' I then realized that religion and sex had to be brought together. I had been a terribly repressed person, so I needed a bit of relief, but going beyond that bit of relief you ended up in the sphere of beginning to make love, and that was a different matter.

You don't find a contradiction between sex and religion?

No, no. Religious people often say that if you have too much sex it will damn you. I don't think it will damn you, but what I do think it can do is trivialize you. You can end up as just genitalia and not much else, and I went through that period myself. After I came back to England I wanted to find someone to settle down with, to have a home with, to recreate my grandparents' house within a homosexual context. It took me a long time to find it. Once again, because I didn't know much about relationships, I would try to turn people into my fantasies, and it took me ages before I realized that people don't change and you have to love what is there in front of you. It sounds a very simple truth but it took me a very long time to like people as they are, not as I would wish them to be. My third really long-term relationship has proved successful, which is what I always wanted.

Adolescence was hell for you and when you made it to Oxford you found you could not cope and you came close to a total breakdown. The suicide attempt you describe – leaping from the top of a wardrobe - seems to have been a bit half-hearted . . . was it more a desperate cry for help?

Yes, it was a way of saying I couldn't cope. And you have to remember at that time, in the late 1940s, early 1950s, counselling was not the norm. Oxford was a place where public-school chaps went for cold showers, and homosexuality was still a crime.

You have been in therapy for more than forty years. Would you say your need for therapy is based on the trauma of your evacuation years, or more on the burden of your homosexuality?

I just don't know. It could even have been a pre-birth problem – who can say? During some of the sessions with the analyst, there seemed to be a kind of birth experience, and I couldn't talk, I could only make baby sounds. My childhood was certainly a complete muddle, but on the other hand, many people have had worse childhoods than me and come out fighting fit and normal. All I can say is my cry for help was answered.

Christianity had attracted you during the wartime years because you hated being the odd man out, because you were in love with the dreaming spires of Oxford and the tolling bells, and not least the seductive figure of Jesus. But your flirtation with Christianity ended suddenly when you were overcome with rage at the appalling anti-Judaism of Christian teaching and tradition which had led straight to the murder of six million Jews. What puzzles me is how your flirtation could have begun in the first place since you must have known all about the Inquisition and the Holocaust . . .

I suppose it just didn't connect up really. And of course Christianity wasn't all anti-Semitism. The Christians I met were remarkably nice and I found them easier to talk to than rabbis. They didn't want my body but they seemed to like my soul, and that was something. There were three or four things I got from Christianity, which even the rage I felt afterwards did not take away completely. One was that I began to see all my problems in a new light. Christians showed me that my problems could also be my spiritual capital, that perhaps the only way I could come to understand compassion and mercy for other people was to suffer myself. Therefore I began to see my problems as blessings, and once you feel that there's a purpose in problems and suffering, then they have a new perspective. The next thing I found out from Christians was that home could never really be in this world, because this world wasn't perfection and it could only be a corridor. Later on I realized that you only get a glimpse of love in this world but the real thing is in a different dimension. It's no accident that heaven is a word which comes into the titles of many of my books, for I began to realize that if you did something for heaven's sake, then heaven happened. The third thing I found was that religion could be a love affair, and also a friendship. I was not interested in a God who was a parent figure because I had enough problems with parents, but I needed a friend badly, so Jesus became my friend, and we used to chat to each other. Sometimes I wondered if I was a ventriloquist's dummy or if I was getting schizoid, but what Jesus said to me made remarkable sense.

Do you still talk to him?

Yes, whoever he is. He's a combination of the guardian angel my Polish–Russian grandmother believed in, and the Jesus whom I met at the Quakers. Put it this way, I have a friend in high places. And that friendship is central to my life. I still go, for example, to a Carmelite priory near Oxford, not to be converted or because I desperately want the ritual; but because there's a lot of space there to go into my inner conversations and nobody thinks I'm a fool – it's accepted. Every so often I get a summons from my friend, and he says, 'Hey, hey, what about me? I think we'd better have our little chat.' Divine friendship is no different from human friendship; you have to invest time and attention a bit.

Going back to the fleshpots of Amsterdam, whatever happiness you found there was human and understandable, but was it not an odd place to discover that you wanted to become a rabbi?

No, because actually I found that after making love people often used to talk to me. Before that, I used to want to get away as fast as I jolly well could after having a climax, but later I used to lie in bed just talking, listening to people. If you ask me where do I find God, I will tell you I find God in people. They bring out the Yiddisher Momma in me and I have a great sense of compassion. I remember there was one particular chap, and after we made love I told him that I was to become a rabbi, and he told me he had been in the SS, and we just lay silently for a while and a great feeling of compassion came over both of us. He wanted me to forgive him and I told him it wasn't in my remit, as it were, that I didn't have powers of forgiveness, that I wasn't a Catholic priest. But I felt for him and I just held him in my arms until the morning. I couldn't have sex with him again – I'm not a sexual prowess kind of person anyway – but hold him in my arms I could. Another time I met a girl in a pub in a German port, Bremen I think, and she was well dressed with a sort of Parisian charm, but she turned out to be a transsexual, and that was the only place that would accept her. I went out with her, we went to the opera together, and once again there was compassion. I had been brought up in a respectable suburban world, and suddenly I was discovering the underside of Europe. My friend from above was with me, and he seemed to take over. I began to feel at last that I could become a minister.

Do you think it was necessary to leave England to discover these things?

I hadn't realized until I went to Holland how mannered a place England was, how one uses conversations not to communicate but really to hide. I liked the way the Dutch called a spade a spade. The thing I must make clear about Christianity and why I didn't become a Christian is that I'd read the Gospels and the New Testament and there were too many things there not for me. But at the same time Christianity did give me a friend and that was extremely important. I remember when my second relationship folded up, a sort of black hole developed, because we'd been together for fifteen years, and I went into a little chapel nearby and asked, where the hell do I go from here? And this voice came and said, 'Look, Lionel, in this world you only get reflections of things, reflections of love, but one day you'll get the real thing.' I took that to mean when I died, so it rather changed the centre of gravity of my life. My boyfriend and I shared a home in North London. We had had an enormous row about who owned this and who owned that, but I remember when I got back I suddenly heard the voice again and I just said to my boyfriend that we should toss a coin about everything to decide who owned it. He said, 'Lionel that's the most intelligent thing you've said for years,' so we went to a pub, tossed a coin, and although the relationship finished in the formal sense, at the same time the affection stayed on and we remained fond of one another.

You tell us that Tina – the woman who ran the sauna in Amsterdam – 'made an honest rabbi' of you... did that mean that you kept your homosexuality a secret for some years after becoming a rabbi?

Oh yes, because it was criminal.

But did this not make you a dishonest rabbi in a sense?

Well, actually I told the senior rabbi and he said, 'Well, Lionel, I can only afford one of you, but one of you I'd better have.' And I told all my closest friends in the rabbinate and even though I couldn't say the whole truth I tried not to lie.

In the Church of England some priests are known to be homosexual, but living with a partner is not officially permitted. Has your congregation accepted your way of life without protest?

Yes, but if I had been an ordinary congregational rabbi it might have raised a lot of problems. I've been a religious bureaucrat; I teach at the seminary, I do retreats for alcoholics, HIV people, that sort of thing, and everyone has accepted it because I don't make my homosexuality a threat to them. If people feel threatened they get angry, but if you don't sort of slap it in their faces they are on the whole quite pleasant about it.

So you've never had any problem with that?

Until 1968 I had to be careful, and with all this care I probably destroyed my first relationship because we had to hide so much. It was too big a strain. I always remember, for example, that during a time my friend was badly ill I had to go to a religious conference. This meant finding a hotel for him nearby, and sort of sneaking out to see him. It didn't make for an easy domestic life.

Deep inside, do you consider homosexuality natural, or is it an affliction?

It's not an affliction. Put it this way, it's a more difficult fit, physically, socially and emotionally, but you get to the same place in the end. You do find real love, real companionship. They are more difficult to get to, but they are there.

At the end of your book My Affair with Christianity, *you say that you do not believe in the Messiah. The idea that 'a Messiah would drop from the sky to sort out our problems' is, you say, 'the illusion of children'. I had thought that the Jewish Messiah, so long awaited, was something more profound than the Mary Poppins figure you describe, dropping from the sky to sort out our problems...*

Yes, that is true. I suppose it was a rather shallow statement. My view is that there is a redeemer in each of us, and that if you are prepared to play the role of redeemer, yes, the Messiahship is open to you if you want it. I suppose I'm too Jewish to think of it in terms of another Jew, or even of another human being, and I don't really think that perfection is possible in this life.

But the way you portray the Messiah does rather trivialize a hope which has been clung to sincerely through two thousand years of persecution...

Yes, but there's a lot in that hope which is not for me. I don't hope to be ingathered to a promised land; I do not think there is a perfect world which is going to come. I went through that perfect-world business when I was a Marxist and saw the sort of damage it can do. It seems to me the best thing to do is to concentrate on the little things of life and make sense of them.

Like so many modern Christian churchmen you say that you believe in looking for God within yourself. You describe it as 'a power of redemption that works through all of us, which brings good out of evil, niceness out of nastiness, bliss out of tragedy'. Are you confident you can always find examples of bliss out of tragedy, and so on?

Yes, I am. That meeting with the SS man is a good example. I don't think he'd ever have been the same afterwards, yet we didn't exactly go through any ritual or anything like that. He'd never have been the same about Jews, just as I'll never be the same about Germans.

In the same book you write: 'When we die, time and space die with us, so there cannot be an afterlife but there is a beyond life, which is the source of our souls and of all goodness.' Can you try to elaborate on that? What could all that possible mean in ordinary language?

Time and space do die with us, and at the same time in this life we already touch heaven, that is to say a little bit of oneself is already invested in it. As I said, if you do things for heaven's sake, heaven happens to you. Heaven happens to me, and I think heaven happens to most people. I met a woman who told me she'd never had a religious experience but then she recounted how she had been in a supermarket and the woman in front of her had muddled up her credit cards, the girl at the checkout was having hysterics, the man behind her was getting so annoyed he was pushing her in the bottom with a loose trolley. This woman I met was about to join in the fray when instead she burst out laughing, helped the woman sort out her credit cards, pacified the checkout girl, even waved her bum about a bit so that the man could have a better target for his trolley. Now, what she was describing for me was a state of grace for someone who's touched heaven.

So when you die, what do you expect to happen?

I think I'm going to meet that voice I've been talking to for years. I will have a sort of appointment. When I die, time and space will die with me, and that is why I call it a *beyond life* because then I will be in territory which my mind cannot grapple with. In my restricted language I can talk about it in terms of a meeting, and I'm looking forward to that meeting because he has been the best friend I've ever had, and even if we just sit holding hands that will be enough.

The resurrection of the dead, like the coming of the Messiah, is a key belief of Judaism. Doesn't a rabbi who abandons key beliefs do so at his peril?

People think of resurrection in very different ways. Some people think of it as just their souls going home. The only thing I'm sure of is that I'll meet my voice. The rest is for me speculative.

In the context of your two heart attacks and your treatment for cancer you have said that you used to be frightened of death but not any more. 'If the worst comes to the worst I don't feel this world is my only home.' I'm wondering where exactly you will go if there is no afterlife...

I will go in pursuit of the voice. The voice is my home. Lots of people who have seen their houses being blown up know that their house is not their final home. The things which look so solid aren't, and the Jewish tradition was that you used to leave a little bit of your house unplastered to remind yourself that this is not your final home. My home isn't here; this world is like a departure lounge in an airport; you make yourself as comfortable as you can, and you get to know people, but at the same time it's not your final destination.

In March 1996, speaking at the symposium on electronic information, you mentioned prayer as a means of communication and described it as 'the divine spark incarnating itself inside myself and others'. Yet in 1998 you told an interviewer that in time of trouble you never turn to prayer and dismiss it as 'pre-scientific ju-ju'. Were you correctly quoted?

Yes. I don't know the context in which I said these things, but prayer in the sense of one saying, I want this, I want that, is nonsense. Think of all the prayers that must have been said in the wagons and the concentration camps; they weren't answered in any way we know of, so prayer in that sense is certainly pre-scientific ju-ju. I gave that sort of thing up when I was five years old. Prayer for me is... let's see, what it would be... prayer for me is the going into another gear, it is just chatting to my friend; it's not asking for this or that. Sometimes you do seem to get what you want, like when I was really at the bottom and I found religion and my analyst – you can say then that my prayers were answered. But there have been too many people who haven't had answers for me to trust prayer. The best thing to do is not to think of it along those lines.

You have jettisoned a great deal of orthodox Judaism. Do you still keep an orthodox kitchen and follow all the dietary laws?

I don't. I'm vegetarian, well, more or less vegetarian, because I do not want to eat battery-farmed animals. I don't want to have battery veal and I prefer not to have battery chicken, so that accounts for an awful lot of it. In any case, it makes life simpler not to be absolutely orthodox. It means everyone can come to eat with me – Moslems, Christians, anyone – and I can also eat out. For example, I'm not going to worry if the person who washes up is menstruating, or whether the plates have had both milk and meat on them.

Do you eat pork?

Not knowingly. The only thing I would eat in that line is breast of chicken, and it has to be free range.

What remains of your Judaism, would you say?

Feeling that Abraham was my great-great-great-great-great-great-great-grandfather and Sarah was my great-great-great-great-great-great-great-grandmother, and that it's my family. Now I might not agree with all the members of my family and I might not like all the members of my family, but it's still my family, and I'm part of it. I've also got to make sure that I convey to the next generation something of the kind of world I was brought into; I have to be a link, part of the chain of tradition.

You have sometimes said that all programmes for human betterment are undermined by human frailty. Is this a way of saying that despite all the technology and electronic marvels we are still beset by the same problems as primitive man – how best to live together and use our tools for the good of the community?

One of the tragedies of modern times is the uneven development of things. The technical part of our mind has grown enormously but the emotions have not grown at the same pace. Take an aeroplane, for example. If you look at the engine, the miracle of technology hits you, the wisdom that's gone into this thing, the exactitude, the respect for truth if you like. But then a man with unresolved potty habits comes along and can hijack the plane and crash it – all because his mother didn't put him on the potty properly.

What do you think gives rise to anti-Semitism? Have you any theories about that?

Jews are a minority and they can't hit back. And also, Jews tend to occupy a moral high ground which they believe they can never be thrown off, and it is dangerous when you start thinking along those lines. What happened in the Holocaust was of a nastiness which was pretty unparalleled, because it didn't just set out to destroy people's bodies, but also their souls and spirits. But I have learned from looking deep into myself that there is probably a bit of a Nazi in everyone, in me too. I remember seeing a fascist procession going down the East End of London and my mother pushing me into a doorway, but I actually wanted to change places with the marchers and have a drum. I was fed up with being on the Jewish losing side, with all the laughter through tears, and the suffering; the pain in Jewish history was sometimes too much to support. So you have to be careful as to what lessons you learn from the Holocaust. I mean, I sometimes sit back and wonder what an Arab child in the Lebanon must think of the Jews, and it frightens me.

You describe your grandmother's 'medieval' mix of superstition, self-sacrifice, piety, mysticism, prayer, faith and food . . . don't most people have that kind of mix, even if not the same ingredients?

I don't think most people have the piety my grandmother had. She was an unreconstructed medieval Jewess and she had the kind of piety which comes from another age. People now are so calculating, because of the society we live in. But my grandmother was not a calculating woman; she made great basins full of soup, and everyone came in, whether it was marching miners or the madwoman who lived on the corner. It was hospitality at its best. It's something I don't do and can't do. I can't welcome all the people in the street to my home; I simply haven't got the piety or the courage to do it. I've learned to be frightened, and she wasn't. That's where the Judaism comes in – this magic of turning a house into a home, relationships into a kind of marriage, poverty into charity. All of that I've seen with my grandmother.

Your book is called My Affair with Christianity, *but it does seem as if you do have a predisposition for affairs – not just Christianity, but Marxism, Quakerism, Anglo-Catholicism, psychoanalysis. Are you sometimes afraid of giving the impression of being a crazy mixed-up kid?*

I suppose people might think so, but in my grandparents' generation what you were born into you stayed in; religion was standing on a fixed point and there you were for ever. People now are not pious battery hens; we're free range, and we make our journeys through the world, like in *The Pilgrim's Progress*, taking in the bad and the good as we go. Judaism is my religious home. Yes, I make all sorts of excursions from it and I bring back things to it, but it's my home, not my prison. I suppose the journey hasn't stopped yet, but Judaism has lasted with me for a very long time.

If you hadn't been a rabbi what do you think you would have done in your life?

If I went back to a job now I think I would be a hospital chaplain. First of all, it would be no great penance for me; I'm not trying to be Jesus on the Cross, because I like hospitals and I've had my happiest times there. My mother liked hospitals too – we both liked the busy wards with all the people going up and down, just like our little street in the East End. The other thing is that when people are vulnerable you see a lot of God in them, and it always surprises me in hospitals, considering what people are going through, how nice they are to each other. It's also a safe and secure environment, and I like that.

INTERVIEW CONDUCTED MARCH 1999

RAYMOND BRIGGS

RAYMOND BRIGGS

Raymond Briggs was born in London in 1934. He went to Wimbledon School of Art and the Slade School of Fine Art. From 1961 to 1987 he was a part-time lecturer at Brighton Polytechnic, during which time he became an author and freelance illustrator. His talent for eccentric comedy was established with his *Mother Goose Treasury* (1966), for which he won his first Kate Greenaway Medal. The second was awarded for *Father Christmas* (1973), which uses the comic-strip format, as do other notable publications, including *Fungus the Bogeyman* (1977), *The Snowman* (1979) and *When the Wind Blows* (1982). His most recent book, *Ethel and Ernest* (1998), is the story of his parents.

From what I've read you seem to have something of a reputation for being gloomy. Would you say that under all the gloom there is a happy man struggling to get out?

There's a happy man struggling to get in, I think. I do feel basically very gloomy about life, I suppose because it all ends in death. Most of my work seems to have a sad ending, so they tell me. But these so-called happy endings like 'they got married and lived happily ever after' are not really endings at all; they're beginnings. An actual ending is always sad, I think.

I have the impression that you hanker after the past and that the modern world is somehow too much for you. Is that right?

That's a question of age. Once you get to sixty you start idealizing the past and thinking, oh, it was so much better in the olden days. Of course, it probably wasn't, although I have to say I do think things have gone slightly mad with technology, which has possibly done more harm than good. In the old days people came into their offices and there was an in-tray full of letters and there would be a few phone calls in the course of the day, but now there are faxes and e-mail and voice mail, and the whole system bogs up. In much the same way, we have all these wonderfully improved communications nowadays and yet you can't phone anybody any more. Where I live in the country we can't phone our village policeman, the local railway station, the local bank any more – all you can do is speak to a girl looking at a screen up in Liverpool or somewhere.

Would you say you are ill at ease with the times in which we live?

Yes, I think anyone of a certain age is. The world is run by people aged between twenty and forty mainly, and by the time you're sixty you feel that your heyday is over. People who are slightly older than me, people in their seventies, won't use an answerphone. If my elderly relations phone me and get the machine they won't leave a message on it. They say, oh, I can't talk to these things, and they put the phone down. That's the way I am with computers.

Your upbringing and background, and in particular your parents, have provided rich source material for your books. Would you say that because of this concentration on the past, as it were, you are someone who prefers to look back rather than forward?

Somebody said that most artists work out of their own childhood, and I think that applies to children's-book artists too. Besides, it's a natural thing to do when you get to my age.

But do you feel old at sixty-four?

Yes. I'm very much aware of the end approaching at sixty-four. My father died at seventy-one, and I remember feeling that he'd had a good innings and that it wasn't a bad age to die. Now that seventy-one is only a few years away, it seems horribly near, and although I don't have Philip Larkin's obsession with thinking he would die at exactly the same age as his father, I don't feel I'm somehow going to leap into some wondrous new existence. I wish I could, it would be terrific, but I just don't feel the same enthusiasm. I've done about twenty or thirty books and I just think, oh, here we go again.

Do you believe that the person one becomes in adult life can be explained entirely in terms of childhood influences and events?

Gosh, that's a difficult question. I don't know that it can be explained entirely, but it is certainly explained partly. There's no doubt that the kind of childhood I and the people of my generation had – playing out in the woods, climbing trees, damming streams and all that kind of outdoor life away from home – doesn't happen any more. Most boys go straight home to their computer screens after school, and that technology combined with this supposed danger of lurking child-molesters at every corner, stops children going away from home as much as they once did. When I was eleven or twelve, we used to come right up into the city from Wimbledon Park and go beachcombing down by the Thames at Blackfriars, and get out on to the roof of St Paul's, where you're not supposed to go – all that kind of thing, which is unthinkable today. My parents would let me go off for the entire day and not expect to see me until the evening.

Was the experience of being an only child ever lonely or burdensome?

No, I didn't notice it at all. I don't think I envied my friends who had brothers and sisters – it just seemed to me perfectly natural. Looking back on it I was rather glad actually, because it meant that I got more attention and I had a room to myself. I've always been very keen on privacy. Being in the army on national service was the worst torture, because I had to share a room with twenty-eight other people. There was never a second's privacy, except in the lavatory.

You described yourself as being an adored child . . . did you ever feel the pressure of having to behave in a way that merited this adoration?

Yes, but not oppressively so. They were very easy-going parents really. Later on when I seemed to be a student forever, my mother kept on at work to support me, so I did feel massively obliged at that time, and that made me work a bit harder than I otherwise might have done. I felt it was a terrific privilege, and I couldn't bear to see other people lazing about at art school. In the army the men thought it astounding that I had reached the grand old age of nineteen without going to work and were quite indignant about it. I remember one Scotch chap who was a friend of mine saying, why the fucking hell should we pay for your fucking education, and I thought, yeah, quite a good point, why should you? There was a grant for all those years at art school paid for by the taxes of working people, and that gave me quite a guilt complex.

Would you say that the important decisions in your life were very much tempered by consideration for your parents?

I'm not aware of having made any great important decisions really. It was more that I had my parents ingrained. The morality at that time consisted in hard work, being respectable, not doing anything too outrageous, and I suppose I inherited that. I mean, I didn't go in a pub until after the army, I didn't drink alcohol until I was twenty-two or so, which by today's standards is incredible.

What about sex?

That came terribly late too. I don't think working-class people of my parents' generation and background were particularly active, certainly not if they wanted to be respectable. And of course in those days there wasn't the pill, so people were kept fairly moral in the 1950s and there was a completely different attitude to sex.

And were you shy with women as a young man?

Oh yes, absolutely. During my five years at grammar school, up to the age of fifteen, I'd scarcely spoken to a girl in that time. I was very undeveloped physically, my voice hadn't even broken, and it was absolutely terrible at school because for the first two or three years I was quite good at sport. But then at fourteen all these people in my class turned into great big men with enormous penises covered in hair, and I was still a little boy. I left school at the height of five foot two with a piping voice, and was plunged into art school with all these gorgeous girls of sixteen and eighteen. This didn't give me much confidence on the women front.

But later on in life, did you consider sex important?

Important, yes, but slightly intimidating. If you're one of these terribly good-looking men, women chuck themselves at you all the time and are quite content to have a fling and forget it, but the women who would go for an ordinary chap like me were usually wanting a fairly deep relationship and had to fall in love. I was always fearful of involvement in that sense.

I gather from reading Ethel and Ernest *that you rather disappointed your parents by choosing to go to art school – they would have much preferred you to have an office job and wear a collar and tie. Did you feel very sure of what you wanted to do?*

Yes, I wanted to be a cartoonist and I was determined to go to art school to learn to draw. I hated the grammar school anyway and wanted to get out of it, so my parents were terribly disappointed. To them art school was something completely foreign and incomprehensible and probably not very respectable. But they did support me, which was very good and broadminded of them.

The idea of being an artist must surely have seemed quite a remote concept, not just for your parents but also for you at that time...

Yes, being an artist in the painterly sense was terribly remote. When I went to art school I hadn't even heard of Van Gogh, in fact I knew nothing about painting at all. My one idea was to draw cartoons. As for my parents, they thought of artists in terms of long hair, drink, nude women and general bohemianism, so it was very noble of them not to make more fuss.

You married Jean, who suffered from schizophrenia. That must have been very difficult...

It's a full-time occupation looking after someone with schizophrenia. Those who suffer from it have a very tenuous grasp on reality, and they have physical seizures, rather like epilepsy. There is also fainting and teeth-gritting to contend with, both of which are exhausting, and they can have delusions, actually seeing things in the room that aren't there – although Jean didn't have much of that. She suffered more from what's called referential mania, where she would see a piece of writing and think it was a message for her of some kind, that someone was trying to tell her something. She saw significance in signs and notices, because schizophrenics are so intent on themselves that everything occurring in the outside world is somehow related to them. People can even think that the twigs blowing on a tree are somehow signalling about them.

Did you have any clear idea of the nature and extent of your wife's mental-health problems when you married?

Oh yes, yes. She'd been like it for some time. Schizophrenia quite often comes in the late teens, which it did with her, but she felt – and that's what kept her going – that there was a cure round the corner. Sometimes it can disappear and then either come back or not come back; some people have florid periods for a couple of years and then no more, but other people suffer all their lives off and on with lucid intervals in between, and it has to be held down with drugs so that life becomes bearable. It's quite a thing to live with. I don't think one could have managed a child with it, quite apart from the child inheriting the blessed thing anyway...

There were ten years of marriage before your wife died. Presumably there were highs and lows in that time...

Oh, yes. I myself think schizophrenia in one sense is a gift, by which I mean that the person is intently emotional and very moved by things. They're the very opposite of boring, because you never quite know what kind of mood they're going to be in, either the depths of despair or tremendous elation, or claustrophobia or agoraphobia – all these things seem to come into it at different times.

How did you cope with the bad times? How did you stop yourself from going mad?

I did get symptoms of fear, which sounds crazy now. I used to think: what are we going to do this evening? How are we going to get through the time from teatime to bedtime, this yawning gap of time? I felt fearful, and I developed slight claustrophobia which I've still got, dating from that time. For example, I don't go on the tube. So you do become affected by it; you don't catch schizophrenia itself, but you get a kind of nervous exhaustion from living with it, which produces its own symptoms.

She was young when she died, and it must have been very hard... was there a sense in which you were able to think about it as a release from suffering?

Yes, I did think that. She was in hospital with leukaemia but continuing to have schizophrenic attacks, and I remember writing at the time that I had never seen such suffering. She had both things going on together, which was appalling.

Your latest book Ethel and Ernest, *the story of your parents, is a way of making quite ordinary lives seem extraordinary in terms of the integrity of their daily existence, the dynamic of their marriage, and the values they embraced. It is also a handsome tribute to them. Was that important to you, to pay tribute to them, I mean, somehow to mark their lives?*

No, I didn't do it with any kind of high-minded attitude of paying tribute to them; I just thought it would be interesting to look back on that time, particularly perhaps the house itself and the fact that they stayed in the same place for forty-one years. I just wanted to relive the whole thing, particularly the building, and of course their relationship. I was especially inspired by the way they met – the fact that my father was cycling along the road and my mum was dusting this big grand house and just walked to the window to shake the duster at that precise moment. It was split-second timing, and if the window had stuck, or if he had stopped at the traffic lights or something, they would never have waved at each other. I always thought that was a marvellous story.

Are you in danger of romanticizing your parents, do you think, or the lives that they led?

No, I don't think so. I don't think I've been sentimental, or idealized their lives. They had their rows and disagreements, but there were never any major breakdowns in their relationship at all, no affairs that I know of. My mother certainly didn't, and my father – well, I don't know what he did on the milk round, but I just think it most unlikely. There's a scene in the book based on a story he told me where a chap asks him to deal with his highly sexed wife, but he politely refuses.

There is a dignity and simplicity about your parents' story which you seem to suggest have all but vanished. Is that how you see it?

It's much more difficult for people today to lead that simple kind of life, partly because of television. My mother had never heard of homosexuality, for example, until she was over sixty, and even then she didn't really quite believe it. Nowadays when marriages are under strain men can get on a plane and go to San Francisco for a business trip, and anything can happen while they're there, whereas if you're only going down the road to deliver milk there's not so much chance.

One gets the feeling that although you profoundly admire what might be called the values of your parents, you do not necessarily share them . . . your world is much larger than theirs, you would not be shocked by the same things . . .

Oh no, very much not. I'm not bothered by homosexuality or what people do at all. I think there was a terrible song and dance made about the Clinton business – it's so boring, so irrelevant and uninteresting. What people do sexually is so desperately unimportant really.

Your parents never questioned anything, they simply accepted their lot and got on with what life threw at them. Nowadays the culture seems to be to question everything, to be concerned with rights much more than with duties. Is that a source of regret with you?

One of the sad things that has happened is if you say the word 'duty' you immediately sound pompous and people start smirking behind their hands at the mention of the word. The theme of the film *Brief Encounter*, for example, was duty; two people madly in love, but they know they've got a duty to their wife and husband and their kids, and so they don't proceed with their affair and ruin the lives of several other people, and I think that was admirable. People tend to laugh at that film now and think it's a joke, but I don't. I think it's a shame that the concept of duty has almost disappeared.

There is quite a lot of political comment in your books . . . are you a political animal, would you say?

Not terribly, other than having been broadly left-wing all my life, I suppose, and now slightly right-wing, which seems to happen to everyone as they get older. I still get incensed about the House of Lords, for example, all these hereditary peers able to contradict what the elected majority want to do. In that sense, I feel fairly in tune with the right-wingish Labour government we've got at the moment. I was passionately against the unions being over-powerful, as I think they were at one time – we used to have trouble even in my profession when the print unions refused artwork unless you had your chapel number on the back of it. I didn't know what a chapel number was, but it turned out that the work of freelance artists was only accepted if you joined their union, which was insane, because they knew nothing about our kind of work. It was simply a dreadful kind of blackmail.

You describe yourself as having 'an obsessive personality'. Has that been an advantage for your work, would you say?

Yes. Unless I'm obsessed, I can't get it done, and if it doesn't obsess me there's no point in doing it, because it means the idea is lukewarm. I've had several lukewarm ideas since I did *Ethel and Ernest*, but none of them has obsessed me enough to make me want to get on with it. I also get obsessions about silly things, you know, like collecting things.

What sort of things?

Electric fires. It sounds lunatic, doesn't it? But they all work, and if they don't I get them repaired, but I've got more than I need to use, so I'd like to have a bigger place where I could use them all. I'd like to display them properly but I haven't got room for them.

I get the impression you're not a religious man . . . do you sometimes wish you could have the comforts of religion?

Yes, but you can't have the comforts without the pain. All this nonsense about having the heaven without the hell . . . well, I certainly don't believe in hell, nor do I believe that the whole construct of the world came from a kind and loving God. If there is a God at all, I always say he must be an absolute bastard. I have seen what he does to people like my wife – all that suffering. Obviously people have to die, but they don't have to die in prolonged agony. God could just let people fall asleep or fade away; they don't have to suffer in this appalling way. So I don't believe in God at all, and I've always disliked Christianity intensely. Indeed most religions seems to produce a state of mind which leads to warfare and killing.

You are quoted as saying: 'Life's ultimately sad, because people idealize their children.' Can you explain what you meant by that remark?

I just feel that when people have a new baby, things are absolutely wonderful, as of course they are, but then it seems to me that as time goes on things become less and less wonderful. The huge event is the birth, it's supremely miraculous that this amazing creature has appeared from nowhere, and then they become more and more pedestrian the older they get. By the time they're teenagers they have become fairly insufferable, and then when they grow out of that stage they turn out to be quite ordinary, like the people next door. So there's a slight anticlimax to the whole thing; you might still love them, of course, but they've become fairly ordinary.

But don't you think we idealize our children because they contain the future, they are symbols of hope? They might not turn out as we hope but if we stop hoping, is that not worse?

Oh yes, it would be awful if people didn't idealize their children – I would be exactly the same and, as you say, they are the future and each generation thinks they are going to get it right. It's just that it doesn't turn out that way.

Do you think you would have enjoyed parenthood?

I think I'd have been all right at it, the worst soppy devoted parent imaginable and inclined to spoil the child. Thinking your children are wonderful is a form of conceit, and since I'm conceited anyway, I expect I would have thought my own children the best. But I certainly wouldn't have sent them away to prep school and public school – that's something I always find incomprehensible.

Your books are also very much concerned with love. Ethel and Ernest, *for example, can be read at one level as a moving love story. Are your books the vehicle for expressing love which you might find difficult to express more explicitly perhaps?*

I suppose that's possible. I do believe that love is a good thing, as long as it's not the kind of love which leads to insanity. The more enduring, prosaic kind of love is terrific and it's what society is founded on really; without that it wouldn't be anything. Love makes life bearable.

How have you coped with the business of being famous, have you found it difficult?

I don't think I'm particularly famous. I'm certainly not famous to the extent that I get recognized in the street. That would be impossible to bear. I simply couldn't cope with that. But the kind of mini-fame that I have is nothing to cope with at all. I did have a stalker recently who came about because of the so-called fame, and he shat on the doorstep when I wouldn't do what he wanted. He wanted me to give him Bob Geldof's phone number, but I scarcely know who Bob Geldof is, let alone what his phone number is.

Several of your books are concerned with the business of death or dying, either in terms of life being lived and coming to an end, as in Ethel and Ernest, *or in terms of death being imposed by war, as in* When the Wind Blows. *Even* The Snowman *is about death. Have you always had this sense that life is a short and fragile thing, which can be snuffed out at any moment?*

I suppose so, but it becomes more apparent as you get older, especially when your contemporaries start dying. People under thirty think they're going to live for ever – that's why they all smoke and think death doesn't apply to them, but when your parents go and then your wife goes, you realize it's very close.

What is your attitude to your own death?

I dread the stuff that comes before, but I don't mind being dead. Larkin said he hated the idea of non-existence, but I can't see what's wrong with it, because if you don't exist you're not aware of not existing. It's the ghastly lead up to death that can be so awful, and I'd like that to be quicker. I am quite a strong believer in euthanasia; when the situation is hopeless you should be able to get the hell out of it. That seems perfectly natural and reasonable to me. I saw a programme on television in which you actually saw the doctor give the chap the final injection. He was in his own home with his wife and he was able to say goodbye, and it seemed fine. We go to sleep every night so we might as well go to sleep for ever.

INTERVIEW CONDUCTED NOVEMBER 1998

LORD CALLAGHAN

LORD CALLAGHAN

James Callaghan was born in 1912 in Portsmouth, where he spent his early years. He entered the Civil Service as a tax officer in 1929 and served in the Royal Navy during the war. He joined the Labour Party in 1931 and entered Parliament as MP for South Cardiff in 1945. In 1964 he was appointed Chancellor of the Exchequer in Harold Wilson's government. He was Home Secretary (1967–70) and Foreign Secretary (1974–6) and in April 1976 he was elected Prime Minister on Harold Wilson's resignation. He resigned as Leader of the Opposition in 1980 and was made a life peer in 1987, the year in which he published his autobiography, *Time and Chance*.

Your extraordinary political career, your rise from humble beginnings to hold the highest office in the land, the only person in fact to have held all four great offices of state – all this is well known and documented. But I'm curious about Callaghan the man – as opposed to the politician. Would you agree that they are not the same person ?

Yes. With close family I don't convey the same impression as I seem to convey publicly, though I suppose the principles and standards by which one lives as a private person should also inspire what one does publicly. I can't say I always live up to that, though I try. The world of politics is rather rougher than the world of the family or close friends, but I think principles and standards emerge automatically when you do something. It is very difficult to disguise them or run away from them.

Would you say that you are gentler in private life than in your political life?

In my early career that was certainly true. In later life, I am so gentle that people often fall asleep when they listen to me.

Would you say that life for you has been defined in terms of politics, or do you regard politics as something apart?

It has been defined in terms of politics. I wanted to live in a way that one would achieve certain aims. Politics is a very demanding mistress but if you are going to be in a position to influence events and do particular things you must give your life to it. We all came back from the war determined that Britain would not be the same place it had been in the 1930s or the 1920s; we wanted to change Britain, and we devoted ourselves to that.

When you became Prime Minister the Sun *newspaper delved into your background and discovered that your father had changed his name and date of birth to avoid being traced when he ran away to sea...*

Yes, I have since been in touch with family members on my father's side. I discovered I had a cousin living in Australia, my father's brother's daughter, and she was able to tell me some very interesting stories. My father, who was by way of being a bit of a joker, used to tell my mother never to look up his family because they were either in jail or had been deported to Australia. He seems to have been right to some extent.

Your father, a Catholic of Irish descent, left the church in order to marry your mother, a Protestant, and you and your sister were brought up as Baptists. The Sun *also turned up a Jewish grandmother, highly unusual in an Irish Catholic family. What effect did this religious mix have on you? Did it make you more or less sympathetic to different religious groups?*

More sympathetic, not so much for religious reasons but because I found the different groups to be attractive people with attractive faiths. I've always admired the Jews who came here greatly to our benefit when Hitler pushed a lot of them out of Germany. In 1938, when my wife and I had been married for only six weeks, there was an appeal to take in refugees from Germany and we were lucky enough to have an editor stay with us. Our families were rather concerned that so quickly in our married life we had somebody in our house, but he was a splendid man and I learned a great deal from him. As for Catholics, I have always admired – perhaps envied is a better word – their certainty, which I must say I don't share myself. And when one comes across a man like Cardinal Hume, one has to respect a faith that produces such a man.

Your biographer Kenneth Morgan describes how as Home Secretary you succeeded in showing understanding of both sides of the conflict in Northern Ireland. He notes that you referred movingly in the House to your own religious background, saying, 'I remember how my own parents regarded the Catholics.' How exactly did they regard the Catholics?

I am afraid we were terribly bigoted. My mother felt very strongly that it was wicked to be a Catholic, and she expressed it in no uncertain terms.

Your biographer also quotes the view of many observers at the time that if you had remained at the Home Office after 1970, instead of being replaced by Reginald Maudling, your combination of fairness and decisiveness might have led a way out of the conflict. Given the evidence during the last twenty-five years of hatred on both sides, is it still possible to believe that?

I admired Reggie Maudling and he was in many ways a friend, but I thought when he went to the Home Office that he was too laid back for Northern Ireland. It needed constant intervention, and I had a man there whose job was to make sure that the channels never got silted up. In terms of the larger question, no, I don't think I would have prevented the developments in Northern Ireland; I might have delayed them, but as the IRA gained strength that settled the issue. Peace might just have been a possibility when O'Neill was the Prime Minister in the 1950s. He had a breadth of outlook which was far wider than a number of Irish politicians on both sides, both Protestant and Catholic, who are terribly introverted, or at least have been in the past.

Doesn't it look as if even the present peace plan has failed?

I think we'd better wait and see. I've never condemned any move that has been made, although I did feel at one stage that every time a British government produced a solution one or other side would attack it. At least we have now got all groups supposed to be working towards the peace settlement, and I wouldn't want to destroy any feelings of hope and optimism that might exist. But it is the most difficult problem for this country, as well as for Ireland itself.

Your father died aged only forty-four when you were nine years old, and you felt his loss deeply. How do you think this affected you as you grew up?

Only in later years have I come to realize that it affected me deeply. Children are extremely resilient and they bounce back, which I did, but I'm sure it did have an effect on me at the time in terms of my behaviour at school, for example. I wasn't conscious of it since one didn't examine oneself then the way that we all seem to do now. What I think I missed was the solace, the comfort and the example that a father would have given me when I was young.

Under the first Labour government there was no pension for your mother. It is almost impossible to imagine how she and others managed to feed and clothe children in these circumstances. Do you remember life as very hard?

I didn't think of it as very hard at the time. When I remember what I had to do, then it can seem rather hard in retrospect. For example, we lived a lot on the charity of the chapel, and when I came home from school on certain days I was told to call in on the fish auctioneer who was one of the chapel deacons. He would wrap up in a newspaper one or two fish that he'd subtracted from his sale, and we would have that. Otherwise our midday meal tended to be bread and dripping and a cup of cocoa made with water, which has put me off it ever since. But by comparison with some others life wasn't hard. I have recently written a foreword for Roy Mason's autobiography. As a young boy of fourteen, he went down the pit, and in a seam two feet high, three foot six inches wide, he would lie on his side shovelling coal. My life doesn't compare with that kind of hardship and I cannot disguise my admiration for him.

According to your biographer your upbringing in Baptist fundamentalism has left you with 'a Calvinistic sense of guilt, inadequacy, inner torment, and almost a neurotic sense of tragedy'. Considering what you have achieved, we should perhaps all wish for such burdens to bear...

[laughter] Well, certainly there is an everlasting sense of guilt, but I'm not sure about the tragedy. My father was evidently an eternal optimist and I think I probably inherited that side of his character. But I do have a feeling that I have not done what I should have done; I've never been able to escape that, even today at the age of eighty-seven. Ridiculous, but there you are.

Did you perhaps feel that it was difficult to live up to your father who had packed such a lot into his short life – running away to join the navy, rapid promotion, a dangerous expedition in Nigeria, serving on the royal yacht, and so on... wouldn't any boy feel that was a hard act to follow?

I wasn't conscious of that until more recently. Today everyone is constantly looking at their navels and I suppose I have fallen into the habit too. But during my active life I wasn't very introspective, and I don't think I ever consciously felt that I had to live up to my father.

Were you conscious of having a special relationship with your mother, as the youngest child and only son of a dead father?

No, I wasn't. It seemed quite normal. I obviously had affection for her, and I know she had a deep love for me, and a great pride in me. Whether I reciprocated as fully as I might have done, I wonder sometimes. When your mother finishes up in a rest home you do inevitably feel you might have done better by her. She would never have said so, however. She was an extremely independent, strong-minded woman.

You became a Sunday-school teacher, and it was there that you met your wife Audrey when she was sixteen. Audrey was your first love, but was she also your only love, or did you go out with other girls before you settled down?

[laughter] Not formally, no. I gather there's an old lady in Portsmouth – she may have died by now – who used to claim that we went out together, but I don't remember it.

You were obviously both religious young people... did you give your children an upbringing similar to your own, or had you both changed your views by then?

My wife really had charge of that side of things, and she had never been as strict or disciplined as I had had to be in Baptist tradition. So the three children had a much freer upbringing than I did. I'm glad to say they are all very good characters and I'm very proud of all of them.

At some point in your political rise to fame you became 'Sunny Jim' to the tabloid newspapers and were accepted as such by the rest of us, yet Kenneth Morgan sees this as 'one of the less appropriate soubriquets for this sometimes difficult and bad-tempered man'. How do you respond to that?

I must have given him some rough treatment when he used to come and see me [laughter]. I suppose I didn't live up to my name. Of course I've got a bad temper, though it is better now than when I was in active life. I couldn't suffer fools if they were people I worked with. If on the other hand it was one of my constituents who was in real trouble and didn't know how to handle things, then of course I wouldn't begin to feel that way. But with my colleagues I would sometimes get very bad-tempered.

Morgan goes on to tell us that you are thought by some to be a bully and that Roy Jenkins has described you as 'an aggressive pike, eating up the minnows'. Do you recognize yourself in any of this?

I only bully people who are my equals; I wouldn't ever bully someone weaker.

You are seen as reassuringly traditional in your views – a monarchist, a patriotic Englishman, slow to see the need for devolution or a Bill of Rights, a conservative with a small c, a man who found himself more in sympathy with some American Republicans than Democrats. Have you found it difficult to accept the idea of change in general?

Well, I can accept some of that. I do need the case for change to be proved. On the other hand, when I entered Parliament I had no difficulty about the change that was necessary in our institutions; nor do I have any doubt about it now, but it's different when change is made for change's sake. I therefore tend to want to see the evidence before I go along with the idea of change. I'm very good at analysis, but not so good at imaginative leaps; that is my weakness, but then I always said I would employ others to do that. My strength is understanding people, knowing what they are likely to react to, winning their understanding, their sympathy, their agreement, and being able to get to the nub of a problem quickly. My weakness is not being able to find solutions very easily.

Were you ever driven to despair by the antics of the far left in the Labour Party, and were you at any time tempted to leave the party?

I despaired very much of the far left, but I did not despair of the Labour Party. I am one who believes that fashions and attitudes swing like a pendulum; they go from one extreme to the other without really settling in the middle. Occasionally they will settle temporarily in the middle, and if you happen to be there at the time then you're very lucky. Did I ever think of leaving the Labour Party? Never. Would I leave my family, would I leave the party that gave my mother a pension, the party that gave me the opportunity of going to secondary school, the opportunity of being a Member of Parliament?

And then to be Prime Minister...

Well, it was actually more important to be a Member of Parliament. When you are young like that, it is the acme of your being to represent people. It was a wonderful thing and I shall never forget it; 1945 was an *annus mirabilis* as far as I was concerned.

Morgan alleges that your old-fashioned beliefs about the role of women may have affected your relations with Barbara Castle, and that your hostility to her plan 'In Place of Strife' may have led indirectly to eighteen years of Tory rule and Mrs Thatcher's destruction of the unions. Is there any truth in that?

No, I don't think for one moment that I have been anti-women. I would like to be careful about what I say about Barbara, because frankly I am now too old to persist in long-standing quarrels and disputes, so I will confine myself to explaining a little of my objection to what Barbara was doing, rather than to Barbara herself. I was also a little piqued at the time since I had been handling the development of industrial relations on the party's line, and then somehow Barbara took hold of it with Harold's encouragement and went away for a quiet weekend with a few people and came up with an answer which was in my view totally superficial. It was intended to deal with unofficial strikes – though it would have done nothing of the sort – and I believed that the argument that was used was shoddy. I don't like shoddy arguments, hence my opposition to what was done. Of course, I suppose I must carry some responsibility for Mrs Thatcher's treatment of the unions, but they carry a lot of responsibility themselves in terms of weak leadership and irresponsible wage claims for thirty-five per cent at a time when I was offering five per cent. Wouldn't they love to have five per cent now! But I should have been quicker on my feet. When I became Prime Minister I was twenty years older than Tony Blair is now, and I think I was getting a little tired.

You left the Baptist church, but did you retain your Christian faith?

I didn't formally leave the Baptist church, I just stopped going. Am I a Christian? That's a difficult question, a very difficult question. I suppose I am, and I suppose I shall be buried as such, but I find some of the tenets of Christianity hard to accept.

Tony Blair is a committed Christian and makes no secret of it. Do you regard this as a strength or a weakness in a Prime Minister?

Whichever way I answer that I'm going to get caught. I don't wish to make a criticism of Tony Blair so I think I am going to bow out of that question.

Well, some people accuse Tony Blair of parading his Christianity and also of being hypocritical in terms of defending the bombing of Yugoslavia, for example, while talking of morals and justice... do you have any views on that?

I don't wish to discuss Tony Blair.

All right.Perhaps you can say what you yourself felt about the bombing of Yugoslavia. Would you have taken the same stance?

I didn't have a moral objection. I had a political objection to it, not to the bombing as such but to the policy that was being followed, and I conveyed my views privately to George Robertson, the Secretary for Defence. The government was faced with a very difficult situation, and this is one reason why I wouldn't utter public criticism, because I think the government is entitled to support in those circumstances. Even if you express privately your own views you should not undermine what it is doing. But I think I would have to say that we are only at the start of this problem. You can relieve the humanitarian distress, but you cannot, I think, resolve it by force.

Anthony Howard has suggested that you have been treated with disdain by some sections of New Labour... is there any truth in that?

I think it is the fate of most people who have led the party to be reviled by their successors. It doesn't concern me really. New Labour had to distance themselves from the Labour government of 1974–9 in order to win an election, but that doesn't leave me with any sense of grievance.

In 1967 with your three children all married and starting families of their own, you and Audrey bought a farm in Sussex. Private Eye immediately accused you of suddenly becoming wealthy because of your association with rich businessmen Charles Forte and Julian Hodge. Although the charges were unfounded, they must have been very damaging. How far did they hurt you and your wife in your personal lives?

I didn't take much notice. I can tell you the simple arithmetic of the situation. We had a house in Blackheath which I sold for fourteen thousand pounds, with a mortgage of course. I transferred the mortgage and added on to it by buying the farm for twenty-two thousand pounds – hardly a big deal. [laughter] One thing that did hurt me was in my connection with Julian Hodge, and that was a budget issue. A motorcycle manufacturer in Lancaster had written to me with a story about the impact of some duty that we had on motorcycles, saying it was killing his industry. I thought he had a case and that this duty, whatever it was, could go. Then about a fortnight before the budget Douglas Jay came to me from the Board of Trade and said that if we were doing it for motorcycles we should also do it for three-wheeler cars since they were always classified together. Of course it had never crossed my mind that Julian Hodge owned the Reliant motor company in the Midlands. The press built a huge story on the basis that I had relieved the three-wheeler motor-car industry because of my close links with Julian Hodge. There wasn't a word of truth in it. I was younger and more sensitive in those days, and I really got angry. When I had been Chancellor for only a few weeks, a short letter appeared in *The Times* which read: Dear sir, Since the war there have only been two kinds of Chancellors of the Exchequer, those who left in disgrace and those who got out in time. Yours faithfully... [laughter]

From everything I have read, you are the rarest of beings – an honest man, in both your private and public lives. Do you, however, believe that the private lives of politicians should remain private?

I wish I were as honest in thought as your question implies. I fear that I am dishonest in thought on some occasions, and I don't live up to the standards that I like to espouse. But yes, I think politicians' private lives should on the whole remain private. I read the other day that three journalists are now investigating Alastair Campbell's private life, which I think is monstrous. What has his former private life got to do with the public interest, or the way he is doing his work? I have nothing but contempt for so much of the press nowadays.

As Prime Minister you took over from a largely discredited Wilson...

This sounds like a very loaded question...

No, his being largely discredited is surely a matter of historical fact. In any case, you yourself said early on that you wanted 'to redeem the tawdriness of the Wilson regime' – these are your own words. Did you regard this as a huge challenge or as an opportunity?

I think all I want to say about it is that I had my own methods of conducting government and Harold had his. Harold had a great many advantages and virtues but we each of us conducted our governments in our own ways. I have no criticism at all to utter.

Let me ask you this then. Do you think historians in the future will be kinder to Harold Wilson?

I said that myself at the cabinet meeting when he retired. Remember that there were occasions, especially over Europe, when Harold Wilson sacrificed his own feelings for the sake of the party. He and I were of one mind about the party; in that sense we were both Disraelians, and the party mattered. We were both determined that we could never go through 1931 again, or anything that gave rise to a split in the party, and Harold at times went through great difficulties which arose from the very creditable view that he shouldn't split the Labour Party. Harold was a kindly man who was surrounded by people who weren't as good as he was. He had ideals, especially about race and about the Third World. He was also a man who liked to please, and perhaps that led him to decisions that he would not wholly have wanted to take.

Your worst time as Prime Minister, and perhaps as a man, came in 'the winter of discontent' when all the essential services were brought to a halt by the power of the trade unions. In Kenneth Morgan's words, you were 'becalmed in a kind of depression, almost ennui'. Do you agree with that analysis?

Yes. It was the only time in my life when I didn't enjoy being in politics. I loved being Prime Minister, I had a whale of a time, but I did not enjoy that last winter. It's fair to say that I became becalmed; I couldn't see my way out of it or find a solution, I don't know why. I was also tired, no doubt about that, and I wasn't nimble enough on my feet.

You said afterwards, 'I felt I let the country down.' Can you elaborate on that?

It was my fault in the sense that I was the leader of the country, I was the Prime Minister, and we had got ourselves into a position that was really disgraceful. It was probably a combination of weak leadership among the trade unions and insensitivity on my part, but I must carry the can. I very much regret it. Even at my present age, if I were to go back and be Prime Minister now I would certainly take more initiatives than I did then.

Was your dismay perhaps also to do with the fact that you had worked for and defended the unions all your life?

Yes, I'm sure that was an inhibiting factor. I cared about trade unionism as an ideal. People would laugh at this now, but to me the way in which men and women had banded themselves together when they were oppressed was a wonderful thing. I always felt deeply about social injustice and about the weak being trodden underfoot. I thought it was a very great movement, and I believed they would reform themselves. After that experience I came to the conclusion that they can't reform themselves; they have to have some external parameters within which they are required to live. The modern trade union leaders do so, but they are a different group of people from those we had then. There were some good leaders in the 1970s, but also some very bad ones.

One wouldn't like to admit it perhaps, but don't you think it was Mrs Thatcher who changed the unions?

I'm not so sure about that. She was a factor, yes, but I don't think she was the mainspring of change. It was a combination of the trade unions themselves recognizing their own excesses and a new generation of younger managers coming up who thought of men and women at work, not as units of labour or resources, but as their most precious asset. That as much as anything contributed to the legal framework which was instituted.

You expected to be accused of nepotism when you appointed Peter Jay, your then son-in-law, as ambassador to Washington, and indeed you were criticized. But you made the appointment on David Owen's recommendation that Jay was the best possible choice, and also because you knew his career had suffered a setback through being related to you. Have you ever, at any time or for any reason, regretted making that appointment?

No, never. I knew from the start that I would be attacked for it, and when David Owen first came to me I sent him away. I said, no I can't do this, you've no idea what people will say, and so on. For some weeks he tried to find somebody else – at least I hope he did – but he came back and said that Peter was the man he wanted. So I said, 'Well, you're the Foreign Secretary, if he's the man you want, you'd better have him.' I don't regret it. Frankly, it was a small incident in my political life.

Your biographer tends to dwell on your feelings of inadequacy caused by the lack of a university education. What difference would that have made, do you think? Do you honestly think you could have achieved more with an Oxbridge degree?

I suppose you can't do more than be Prime Minister, can you? [laughter] No, what I regret is not lack of achievements, but the fact that I don't have a trained mind. I recognized that my contemporaries – people like Tony Crosland and Healey and Jenkins – had experiences opened to them that were closed to me. They were discussing social, moral and political questions when they were eighteen, nineteen, twenty years old; they were reading accordingly, enlarging their minds, discussing large questions, and they were able to do this effortlessly because university had trained them to do so. I had the advantage of living life in the sense that I was in the navy and so on, and that probably made up for university in practical terms, but I did envy many of my contemporaries. With me it was a laborious process of catching up, and frankly I am still catching up, still learning new things, still finding new truths.

You have lived to see your reputation, if anything, enhanced in retirement, which has not always been the case with former Prime Ministers. Do you attribute this to good luck or to good judgement on your part?

If I were to say good judgement, you would say, what a vain character he is, and if I were to say good luck, you would say, well, that man's got no judgement. I think we are all evaluated as time goes by and I should not be the slightest bit surprised – though I shan't be here to see it – if there is another evaluation after I die and people come to the conclusion that I was the worst Prime Minister since Walpole.

How would you most like to be remembered?

In the simplest way. As somebody who, despite his faults and his mistakes, really cared about ensuring justice, a measure of equality and compassion in what he tried to do. I am not a great man, but I would like to think people felt that I cared and I tried.

INTERVIEW CONDUCTED JUNE 1999

SIR FRED CATHERWOOD

SIR FRED CATHERWOOD

Fred Catherwood has been president of the Evangelical Alliance since 1992. He was born in Co. Londonderry in 1925 and educated at Shrewsbury and Clare College, Cambridge. His public service has included being chief industrial adviser to the Department of Economic Affairs and chairman of the British Institute of Management and the British Overseas Board of Trade. He was MEP for Cambridgeshire from 1979 to 1994 and he is the author of many books which include *The Christian in Industrial Society* (1964), *God's Time, God's Money* (1987) and his memoirs, *At the Cutting Edge* (1995).

As an Ulsterman whose forebears landed in that part of Ireland in the early seventeenth century, you have known what it is to live among people who consider themselves to be the dispossessed natives, with you the interlopers. How far has this set of circumstances helped to form your character and shape your life, would you say?

As a family we lived on both sides of the border. When I was fifteen we moved to Donegal where the Irish were in power, and we lived perfectly happily with them. My father knew the politicians from both sides but the Catherwoods, if anything, were against the Unionists because they nationalized the family business. We realized then what it was to be faced with a one-party state, there being no appeal against the Unionists, so I think we were rather sympathetic to the minority in Northern Ireland.

Ulstermen, as Unionists, are British, and you yourself had an almost totally English education. Do you feel yourself to be Irish in any sense, or do you never describe yourself as an Irishman?

I was brought up to dislike nationalism because it divided Ireland. I am a Unionist in the sense that I believe in a union of four different races in one country and all of those four races should be equally treated and equally respected and equally British if they want to be. The bane of twentieth-century life has been ethnic nationalism. That's certainly been so in Ireland, and it is now a real danger in England. It started with Mrs Thatcher and the extreme hostility she showed to our near neighbours on the Continent. I believe it does immense damage to them, to us, to the European enterprise, and to everything I hold dear.

You speak of attending Sunday services in local brethren assemblies, and you say what struck your childish mind most was the sincerity and passion of the speakers. Did you ever reflect in adulthood that sincerity and passion were perhaps not adequate measures of morality – indeed they could be used for evil ends?

Oh yes, but we have the Bible, we have the great creeds, our Christianity is all clearly spelt out. If a particular sect goes in the wrong direction you very quickly become aware of the fact that it is wrong. You have a basic written faith on which you can fall back.

But don't people interpret the written word in different ways?

Of course they do. What happens when people go wrong is that they step out of the mainstream of interpretation over two thousand years. But there has been a fairly steadily agreed interpretation from the time of the apostles through the great Augustine, through Luther and Calvin, up to our present day.

You say in your autobiography: 'If youthful indoctrination were the golden road to faith, then the twentieth-century churches would never have emptied as they did.' This rather argues against the 'accident of birth' theory of religious adherence, but surely there is a sense in which we inherit our faith . . .

No. The mainstream Christian doctrine is that you do not inherit your faith. The faith you have is a gift of God, and no parents can ever assume that their children are going to be Christians. What you have a duty to do as a parent is to teach your children what you see as the truth, to bring them up in the faith, but they may not accept it. So I stand by what I said.

Calvinism with its emphasis on hard work and the duty to make the most of God-given talent is the bedrock of your Christian faith. Surely you would concede that this was the culture into which you were born – in other words you didn't just happen on these principles; you grew up with them, you imbibed them, and in this sense you didn't consciously choose them . . .

Faith means trusting that Christ died for your sins and that you are redeemed through the gift of faith. That is your relationship to God. The outworking of your faith is something which gets into a social pattern – in other words, it may well be that your children do not have a personal faith, but they can still inherit the idea of the social rights and wrongs that you teach them. They may not be Christians but they can go on doing things that Christians do, at least for a generation or so. What then happens is that it fades out, and that's what's happening here. This country was built up on a Christian conscience, the outworking of the Christian faith; it has now lost its basic Christian faith and therefore the culture and the social standards are coming apart.

Do you believe that had you been born into, say, a Moslem family, or even a Roman Catholic family, you would still have arrived at your present system of belief?

Yes, because it's a much too Anglo-Saxon or Eurocentric kind of view to think that only we in our part of the world can arrive at these kind of beliefs. For instance, at the moment, the Chinese church is the biggest in the world; it has at least fifty million adherents. China will be transformed by Christians working out their faith in the Chinese context, and it's the same with many other countries where the Christian faith is growing. In Eastern Europe, for instance, Communism is gone and hardly anybody in Eastern Europe who is a Christian has been a Christian for more than five years. But they believe what I believe, and when you talk to them about working out their belief you discover that we work it out in the same way. God gave us talents – we have to use these talents. God made us to love our neighbours as ourselves – we've got to do that. The moral order that has helped this country so much will, I hope, help those countries too.

At the age of nine you were sent off to boarding school in England, a long way away from home, and although you mention briefly the feeling of separation from your family, you accepted stoically what others have described as traumatic. Is this reticence on your part, or an accurate account of the way it was?

It's an accurate account of the way it was. Children do accept things – this is part of the tragedy – and so you do things to them which are not right, but they still accept them. To be fair to my parents, they had not much experience. My father was sent away for his secondary education, and he just thought that education over the other side was best. He took the decision in ignorance, if you like. We didn't send any of our children away because we believe the family is the basic unit of society and that it should be kept together. Children should come home every night and we shouldn't farm them off for other people to look after.

At Shrewsbury you were in a very alien environment. Everything about it, from the fagging system to the fact that independence of thought and action were discouraged, went against your upbringing. Did you never openly rebel against those in authority?

Well, it was wartime, and the authority of the school was reinforced by a nation at war, so it was not the kind of time when people were tempted to rebel. I was rebellious in the sense that I absolutely refused to accept their standards, and I didn't measure up to the perfect model of a public schoolboy.

It was the son of a clergyman who tormented you for reading the Bible and for refusing to swear. You prayed for help and the fact that your prayers were answered immediately greatly strengthened your faith. In what ways were your prayers answered?

This boy was trying to stir up other people against me, and he absolutely failed to do that. I prayed that he wouldn't succeed, and my prayer was answered.

I'm interested in the business of prayer because it seems clear that many prayers remain unanswered, even for those in desperate trouble. How do you account for this?

Well, God doesn't promise to give you everything you ask for. Nowhere in the Christian faith are you promised an easy ride. If you read the epistles of Paul the Apostle, he promises only that if people do what is right, God will reward them.

But what is it exactly that we do when we pray? Can it really be that God can be prevailed upon to change his mind?

What God does is to tell us to pray as a child would ask his father, but the father knows ahead of time what the child needs. So yes, God does want you to ask for something, but he does not change his mind, so to speak.

But how do you know all this? How do you know what God thinks?

Because the Bible is full of prayers. The psalms of King David, for example, are full of prayers and responses, showing us through a dialogue with God what happens when the immediate prayer does not seem to be answered. I empathize with David in those psalms and all the prophets in the Old Testament. They pray to God that he will deliver his people, but the answer comes back: 'No, because the people are wicked, they have turned their back on me, I cannot deliver them.' And then you find another passage in which the prophet recognizes that God's holiness is more important than the comfort of the Jewish people who turned their backs on him. So the pattern of prayer is established through the Bible and you know your own prayer is valid because you are praying exactly the same way as David did or as Isaiah or Paul did. Paul prayed that God would remove his 'thorn in the flesh', which God refused to do so that Paul might realize that he was dependent on God and not on his own strength. It's all there in the Bible, even if people tend not to read it nowadays.

So you base everything on the Bible...

Yes. Christ came and rose again from the dead, publicly acknowledged in front of hundreds of people, and so authenticated himself as the Son of God. What he says is valid. He then authorized the apostles to speak, and what they say is valid. The Bible is an authentication by Christ. I'm a Christian, I believe in Jesus Christ, and therefore I believe in his authentication. Furthermore, I am now seventy-three years old and I've been a practising Christian since the age of nine, and I don't find anything written anywhere else that is as true to life as that which I find in the Bible.

But how do you know that the Bible is genuine, that what was written later on is what happened then?

Because of all ancient manuscripts, the Bible is far and away the best authenticated. The Jews are notorious for having preserved their scriptures, generation after generation, so these scriptures are absolutely valid. Nobody would deny that, and the most ancient manuscripts of the New Testament are the most valid ancient manuscripts in history, and they go right back to the time when people were alive who could have denied them if they had been wrong. They got the circulation they did simply because the people who knew the apostles knew they were right.

You never succumbed to the public-school system, largely because of the friendship and influence of a man called Robert Laidlaw, an army scripture reader. Your discussions with him laid the foundations of your belief in upholding the highest standards of Christian ethics in business and other areas of human activity. Looking back, do you think your life would have turned out differently if he had not been your role model?

Well, that's a hypothetical question which is extremely difficult to answer. All I know is that he is the most vivid influence in my memory. He stayed behind in Britain when he could well have gone to the safety of New Zealand, he was a millionaire and yet he operated as an army chaplain, and he lived through the Blitz, and so on. So what boy could not admire him? He was understanding, funny and very wise, and I felt extremely fortunate to know him. I just feel the Good Lord sent him along...

I'm interested in how much of your life you think was predetermined by God. If Robert Laidlaw was given to you by God, did you think you had been singled out for a special purpose?

Not exactly a special purpose, but I think God has a task for you to do and he sends along to you the people who are going to help you in the task he has in mind.

Are there not inherent dangers in thinking along these lines? Could it not turn out to be a terrible self-delusion with unhappy consequences? I'm thinking of gurus and self-appointed spiritual leaders, many of whom turn out to have feet of clay...

Oh yes, but what you're leaving out of account is that if you are a Christian you believe in the corpus of what is written in the Bible. If you believe what Robert Laidlaw believes you have a common position and that common position would avoid his exploiting you. I mean, he was a good Christian and an honourable man, and you accepted him because he put himself within the framework of the Christian discipline and wouldn't move outside it. You were safe with him.

But how would you know that as a boy? There are some things you can only judge as an adult...

I was sixteen and I had been brought up as a Christian. Robert Laidlaw was a chaplain, I had read my Bible, and I just knew I was on safe ground.

Robert Laidlaw explained to you why he found Darwinism incredible and you say in your book that you 'had to agree with him'. Is this still the case? I mean, do you completely reject the theory of evolution and the descent of man?

My view is that the theory of evolution is just that: a theory. I find it almost impossible to believe that the human eye, for instance, was not *designed*, that it just happened as an accident. It can focus and adjust to light, tears come automatically, it self-cleans, it sees in colour – it seems to me that if anything was designed, the human eye was designed. Even Darwin accepted that the human eye was a big barrier to his theory.

Do you reject Darwinism out of hand?

I read history at Cambridge under the Regius Professor Sir Herbert Butterfield who happened to have written *A History of Science*. Butterfield made the point, which I think is absolutely critical, that the scientific method was formed by people who were believers – the Puritans, the Huguenots, the Dutch Reformed, and so on. They believed in a creator but they also believed that he had given us a world in his image. It was unitary, that is to say the melting point of steel would be the same wherever you found it; it was orderly, i.e. you would find an order in nature; it was rational, i.e. it had systems in it; it was stable because God promised that it would be stable; and, finally, it was benign, subject to the fact that the world was in rebellion and therefore it was no longer perfect. Those are the five foundations of the scientific method, and you cannot have a scientific method without them. None of those assumptions can be proved, but they're all Christian assumptions. Now, it was Francis Bacon who urged that science should stick to what could be proved and should not enter into metaphysical theories about origins which could not be proved. So he detached practical science for the good of man's estate from theoretical science, and it was the practical science that took off, but it only took off because it rested on those assumptions. If you cease to believe in those assumptions you will find that the scientific method crumbles, and indeed in our country at the present time it is crumbling. I mean, post-modernism is a refusal to believe in the scientific method, so once you put Christianity out, you put the scientific method out and you get to post-modernism which doesn't believe that there is any firm yes, no, proved or not proved.

Do you believe in evolution for animals?

You ask me if I believe. I'm perfectly prepared to accept anything that is scientifically proved before and after, but that's got to be within the framework of what can be proved, and I think there are kinds of evolution that can be no more than theory and there are changes which occur through breeding, and so on. I believe that there is what I would call change and difference over the centuries within the framework of particular species, but I only believe that if it can be proved. I don't believe in it as an article of faith.

For instance, there is a particular species of wasp which lays its eggs inside a caterpillar, so that when the eggs hatch they have the flesh of the caterpillar as ready food. The caterpillar is first of all paralysed and then kept alive so that the meat, so to speak, will be fresh. All of this is of course perfectly compatible with evolution, but how is it compatible with a loving God?

If you go back to the first part of Genesis you see that God created the world perfect, but then there was a rebellion and into that rebellion came death and suffering and everything else. From then on it was a suffering earth, but he didn't create it in that way.

Do you see science and religion as irreconcilable?

Not at all. My religious beliefs are prior to my belief in science, but because I am a Christian I believe in the scientific method. Were I not a Christian, then I would be taken in by post-modernism, which does not believe any longer in the scientific method. For instance, when you go through an airport waiting-room, the pictures on the wall are post-modern, they're all chaotic because they represent the view that there is no rhyme or reason, there is no truth, there are no absolutes. But when you get on to the aircraft you are extremely glad that the aircraft is built on the scientific method, not on post-modernist principles. Unfortunately, our society today is dominated by post-modernist destruction which is taking apart the social order on which Christianity has had such a huge influence. The moral order behind it is being deconstructed, and we are therefore living in a chaotic society which doesn't know whether it's coming or going.

You seem very critical of what you call 'pietism'. I thought pietism was a term for exceptional devotion to religion... can you clear this up for me?

There is a theological pietism which concentrates on the personal feelings of the individual Christian; it's inward looking, and it doesn't care for its neighbour as much as it should, and it doesn't care for the objective doctrine as much as it should. Those who practise pietism go to great conventions which make them feel good. To me that is not Christianity. You have to teach what is the Christian faith, and pietism doesn't.

You trained as an accountant and embarked on a spectacularly successful career in business management, eventually becoming managing director of British Aluminium, as well as holding high office elsewhere. How difficult was it to maintain Christian standards in such a worldly and materialistic environment?

It depended on who your boss was. It was difficult with my first boss, and that was why in the end I left and took another job. My second boss, Edwin Plowden, was no problem at all. He was one of the most distinguished public servants in Britain, and his ethics, integrity and relationships with people were absolutely superb.

Were you ever tempted to lower your high ethical standards in business?

No, because as you must know, business is very much about trust. I was brought up to believe that you do business with people you trust, and with people you don't trust you don't do business. And also, because we were looking after other people's money, we had a fiduciary relationship which we had to keep to. Post-war standards in the City of London were extremely high, and I was very happy with that.

Can you be confident that you always preserved an ethical balance between the conflicting needs of workers on the one hand and management and shareholders on the other?

Well, who could be absolutely sure of that? All I can say is I tried.

When Labour won the general election with a slender majority in 1964, you were invited by George Brown to become the government's chief industrial adviser. Wasn't that a very risky job to undertake for a man of your standing in the business world, especially as a paid-up member of the Conservative Party?

I may have been a paid-up member of the Conservative Party, but I resigned from the party when I entered public service because I went in at a rank where you couldn't have anything to do with politics, and I thought it was best not to belong to the party if I couldn't do anything about it. Edwin Plowden said to me that there would be people in the City who would never trust me again because I had worked for the socialists, but I believed it was the right thing to do.

What did your Conservative friends think of it, and your decision to suspend your Tory Party membership?

I was not an active member of the Tory Party...

But you were advising a Labour government...

Well, nobody seemed to notice. I only once took an active part in my local party, and that was over Suez, and so I really wasn't known in the party except for that one occasion.

Were you for or against Suez?

I thought it was a ridiculous idea. I found it extremely difficult to see how, if the Israelis and the Egyptians were both east of the Suez Canal, it helped matters to send the army down the Suez Canal and separate them. The whole thing was so clearly phoney.

You thought highly of George Brown, who seems to be remembered mostly as a joke figure, a drunken embarrassment to his own party. Yet you say he simply had a very low alcohol tolerance...is this remark based in Christian charity rather than reality?

No, it was a fact. He would get drunk on sherry – that was the problem. He was always very friendly and we had very good relations. I respected his political clout and he respected my ability to carry business with me, so that was the deal.

It is noticeable that although you may criticize policies, you never speak ill in personal terms of anyone. Is this a deliberate decision prompted by Christianity? Have you privately felt dislike, perhaps even hatred, for people in the course of your life?

Christianity is a faith which emphasizes love, and it tries to eradicate hate, irritation, and all of those kinds of things. If you're a Christian for a long time you feel an affectionate relationship comes more naturally to you than irritation, and you try to see the best in people. And if you act with Christian love towards them you get far more out of them.

And yet you say you're impatient by nature...

Exactly, but one of the things that the Christian faith does is help you to overcome your natural tendencies. You have to work hard at it.

Is there any politician, whatever his religion or lack of it, in whom you have recognized true goodness, a person of whom you might have thought, this is a better man than I am, to paraphrase Kipling?

There are a great many very good politicians, yes. For example, Alec Douglas-Home was a very good man – he may have had his limitations, but as an honourable man he was first class. And I liked old Jim Callaghan too – he is a good man.

In view of the peace agreement, are you now optimistic about the future of Northern Ireland?

Yes, I am. I have been in and out of this for thirty years and I now believe an enormous step forward has been taken. My own feeling is that once there is an assembly set up and once local politicians have got a stake in that assembly – I'm thinking particularly of the Unionist side – then it will begin to gain a momentum of its own. Once the cross-border bodies get going it will be seen that there is not the slippery slope that the Unionists fear. The main problems at the moment have to do with how you get the IRA to give up their weapons without this being an acknowledgement that they have been defeated. In their view only defeated armies give up their weapons, it's an act of surrender, but we can't go on having the perception that if they don't get their way they can go back to the gun.

If for some reason in the future – demographic changes, for example – the six counties joined the twenty-six and Ireland became united, would that worry you?

No, it wouldn't worry me unduly, not if there were a majority in favour.

Many Unionists have resisted the very idea of a United Ireland for fear of being subjected to the same restrictions on their personal lives as those imposed by law in the South: no divorce, no artificial contraception and no abortion under any circumstances. Yet these are rules of which you might approve, are they not?

The impression I get from the Irish Catholic hierarchy and from my colleagues in Ireland is that the church no longer has any clout in the South. The South of Ireland is becoming a very secular country, and the church has scarcely any power left.

Your uncle and namesake emigrated to America in defiance of his father's wishes and died there without reconciliation. It was a blow from which your grandfather never recovered, but you suggest that his mistake was in not realizing that a child is as likely to react against his parents as to follow them, and that each must answer for himself. If your own children had rejected everything you stood for, including Christianity, could you have let them go without blaming yourself, taking comfort in 'each must answer for himself'?

Well, it's the only comfort you have. When it happens to the children of our friends, that's what we say to them. You do the best you can and that's all you can do. You shouldn't blame yourselves. With one of our children we certainly had a very sticky patch and all we could do was to go on loving and caring and being good parents. You can't do more.

The Catherwoods, parents and children, seem to epitomize the doctrine of Calvin, that virtue should be practised for its own sake, without hope of reward or fear of punishment, and provided that is done, prosperity will follow. Do you agree with this observation?

No, I don't agree prosperity will follow. Our daughter and her husband are both teachers and prosperity certainly doesn't follow in their case, and it is the same with our son, who is a lecturer and writer. It's true that our older son is doing very well, at least so far.

Would you allow that many have led a virtuous hardworking life without reaping obvious rewards?

Yes, of course, but it's done for its own sake, it's not done for rewards.

Modern capitalism is said to have arisen from the widespread influence of Calvinism, and it underpins the best of Conservative thought, but we now have a Labour government which seems to have embraced much of its doctrine, a churchgoing Prime Minister and a Foreign Secretary who advocates an ethical foreign policy. Do you feel less pessimistic now about the state of the country?

Let me correct one of your primary assumptions. Capitalism has been there since the beginning of time; what Calvinism did was to produce a scientific method which meant there was a colossal technological breakthrough, together with a doctrine of hard work and the use of the talents which produced professionalism. It is science and professionalism which together have created wealth, so I don't say that Calvinism equals capitalism; it doesn't. My definition of Christianity is love for our neighbour, but in British society there is no care for those who are below a certain line. Now that was not the way I was brought up, it was not the way the Labour governments used to be, it was not the way the Tories used to be, but since the 1980s that is the way it has been. Sadly, Blair has not done anything about that, so the rich still get richer and the poor still get poorer. I'm extremely disappointed in Blair.

How do you view personal standards of behaviour in political life – the so-called sleaze factor which haunted the last government?

It is just one highly visible part of the deterioration of moral and social standards. The other thing that Calvinism contributed was honesty; banking and trade prospered because people who didn't know each other could trust each other, and indeed democracy grew up in so far as it did in the nineteenth century partly on the basis of the feeling that all men were equal and partly on the basis of certain standards in public life. If you take away the moral underpinning from society, as we have done, you can't expect that the police will not become corrupt, that politicians will not become corrupt. It is a natural result of saying that there are no absolute moral standards.

You see unemployment as a great evil, partly responsible for the moral decline of the nation...but can Tony Blair do very much to solve the problem? Governments don't actually create jobs and there is not much point in training schemes if there is no job at the end. If you were asked to be Blair's adviser what advice would you give him?

I actually wrote a letter to the *Independent* giving the Chancellor a bit of advice. British industry lives on its wits, and in a world that doesn't owe us anything, we have to sell more than we buy. That's the only way forward for this country. Services are important, but not as important as industry and they're also more volatile, so you need to make absolutely certain that British industry expands at a sufficient rate to create the surplus that enables you to expand the public services pro rata. At the moment, it costs a British company fifty per cent more to put down new capital than it costs a continental company because our interest rates are that much higher. Our interest rates are higher because the government came in with a pledge that it would not raise taxation. If you can't adjust the economy through taxation you have got to adjust the economy through interest rates. To say that you can't have a penny or two adjustment to get interest rates down in order to make British industry competitive is absurd. We are in the single market and British industry is faced with competitors who for the next generation of every product can put down fifty per cent more capacity than we can. The government is entirely responsible for that, not to mention the resultant loss of jobs and loss of hope.

What would you say are the moral absolutes nowadays?

We have the Ten Commandments, you know. They are the moral absolutes, and we don't keep them.

Do you believe in capital punishment?

I believe in capital punishment subject to the qualifications that a Christian puts on it, which is that you have to be absolutely satisfied on the evidence of at least two people.

Can you ever be?

Well, that's a difficult question . . .

Do you believe in hell, and if so, do you see it as the biblical place of fire, or simply as banishment from the presence of God?

The latter, but having said that, we underestimate the awfulness of banishment from the person who is the source of all good.

Do you believe that anybody, however wicked, should be punished for all eternity?

The Christian concept of heaven is the concept of being in a place of absolute good, with a good God who is honoured and respected and obeyed by everyone who is there. If you bring in a rebel, for however long, he is still a rebel. That introduces a flaw – which is how evil began in this world. There was a paradise, there was a rebel, and there was a flaw, and once you had that there was no longer the relationship with God. Heaven is a place where there is complete trust because there is complete obedience to God, and you cannot have heaven flawed. I don't know what heaven is like and I don't know what hell is like; all I know is that heaven is a place of total good and total obedience.

Is there salvation for those who cannot accept the truth as you see it?

There is salvation for everyone. What happens is that people either come to see the truth, or they don't. But the reason that people do not become Christians is that they are not prepared to subject their right to decide what is right or wrong to the view of God who made them.

You say that Christians must have more than mere inner convictions: 'We have to show that the God revealed by Jesus Christ was the one true sovereign God who created the universe and that that message was the only valid analysis of the human condition.' I ask this with great respect, but how can you hope to show that? You may believe it and preach it, but how do you show it to a Darwinist, an atheist or even to a Buddhist, or a Hindu?

I am in favour of freedom of religion, because in the free market of ideas Christianity is usually most successful. The Christian church in China now has between fifty and seventy million people who grew up during the Maoist terror. Eastern Europe suffered seventy years of anti-Christian propaganda, but everyone has now forgotten the Communists and the Christian church is rising again, and it's exactly the same in Central Europe. The Christian church is the belief system most widely accepted in the world, and one cannot therefore say other than it is valid for every people, race and nation.

Would you say you were puritanical when it comes to sexual matters and religion?

No, I'm a Christian, and I practise what the Christian faith says. The proper place for sex is within marriage.

But most people have sexual intercourse before marriage...

Well, your asking me what I believe, not what happens with most people.

Do you believe that sex is also a gift from God?

Sex is a gift from God but the family is also a gift of God, and sex is meant for the family, not outside the family. If you went round the inner cities of our country at the moment and you saw the estates where most of the children are brought up with no father, you would conclude that the family where a man was committed to bringing up his children was a good thing, and you would not think that promiscuous sex was helpful socially. We are breeding a generation of unloved and unwanted children who are the loose cannons of our society. It is truly appalling.

Would you agree that the language of faith is very imprecise, that it's almost impossible for one man to know what another man means by God or salvation or divine mercy?

That's what churches are for, to explain to us what these things are. It's not that there is a mystery about them, but that there is a theological system to explain everything to people. But once you become a Christian and you practise it, then it's like driving a car. At first you think, how can anyone understand how to make all these gears and pedals work, but once you're in the driving seat you've committed yourself to it and you understand what responses you get. You know you're in a workable system and you know how it works.

You say that eternal salvation matters more than anything in this life... is that not an almost impossible message to get across to people today, particularly to the young, who have grown up with very different values in a rather fragmented society?

The average age in our church is about thirty. I think we have about a hundred and fifty students, all highly intelligent, all very young, and the message certainly gets across to them. The fact that this is not recognized by the rest of society doesn't mean it doesn't exist. The church is there, it is extremely active, it appeals to the young. Society has this image of Anglican churches being inhabited by three old ladies, but that is not the case. Far more people are interested in the Christian faith than are interested in politics, for example.

Yet statistically there is a decline in people going to church...

Yes, and that decline happens because in a great many churches the liberals went along with the humanists. The liberals took over and since they didn't believe in any absolutes they began teaching people that you don't have to believe anything, so they didn't go to church any more. Liberal churches have gone into perpendicular decline, but the vast increase in the evangelical churches where people still hold to the orthodox faith has made up for that decline.

Do you believe that the churches should be moving with the times, so to speak, trying to adapt to modern society, or are you in favour of the church sticking to the old truths which are immutable and not to be diluted to suit modern times?

There is such moral and social and economic chaos in our cities today that you cannot put your trust in the deconstructionist society that we have now. We are told we cannot believe in any absolutes any more, and so all the bonds that keep a society together are dissolved. Our society is in decline and we cannot have any faith in modern Britain.

Obviously you believe in an afterlife, but do you fear death itself?

To the Christian death is particularly awesome, because you are not just snuffed out – death is not the end. It is the time when you finally account for all you have done and it is a very awesome thing to come to your judge. Therefore it's not so much that you fear death, but that you don't lose the sense of awe about death.

INTERVIEW CONDUCTED JUNE 1998

MARGARET DRABBLE

MARGARET DRABBLE

Margaret Drabble was born in Sheffield in 1939 and educated at the Mount School, York, a Quaker boarding school. She won a scholarship to Newnham College, Cambridge, where she achieved a double first in English. She published her first novel, *A Summer Bird-Cage*, in 1962. This was followed by other novels including *The Garrick Year* (1964), *The Millstone* (1966), *The Needle's Eye* (1972), *The Radiant Way* (1987) and most recently *The Witch of Exmoor* (1996). She has also published biographies of Arnold Bennett and Angus Wilson, and she is the editor of *The Oxford Companion to English Literature*.

For most writers childhood is fertile ground, particularly, it seems, if it has been unhappy, as yours was by all accounts. Do you think the unhappy childhood, however clichéd, helps the creative process?

Yes. An unhappy childhood gives you a lot of material, and it's much easier to remember unhappiness than happiness. Some writers have had very happy childhoods which give them a sort of golden time to write about, but for me personally it's been very useful to have had a lot of grievances and miseries to look back on. They may be exaggerated in later life but they give you an argument with the world.

It is only comparatively recently that you have felt able to talk about your rather dark and troubled childhood that was tyrannized over by your depressive mother. Have you managed to lay the ghosts, would you say?

I've just finished a novel about my mother, and I found it really hard to write because she is a difficult memory. While she was alive I was always thinking two ways: that I must keep her happy and that I must try to keep things going. And it's taken me all these years since she died in 1983 to come to terms with everything.

Do you miss her?

I don't miss her at all. While I was writing the novel I thought about her a lot, on the whole quite miserably. But just occasionally I would have a dream in which she was happy and we were having a nice time. Then I really felt that I was redeeming things, but that happened very rarely. I miss my father, but that's another matter.

Did your mother have any qualities that you admired?

Yes, she had many admirable qualities. For example, she was very honest, not about herself, but about other people; she wasn't a deceiving woman, and she was very proud of her children. But she also had this depressive, manipulative quality which made dealing with her extremely difficult. It was so hard for my father, and for all of us. She imposed her sense of what was wrong with the world on those around her, and it cast a big shadow.

How did your father cope with her?

He was always trying to placate her, to make life pleasant for her, but it was never enough and he never succeeded. They both came from very humble backgrounds, but he did well in the world, becoming a barrister and then a QC, and he was always so careful to get good domestic help, but it was never quite enough for her. He took her on holidays but she always wanted a bigger or better holiday – she could never be satisfied. My theory is that it was because she had no career. She was a clever woman who had lived in the period when you didn't do anything but look after your children, and I think she must have resented us very much. She never said she did, but I do think that if she had been born a bit later she would have had a better time.

Your childhood is generally packaged by journalists into a neat tale of sibling rivalry with your older sister Antonia Byatt. Is the truth more complex than the stuff of journalism?

Much more complex. There was rivalry in the sense that Antonia was very jealous when I was born, but that is an absolutely commonplace situation, the older child being jealous when the second is born. What the journalists never comment on is that I have another sister and a brother, so the situation extends beyond the two sisters who happen to be in the public eye. We were a family, and I think my sister, indeed both my sisters, would agree that the problems were with our mother and not with each other. My mother was a very ambitious woman for her children, and if we slipped a bit or didn't get the top A grade, she was very critical. There was a sense of having to do the best all the time, which is very difficult with siblings, even when they're close and supportive of one another. A competitive situation can be made worse by praising one child at the expense of another, and that certainly went on.

But was there a time in your life when you and Antonia had a warm relationship?

Oh yes, we were very close. As the younger sister, I adored Antonia. I thought she was wonderful and I used to listen to her as if hers was the voice of the Lord. We used to play amazingly complicated games, with my younger sister as well, and it was only when we grew older that we split. But that again is normal; children do grow apart when they get older.

The family feud theory is one that appeals to those interested in the private lives of authors, but how much of the so-called 'rift' between you is to do with family reserve and a way of coping with fame in the same field?

Coping with fame in the same field is certainly difficult. I think Antonia said at some point that she really wished that I had stayed being an actress because it would have been much more convenient for her, but unfortunately that's not what I ended up doing. I wanted to be a novelist and so did she, and in those early years she saw us very much in competitive terms. However, being in the same field isn't necessarily difficult for people. For example, my first husband was an actor and his brother also became an actor. There has been the occasional mix-up when they have been cast by mistake for each other – a potentially nightmare situation – but those two brothers are so close and good to each other. I wish my sister and I could have been a bit more supportive rather than allowing ourselves to be set in opposite camps. It's a pity. I do greatly admire my sister's work and I am always very excited when she rings me up.

You say that you and your sister followed unquestioningly the pattern which your mother had mapped out for you both. Were you aware of that at the time, or was this something that became apparent only in retrospect?

It became apparent in retrospect. At the time I was quite happy to go along with the programming. My mother wanted us all to go to Cambridge University, so all four of us went to Cambridge University. I now see I should have gone to Oxford, and if I had, then all might have been different. Antonia and I would have belonged to different worlds – she would have been a Cambridge writer and I'd have been an Oxford writer. But I wanted to please my mother because she was unhappy.

How did your younger sister and brother fit into the family situation? Were their lives also mapped out?

Yes, they were. My younger sister was also sent off to Cambridge, but she made the big decision after her first year to change from English literature (which my mother had read) to art history. It was very sensible and she became a very successful art historian. My brother had the advantage of being programmed by my father. He went to Downing, my father's college, and he became a lawyer and later a QC. He also had the good luck to be at university in the 1960s when everybody was rebellious, so he had a slightly different experience of Cambridge from the rest of us. It has worked out fine for Richard, although he had a difficult time with my mother, being very much the youngest and isolated with her for years because of the family structure.

Why do you think that you, the second daughter, became your mother's favourite? Did the fact that you seemed to have inherited her tendency to depression have anything to do with it?

That's a very interesting question. I never thought of it that way, but it's possible, yes. Both Antonia and I were quite highly strung. She was a delicate child, quite dangerously asthmatic as a little girl, and I was depressive with a bad stammer, so we both had problems. My mother's line on my sister's asthma was very unsympathetic. She was quite Yorkshire and she just said, well, you've got to learn to live with it. She was hard with both of us and I really don't know why I became the favourite. Perhaps it was because I was more patient with her, whereas Antonia got really fed up. I paid her more attention, and that lasted until she died.

Have you tried to avoid having a favourite child of your own, and have you succeeded?

I have tried passionately not to have a favourite child, and I can honestly say that my favourite child alternates day by day. At times I feel my eldest is closest because he's intellectual; then I think my daughter's the closest; and then I think my youngest boy with his little children is my darling.

Your mother suffered very severely from depression, yet you say you were able to control yours and even to forget about being depressed. This does not sound like clinical depression – was it perhaps straightforward unhappiness with you?

It's possible. It's also possible that my mother wasn't clinically depressed; she just had no outlet. When I was at Cambridge in the late 1950s the world was just opening up in the most thrilling way, not only for women but for young people generally, whereas when my mother was at Cambridge things were difficult. She couldn't get a job, and so she was driven in on herself. I think I am depressive by nature, but I'm never manic. I just go through black patches when things don't seem worth doing.

Do you agree with your mother that you suffered because of a heightened awareness, or do you think it is to do with a chemical imbalance?

I really don't know. I feel in my case it is something much more spiritual, a sort of melancholy that comes over me.

You attended the Mount School in York, a Quaker boarding school. Was it something of a relief to be sent away to boarding school, would you say?

Yes, I loved it, and I was very happy there most of the time. It was a good school and I had good friends there, one or two of whom I still see. There were things that I didn't like about it, but by and large it suited me very well.

Why were you sent to a Quaker school?

Very complicated reasons. My parents were quite left-wing and didn't want to send us to a snobbish girls' school where you learned to be a lady, and also they quite liked the moral seriousness of the Quakers and the egalitarian idea of decent people together. They wanted the best of both worlds really.

You have described your father as 'a very good man'. What does that mean in your terms?

He was kind, he was fair, he was generous, and he was sensitive to his children. He was a completely unpretentious man, he thought a great deal about social issues, he believed in a better world, and he was always worrying about other people. He was also a gentle man, too gentle perhaps.

Your criticism of your mother is understandable, but have you come to feel compassion for her, perhaps as you yourself have got older?

In a way I have always felt compassion. I have always believed that she had a bad deal, both historically and personally. But, yes, I think I now understand more what it was that she suffered from. The actual causes of her feeling so unhappy are clearer to me now than they were; but I always felt sorry for her, always.

How difficult has it been to avoid becoming *your mother? Is that something you have consciously resisted?*

I've tried to, but I now hear myself saying some of the things that she said. However, I honestly don't think I impose my will on my children in the same way – maybe if anything I've gone too far the other way. I think I should have watched them a bit more closely at certain points and been a bit more pushy on their behalf.

You describe marriage at twenty-one as being 'the only way to make one's sex life acceptable to one's parents'. Do you think the reasons for marriage nowadays are any more soundly based?

Yes, I think that people who choose to get married have thought quite seriously about why they want to enter into this state and what it means to them in terms of commitment. A lot of my generation married just to get away from home, but marriage now is much more of a choice than an escape hole.

Your first novel, you say, was the result of loneliness and joblessness. Do you believe that if you had had an interesting job and felt completely fulfilled by marriage and motherhood that there might have been no novels?

It is perfectly possible. If I had found employment as an actress or if I had been perfectly happy and busy I might never have found time to write a book. My first husband and I were both in love with the theatre in those days. We actually met in an amateur production of an Ibsen play at Cambridge – he became a very good actor and I was not a bad actress. But there were far fewer parts for actresses; it was a much more difficult career than being an actor.

Your early novels are very strong on portraying the complexity of feelings accompanying motherhood, which is presented with all its conflicting demands and frustrations. And yet you say somewhere that motherhood for you has been 'the greatest joy in the world'. Is this a feeling which came retrospectively, as it were, once the early experience of motherhood had been lived through?

No, I think I felt it all the time. I wasn't very keen on being pregnant, it's true, and I thought the whole thing was a big mistake, but as soon as I saw this little creature I was completely enraptured and have remained so ever since. Of course, there are difficulties, and my early novels were written to cater for a clientèle of mothers who were having a terrible time, but even the mothers having a terrible time are also having a wonderful time. What I felt when I saw that first baby was always with me; it was always the most important thing. And this is true for the majority of women – it's the most important experience of their lives.

The heroine of The Millstone *describes the experience of pregnancy and motherhood and says at one point, 'I am sure that my discoveries were common discoveries; if they were not, they would not be worth recording.' Was that your own experience too, that the new things you discovered about yourself were part of something universal?*

Yes, it was like suddenly being part of the human race. All the way through school and college, I had been pushed into some special position and told to be different. But suddenly there was this totally common bond.

Time and again in your novels there seems to be a concern with the most ordinary experiences in life ...

Yes, I think extraordinary experiences are interesting, but ordinary experiences are what make us what we really are.

Is there a deliberate attempt on your part to 'de-intellectualize' the business of living, to demonstrate that the truth is all around us, not simply in the scholarly pursuits?

That is absolutely correct. It's not that I don't respect scholarship, it's just that I feel a lot of what is very important is not understood by scholars, not accessible to them. I particularly value the common bonds rather than things that set people apart.

Your heroine in The Waterfall, *Jane Grey, says at one point: 'I could have turned myself into one of those mother women who ignore their husbands and live through their children. But with me, this did not happen; my ability to kiss and care for and feed and amuse a small child merely reinforced my sense of division – I felt split between the anxious intelligent woman and the healthy and efficient mother.' How much do these words reflect your own experience of those days?*

They certainly reflect a period in my life when I felt that my entire milieu was being used up by children, and that the woman in me was not being allowed to speak at all. When you are a young mother there are a lot of conflicts; you can't be sexually attractive, look after a baby, clean the house, and in my case write a book all at the same time. It's less of a problem for women now than it used to be, because women are allowed more roles, more freedom than before.

Jane Grey is an example of what has been referred to as 'the brains and breast dichotomy' – this was presumably something you yourself experienced rather acutely. Do you think it was resolved satisfactorily in your case?

It was resolved, yes. I have had a perfectly satisfying intellectual life and a perfectly satisfying physical life, so I guess I have no complaints at all. I think I had the capacity to be a don, in which case I would probably have read a lot more books and been able to understand deconstruction and all the things that I find quite difficult intellectually; but I don't regret not being a don, because I have had so many other things that I might not otherwise have had.

Do you believe that what can perhaps be articulated and resolved in fiction often remains inexplicable and unresolvable in life, and in oneself?

Yes. Quite often in fiction one is describing a dilemma that is a perpetual dilemma, and one invents characters who solve it and you can feel as a result that you've solved it in life, but in fact it comes bouncing back at you. The business of my mother is a case in point; through fiction you can make a shape out of it that satisfies you for a while; but you can't really resolve it.

Doris Lessing, whom I know you admire, said, 'There is no doubt that fiction makes a better job of the truth.' Are you inclined to agree with her?

I know what she means, but on the other hand I am also quite interested in the truths that you can't fit into fiction. I know Doris found her mother just as difficult as I found mine, and she eventually came to the conclusion that her mother had been driven mad by the First World War. That situation fuelled all her fiction, but it was only in writing her two volumes of memoirs that Doris discovered what her mother was really like. So there is fiction, but there is also fact, and it's very strange when the fact seems to contradict the fictions that you've made out of it. It's a very rich area and a constant two-way process.

You are described in your own Oxford Companion to English Literature *as being associated with early feminism. Can you perhaps elaborate on what you understood by feminism then, and what it means to you today?*

With early feminism it was a question of equal rights, educational opportunities, equal pay, access to the professions, and also, absolutely crucially, it was to do with nursery-school provision. When I had my babies there were no state nurseries at all. This is still a problem but at least we know that we are thinking about it. A lot of the issues to do with providing mothers with support are exactly the same, but the process of feminism is completely irreversible – I don't think we will ever go back. Every now and then there's a backlash and we are all told that it is very bad for mothers to go out to work; well, all mothers know that it is bad to go out to work in some ways, but we are never again going to see women staying at home in the way that my mother stayed at home. The future of feminism is making it happen for the benefit of everybody, for women, for children, and for men, so that they don't feel pushed out of the side of the frame. When I was young, feminism was very much a sense of wanting to choose your own life and that has now happened to a large extent.

But do you think it is still a man's world?

Not totally. It seems to me that young men, my sons and their age group, are very helpful in ways that husbands used not to be, so I think that women have much less to complain about. Women are taken into account much more than they used to be.

Do you dislike what Doris Lessing called 'the shrill voice of feminism'?

[laughter] Doris has been very much got at by feminists who tell her that she ought to agree with everything they say, and being a very independent-minded woman, she doesn't agree with everything they say. I myself certainly get very irritated with feminist literary critics who tell me how to write my books, so that particular kind of shrill voice I dislike very much.

There is a high degree of social comment in your novels, and a concern with moral problems. Do you think that writers have a moral responsibility towards their readers?

I greatly admire writers like Proust and James Joyce, and they have no sense of moral responsibility whatsoever. I am more in the mould of the writer who worries about social inequality and the disadvantaged. I was brought up to think about these things, and to me it is a natural way of writing, to try and include in my fiction a sense of the world we live in and the injustices in it. But I don't go to extremes – I'm not a didactic writer like George Orwell. I am a bit of a moralist in that I am always looking around and wondering if things could be better; that's all really.

Your 1996 novel, The Witch of Exmoor, *is concerned with the possibility of social justice, touching on racial prejudice, greed, factory farming, and so on ... it is quite a bleak picture you paint in some ways ...*

That novel is a sort of satire really – it is meant to be more funny than bleak. It caricatures a number of ridiculous things that go on in our society. And I must say that I found the BSE business really shocking and completely fascinating. The whole saga was very much a product of greed, and it probably needs a real satirist, a Jonathan Swift, to deal with it. But I don't take a bleak view at all. I think that life is very much pleasanter in Western democracies for most people than it was twenty, thirty, forty years ago; not perfect, but better.

Has New Labour done anything to alleviate your concern about social inequality, or have you been disappointed in the government?

I was very disappointed to begin with because I felt it was all talk and photo opportunities, but they have in fact increased the minimum wage, and it was they who introduced it in the first place. I feel that I now have more faith in their long-term agenda than I did at the beginning. Gordon Brown is being very clever in redistributing wealth to some degree, something which is much needed because in certain parts of England poverty is absolutely endemic. Tony Blair says there is no north and south divide, but he should go and have a walk round South Yorkshire where my parents came from. It's dismal there, and the depression is emotional as well as economic. There are no jobs and life is quite without prospect for a lot of people. I can't stand the jargon of phrases like social exclusion, but nevertheless they do mean something. This government is at least beginning to try to bring people into society again. So I'll give them another term or two, and I wish them well.

According to Roy Hattersley, in a recent Guardian *profile, you rejected the idea of a fellowship at Newnham because the cleaning woman who made your bed every day and laid your fire would have been on your conscience for life. Some people might think this a kind of snobbery masquerading as egalitarianism...*

I don't think that's quite what I said to Roy. What I meant was that a fellowship was so seductive that if I accepted I could see myself never being able to get out of my ivory tower. I'm sure that if I had taken it I would never have written the novels, because I would only ever have seen the world with my made bed in it and my laid fire. I was really talking about the dangers of being cosseted to the extent that you can't see what the world is made of.

The heroine of your novel The Needle's Eye *sacrifices her own happiness 'for the sake of the children' – that well-worn phrase – and the novel deals in depth with the lovelessness that often passes for marital love. Do you think the moral problems presented in* The Needle's Eye *remain as relevant today as thirty years ago?*

Even more relevant, because fortunately it's easier to get divorced than it used to be. Sticking together for the children is not always a good idea. I know a lot of people disagree with me, but having been divorced myself, and being on excellent terms with my first husband, I just know that it was right for us and the children.

Some feminist critics, were disappointed in the message of that novel – they saw the heroine choosing self-sacrifice over self-knowledge. Would you write it differently today?

I do think today that she probably wouldn't have made that decision. But she was a slightly masochistic character actually; she suffered from guilt through having far too much money, so psychologically it was a perfectly convincing portrait.

I think it's fair to say that your novels are concerned with moral problems and ambiguities. Do you believe that there are any moral absolutes?

I feel very strongly about one or two issues – capital punishment, for example. I believe that the state should not kill. I also feel very strongly about cruelty; we should not ever be cruel physically to anyone, and we should try not to be cruel mentally either. The trouble is that life is full of ambiguity, and cultures are all relative.

What are your own guiding principles?

Oddly enough, one of my guiding principles comes from my Quaker background. I'm not a Quaker myself, nor even a believer, but I do agree with the Quakers when they say there is the light of God in every man. I do believe that there is arguably in every human being something good or redeemable, and if you treat people as if there is something good within them, you get on a lot better than if you treat them as contemptible or negligible. People become better if you believe they're better, and I suppose that's something I've clung to.

Your mother was a declared atheist, and your father a half-hearted Church of England adherent. What effect did this rather mixed-up religious background have on you?

My father did have quite a religious temperament actually, and in fact both my parents became Quakers later. And a lot of Quakerism does appeal, but it's a very sad matter to me that I can't believe in the Almighty God. Just occasionally I have moments of apparent certainty when I think that perhaps it isn't just black space, and I think this comes from the Quakers. They have no dogma, just the idea that you keep striving, and any kind of movement towards the spirit is considered good. The other day I was listening to Handel's *Messiah* on the way up to Sheffield, and I just *knew* that there was a God, and then of course as soon as the music was over, it was gone; but there are moments of profound conviction.

Do you pray?

Yes, I do, but I don't know who I'm praying to. If I think something bad is happening to the children, then I do look upwards and say, let it not happen, but I don't try to make bargains the way I used to.

As a child you managed to convince yourself that you had committed what you called 'a sin against the Holy Ghost' – where did this idea come from?

I just don't know. Children used to be tormented by hellfire a lot in those days, but I certainly didn't have that at school or at home, so I don't know where I got it from. It could have been an overactive imagination, I suppose, but I really did feel terrible for quite a long time. I had this sense of profound guilt and sin, which I never have now.

Don't you ever suffer from guilt now?

Only perfectly justified guilt, when I've done something awful, but I never feel that sense of overwhelming guiltiness.

Have you ever had any kind of what might be termed a religious experience, any sense of the numinous?

Yes, I have that from nature. If I go for a walk in the country, I can feel completely overwhelmed by the beauty of the world. There's a walk I do regularly in Somerset, up the back behind our house, and in the evening it is just amazingly beautiful. Your heart stands still and you feel that the whole world is full of design and beauty and order. It also gives you a sense of eternity because you feel that when you are gone this beautiful world will still be here.

Have you ever longed for what are usually referred to as the comforts of religion?

No, because I suppose I have always felt that people who seem very secure have probably been through doubt. The religious people I respect most, like the Bishop of Edinburgh, are rather full of doubt themselves. I know that there is comfort in the natural world so I don't want the comforts of religion. We must all find our own spiritual comfort where we can, and I can't find mine in any kind of creed or ritual.

The Guardian *reports that you have become detached from the world's vanities, refusing to be nominated for prizes, finding little interest in reviews and giving support to worthy causes. Is this the result of a happy second marriage with your husband Michael Holroyd?*

It always sounds better than it really is, because there are days when I'm absolutely full of rage and irritation and overwhelmed by petty, petty feelings. But on the whole I am much calmer than I used to be, and Michael has been a very good influence because he takes the longer view on things. When I get very upset and overwrought, he points at something just slightly beyond it, and that's very good for me.

You have described the times in which we live as 'a particularly pointless age'? Can you elaborate on that?

I must have said that when I was in a bad temper because I don't feel that at all. I actually think it is rather an exciting, positive and open age. I'm a disappointed optimist in that I thought by now we would have a more even society, that the poor wouldn't be so poor, that we wouldn't have sink schools or terrible children's homes. I thought all that would have vanished by now, and we would all be living in a much more egalitarian, happy, sharing world. That hasn't happened, but on the other hand it hasn't turned out too badly either.

INTERVIEW CONDUCTED FEBRUARY 2000

PAM GEMS

PAM GEMS

Pam Gems was born in 1925 and grew up in the New Forest. She began writing for the theatre in the early 1970s. Her first commercial success was *Dusa, Fish, Stas and Vi*. In 1977 *Queen Christina* received its première with the Royal Shakespeare Company, as did *Piaf* in 1978 and *Camille* in 1985. She is also author of *The Danton Affair* (1986) and *Marlene* (1995), and her play about the artist Stanley Spencer, *Stanley*, won the *Evening Standard* Best Play Award in 1996 and the Olivier Best Play Award in 1997.

Your father died when you were only four years old, an event which was
traumatic in its consequences for you. Do you have any memory of your father
or of his death?

Yes, I do. I was the oldest of three children and I have memories of him
playing with me. The next child, my brother, was asthmatic, and the baby
had a heart defect, so they were invalids. I remember how my father could
open a parcel without cutting the string, and peel an orange without
breaking the peel. When he was dying they put him into what we knew as
the workhouse, but the name had been changed to the infirmary. He was
dying yet we were not allowed in to see him because we were children, but
there was a kind nurse who would wheel him to the window and because
I was too small to reach my mother lifted me up so that I could kiss him.
One day he gave me a lozenge – he had nothing else to give me – and of
course it was hot in my mouth, and I was very puzzled as to why my father
would want to poison me. When he died he left me his war book which I
used to read in bed by the light of a candle – we didn't have gas let alone
electric light. I loved it because he gave it to me, but it was terrifying –
there were cartoons of the Germans as boars with traps on their noses
which ran with blood. I loved my father dearly, and no other man ever
compares.

Did you get on with your mother?

No, I was the cause of her downfall. You see, my mother was one of six
children, three of whom won scholarships, but it was not possible to take
them up because the family had to eat. Both grandpas went in the First
World War, so there was terrible poverty. My mother was very bright and
she went to work as a maid for the woman who had been the mistress of
Edward VII. When she heard my mother sing, she said that her voice must
be trained. Unfortunately my mother got pregnant after falling in love
with my father who was a soldier, so that was the end of her possible
career. She was very bright but she had no education, although she read
four books a week from the library and listened to classical music on the
gramophone. I was made the scapegoat for all this and I had to bring up
my two younger brothers because she was charring all day in the big
houses where they wouldn't even give you an orange. That early
experience has given me very strong feelings about class.

Your father's death caused your mother to become – in your own words – a melancholic, someone of whom you were frightened, who had to be placated. And yet you say that you and your brothers were somehow in love with her. Can you talk about what gave rise to all those conflicting feelings?

Well, there was the fact that she was a widow, and a younger widow than the widows from the First World War, so that in itself gave a little cachet – 'my mother's a widow, you know' – but it wasn't just that. Unlike me, she was tall and thin with blonde hair and pale blue eyes – frightening they were. We would hear people whisper in the street that she looked like Greta Garbo, and being very vain, she did her mouth and her eyebrows like Garbo. She was stunning, and during the war when she used to work as a hat-check girl in the local officers' club, she had many opportunities to marry – men fell in love with her all the time. But she never got over my father. She never even looked at another man, and we had to suffer for that.

Your grandmother had a very strong influence on your life, much stronger than that of your mother. Was your mother jealous of that relationship, do you think?

I think she was, but of course everything is so puzzling for a child. We would go to my grandmother every Sunday, three miles there and three miles back, the youngest in the pushchair, the other two walking. My grandmother fed us, she gave us what little money she had, and also clothes she had been given by the gentry. My mother never had a good word to say for her, nor indeed for my Aunt May who was married to a successful man in the army and therefore had money. It wasn't so much jealousy, more the poverty; it makes people full of hate.

You once confessed to neglecting your mother. What did you mean by that? And have you felt guilty about it?

Yes. I couldn't wait to get away, you see. I joined up partly because of that, partly because of D-Day plus 2, when a lot of the chaps who were billeted on us got killed, and I had a rage and joined up. But it was mainly to get away from my mother; the house couldn't contain the two of us. I was beginning to go out and have dates, and the atmosphere was diabolical.

Was she jealous of you when you went out with boys?

Yes, I think it had to be that. She was suppressing so much in herself. But we did adore her; it was like living with a goddess. And she was generous. The first fifty pounds she ever got, which was from singing at the night-club plus tips, she bought an upright Bechstein piano for my brother to play.

Did you mean it when you said in an interview I read: 'I was the plain daughter of a beautiful woman... my father's family were short and fat – I took after them, for which she never forgave me.'

It's quite true. I remember walking across the recreation ground with her one day – I must have been nine or ten – and she said, 'Walk in front of me or behind me. I don't want to be seen walking with you, you fat thing.' I also had cross eyes and glasses, which didn't help. [laughter] It was pretty hopeless.

But despite all you say, you seem to have been successful with boys...

Darling, you couldn't not be. I was fifteen when the war came. There were more men on the street than sand in the gutter. We used to get engaged all the time and wear the rings around our necks – I had five or six – and if one got killed we threw that ring away.

You were born into extreme poverty and now, through your own talents and hard work, you are successful and relatively affluent. Is childhood hardship character-building, would you say?

I don't think you can generalize. Some people go under, others thrive. As a parent you try to protect your children, but even in a happy, affluent, contented family you can't ever offer complete protection. I'm inclined to think that success is far more dangerous, more corrupting, than hardship. One of the reasons I have never gone in for publicity, which I could easily have done, particularly when I was younger, is because I thought it would be bad for my children. I've seen the children of people who are famous, and they don't do well.

Would you have been a very different person if you had been born into the sort of family whose houses you and your mother used to clean?

I think I would have been ghastly. I'm a bad enough snob as it is, simply from growing up in the kitchens of these people. The woman whose coachhouse my gran lived in had six indoor servants, not to mention two or three outside – imagine, all those servants for one woman! And when there were guests, my mother used to have to crawl in with no shoes and pads on her knees to light the fire so it would be glowing by the time the people woke. I've done that too. Crawling is not nice. I hated these people though I also thought they were wonderful, because they smelled so nice. My Aunt Ruby was private maid to a woman who was known as the Rose of Devonshire, though she was a drunk by the time we knew her. She used to take my aunt to Biarritz, and give her wonderful, handsewn silk underwear, which of course Ruby never wore. It was just brought out to be shown from time to time. And this while we were starving. Nowadays poor people can live off the detritus of others – there is so much. But in those days people had nothing except what you could poach and what you could grow yourself. I'm inclined to believe that a lot of the food was a good deal safer, but we were all so ignorant. We were brought up on white bread and sugar. People said, 'Oh, you can't give her meat, it's much too strong for that little stomach.' We were quite uneducated.

You won a scholarship to a grammar school and even working-class locals thought it was a waste for someone of your background. How hard was it for you and your family to take up that scholarship?

I had two chances at the scholarship, because my birthday was on 1 August. Technically I shouldn't have been taking it the first year, but I was bright and my headmaster put me forward. But I was left-handed, and my writing in ink in those days was very bad, so when the letter arrived saying that I had won the scholarship, I thought, well they've made a mistake, and I just put the letter up behind the clock and I don't think we looked at it for a couple of days. Then my mother read it and she said, memorably, 'Well, you can't go of course, but you have had the honour of winning.' Fortunately she mentioned it to the relieving officer – that was what we called the man from social security. He was very nice, one of those lost-generation men, crippled in the war, and when my mother told him he said that I must be allowed to take it up. He went to the British Legion, and they paid for my uniform and my books. I will always be grateful to them. So I went to grammar school, thanks to the fact that my mother was so frightened of this middle-class man, the relieving officer. When you were working-class in those days, you were very obedient, often for fear of losing your job. You did as you were told.

How did you fit into grammar school? Did you feel you were in the wrong place?

Fortunately there were a number of scholarship children in each form. We had the mark of Cain, of course, and the teachers treated us differently, and we weren't asked to the class parties. I remember a girl called Amy May, the daughter of the headmaster – she was in my form and she palled up with the scholarship girls, partly because we were brighter and more fun, and her father hated this. He was a very cruel man. But some of the teachers were helpful and gave up their time to teach us how to say 'how now brown cow', instead of 'heow neow breown ceow', which was realistic of them. They knew we'd never get on in life, speaking as we did.

As a child did you feel any bitterness?

No. I think you're so full of life, and there is so much to do, that there's no time to feel bitter. I didn't realize until many years afterwards that I had been quite stressed.

You say, 'I never wanted to become a writer; I always was one.' Did grammar school strengthen this self-belief?

I don't think it needed to be strengthened. I wrote my first play at the junior school, when I was eight. Again I was lucky, for I attended a wonderful church school with a headmaster who'd grown up in Stratford-on-Avon and who spouted Shakespeare all the time. My first play was a fairy play for the seven-year-olds, and I remember being extremely angry because Mrs Collins, their teacher, cut some lines, and I didn't realize you were allowed to do that to the author. I've never got over it. [laughter]

Writing came naturally to me – it wasn't something I showed off about any more than I showed off about my fat legs.

Is the creative impulse every bit as strong now, or is it diminishing with the passage of time?

Sometimes when I look at something that I wrote ten years ago or so, I think, 'God, what energy!' and I don't think I have that now – it's almost a kind of sexual energy. But I come from a family who mature late, and I think that perhaps what I lose in energy I gain in profundity and wisdom.

Why did you choose to study psychology at university? Did you expect it to be a help in creating characters?

I didn't know what psychology meant. I went up to university to do English, and when I got there the queue was round the block. I met and talked to another girl who was ex-navy like me and she told me they were going to sling a lot of people out at the end of the first term because they were oversubscribed. We service people were used to swinging the lead, so we went to find a short queue, thinking we'd be sure to get in. The shortest queue was psychology – it only had four people not counting us. 'What's it about?' I asked her, and she said, 'I've bugger all idea,' but we signed up for it anyway.

And having signed up for it, did you enjoy it?

No, I hated it, because we were all more stressed by the war than we knew. I had been in the Fleet Air Arm where we lost far more in training than we ever did in combat. We used to put the aircraft up, then the ceiling would come down and they'd go into the nearest hill, partly because they were kids, partly because they were in bad aircraft – the good aircraft were on carriers. So we were quite stressed, indeed a lot of us were very damaged. Besides, I didn't agree with Jung or Freud, who were the gods there. It was all middle-class, Jewish, Viennese, *fin-de-siècle* stuff. But I was a farm girl; I had stood and watched the horses being served, and I couldn't subscribe to the Freudian basis of RIS, repressed infantile sexuality. Come off it, not where we came from. Also we had to visit loony bins, and they were terrifying then. All the boys used to faint. I'm afraid I have kept my hatred for a lot of psychiatry.

At one time, as a wife and mother, you apparently kept open house for troubled adolescents who had fallen out with their families. Was this as a result of your interest in psychology, or was it a purely human response?

It was simply because I'm a country peasant at heart and I always thought it was better to have the children under my roof and keep an eye on them. We had a huge house in Kensington when my children were adolescent, and they always had friends who were in trouble. One girl came for a night and stayed for a year, and brought her friend who was also heavily into drugs. In fact she died. I had such compassion for adolescent boys. I know it sounds rather doubtful, but having two younger brothers, both invalids, I get very affected when I see boys in trouble. Adolescent boys have more problems than girls. Girls know who they are; boys are never quite sure.

With all these troubled adolescents in the house, did it ever occur to you that you were perhaps venturing on dangerous territory? Were you never confronted by an angry parent, for example?

Oh yes, more than a few times. One woman got very upset because her daughter ran away from school and ended up with me, and I had to front for her when the police arrived. And somehow it all became my fault because I had given her house room. What was I supposed to do? Turn her out into the street? I also remember one upper-class boy whose family would be well known to you, and once he got into drugs and started on the needle, they couldn't get rid of him fast enough, they simply didn't want to know. But of course aristocrats don't rear their own children; they're reared by servants.

Turning to your plays, you are a feminist and your work has often shown women as victims, fighting for independence in a male-dominated world. Yet lately your tone has changed. Although you were never a man-hating feminist, you now actually see men as victims in the sex war, riven with fear and even hatred of women. Can you talk a little about how this has happened and what you think it means for the future?

That's a big question. I think the problem started perhaps with the industrialized nations of the world moving from heavy industry to light, with the result that medieval notions of honour being invested in male strength began to go out of the window. By the end of the nineteenth century the typewriter had been invented, and women with their smaller fingers suddenly became viable commercially, and that has gone on and on through the computer age. When neo-feminism became a force and women began to assert their rights, they started to encroach on areas which had up till then been exclusively men's. I know this sounds patronizing, but I feel a deep, almost maternal angst about men. I have three wonderful uncles, two wonderful sons, a wonderful grandson, and two wonderful brothers, and I do not believe you can have a society where men are demoted in this way. The breakdown of marriage has threatened the old notion of a man as the head of his family. It's a man's nature to be protective, and when he's denied that he becomes baleful and angry, and I think it's wrong. I believe in the family and I believe in the protection of the family, that women have a right to have children in a protective situation. I lost my father and I know from bitter experience what it's like to be without a father. A father is a lovely idea, and by God, let's save it. But to do that we have to have men who have self-respect and good jobs.

What does being a feminist mean in your terms nowadays?

It means what it always meant for me – fairness for every citizen, male or female, young or old. It doesn't mean to say that women have to wear suits and behave like men. It means that every commercial building should have a crèche in it, because men and women should see their children. The old commuting thing where men left early in the morning and came back late at night meant that they might as well not have been fathers at all. The reason I love Steven Spielberg – though I'm not a fan of most of his films – is that I'm told he has a crèche with glass walls at his place, so that the people who work there can keep an eye on their children. That's the mark of a civilized man.

You claim not to have known there was a middle class in Britain until you joined the Wrens, on the outbreak of war. Until then in your experience there had only been upper and lower classes. Are you still very much aware of class distinctions?

Well, legislation and time and habit are chipping away more and more. For example, when I was a child people spoke in an absolutely ridiculous way, a bit like some of the royal family speak now, you know, those tones which seem to suggest, 'I'm very cross with you.' Even the received English of the newsreader in the 1940s and 1950s, now sounds slightly ridiculous, so we're modifying all the time to the point where the 'in' dialect is now Essex. But while we still have a formalized aristocracy, that is to say, dukes and earls and the royal family, then we are still pegged in. We still have the public schools which were really created as breeding grounds for people to go out and run the empire and to govern. And that ethos still exists, that some are naturally born to govern.

Speaking, I think, of modern times, you say that the true artist addresses a classless society. What do you mean by that?

Laurence Olivier put it very well when he said that drama is an affair of the heart. To me, it's quite simple: to write plays is to pierce people. Descartes said that feeling is thinking, and that is my criterion. You can become a politician and try to change things by putting an amendment, or you can be really subversive and write a play. It was fashionable in the 1970s, when there was all that pseudo-Marxism, to claim that plays don't change anything. Well, if they don't, I might as well shoot myself because I've been wasting the last thirty years of my life. The thing about drama is that it subverts; you can change the climate of opinion by telling jokes, or by using sexuality, suspense, or any of the other tricks of the trade, providing you manage to keep people sitting forward. Once they sit back you might as well give up. I am an anarchist by nature, in the true sense of the word, not in the sense of blowing things up, but by devolution of power from the centre.

Do you agree with Tony Blair's recent claim that the class war is over?

No. The dear boy is being misled. However, he would be right to say that the upper classes no longer dominate in the way they did a hundred years ago. They have a certain cachet in certain quarters, but that's all; real influence and power they don't have.

You were well into your forties before you realized that – as you put it – to expect sexual loyalty of a man was to expect an abnormal man. Was it a shock and disappointment to discover this?

I suppose it was. First loves are romantic loves, and you pledge fidelity, but then of course you get wise and you realize that your own energy gets deployed in rearing the children, that desire wears off, and that everything changes. I have known a man and wife to be completely faithful, sometimes in cases where they don't have a very strong sexual urge, for example, but I can't believe that passion can last for seventy years. In cases like that they just become loving companions.

You have had a long and stable marriage to your husband Keith, but you think that women should accept that total fidelity to one woman is impossible for a man. How hard has it been for you to accept that?

Intellectually not hard at all, but emotionally it is rather different. As Lady Longford said when she was asked if she ever thought of divorcing her husband, 'No, never, but I have often thought of murdering him.' That's my feeling too.

You've always said that it is the deception you hate... why is the deception worse than the infidelity itself, would you say?

I've tried to think this one through, and I believe it may be something to do with the secrecy. If your husband comes back and says, oh, I saw Jeannie today, she was looking well but she's having trouble with her left toe, I would say, fuck off, I don't want to know about your bloody mistress, she's boring anyway. On the other hand, if I see my husband going out with a certain look on his face and I know he's up to mischief, I resent it.

Do you accept that some women might prefer the deception?

I think a lot of women would rather not know, because once you know you're exposed to murderous feelings, however noble you try to be, however much you might want to rise above it.

You express tolerance of male lust, but contempt for male dishonesty; yet you say of Stanley Spencer, about whom you have written the play Stanley, *that his mistake was to try and bring the truth of his art into his private life. Is this a change of mind, or a resigned acceptance of the way of the world? Why do you think he was mistaken?*

Because he made an awful mess of it. It proved that whatever he did, it was wrong. It was naïve and innocent of him to imagine that the standards of total truth that have to apply in art could apply in real life. We're all sinners according to Christian belief and indeed most other beliefs, and I've had to learn, as I suppose every woman has had to learn, and not a few men, that what can't be cured must be endured. And, you know, if the price of fidelity is to have some boring guy under foot all the time, well, who needs it? We live so long now, which makes marriage for life even more impossible. People used to die by the time they were forty.

But why do you think women feel so strongly about sex? A woman can be married to a man for twenty or thirty years, have children with him, a happy life, security and everything, but when she hears that on a trip to New York he bedded another woman she goes out of her mind...

I've known friends who have done just that. I just hope attitudes can change.

The point is it often means nothing to the man – his willy goes up for one night and then it's forgotten about. He still loves his wife, in fact probably he feels even more loving to his wife because he betrayed her...

Yes, the little present is nicer than usual, and everybody wins. On the other hand, when everything is invested in the marriage, women are very vulnerable.

You have always been fascinated by the business of lying and truth-telling, and the dilemmas surrounding them. You say: 'We live on lies – we'd kill each other if we didn't lie.' Could you elaborate on that perhaps?

We lie to each other all the time. We suppress information, we act out different parts to different people – our children, our business acquaintances, our close friends. And it's a loving thing. You can't go into a room and say to your dearest friend that she looks flabbier than ever, even though that may be what you think. Of course, there are vile lies, vicious lies, but not so many; most people lie to protect themselves and to protect others.

What about the Jonathan Aitken lie? What about the Jeffrey Archer lie? Are they to be morally condemned, or are they just examples of frail humanity?

[laughter] Oh, you do ask difficult questions. Their behaviour is quite disgraceful, but I have no desire to wag the finger at those two boys. I mean, everybody knew at the time that Jeffrey Archer was lying. Why else give two thousand quid to a tart? It's so silly. You know what I think? I think he won his libel suit and got the five hundred thousand pounds because that judge was effectively saying to tarts, 'Just don't even think of it.' If Jeffrey Archer hadn't won, then every tart could go to the *News of the World* and say, 'I was with such-and-such a judge last week.'

In your thirties you realized that you had always been attracted to men who were rather repressed, the kind of men who grew up in the big houses you worked in... 'England,' you say, 'has always been in a mess sexually, we send our boys away to school and all that.' Have you analysed what it is that attracts you to this type?

I think that my attitude to men is extremely maternal, being the older sister with two younger brothers. My bowels turn over for some men, particularly when they've been damaged psychologically. It's worse than a physical ailment which you can more easily survive. But when your soul has been damaged by a cruel mother, it's quite different. I had a cruel mother, and that can be worse than being hit, you know.

Your youngest child was born with what's normally known as Down's syndrome, but you prefer the word Mongol, believing that to be called one of a race, however inaccurately, is better than being a syndrome. Do the rest of the family agree with you about this?

I don't think they have feelings either way, because we never refer to her as either. She is Lalla, our daughter, sister, darling one.

You speak of your daughter only with great fondness, but caring for her must have made life more difficult for you as a mother, especially when you found that friends deserted you. How did it affect you and other members of the family?

The children were always very protective of her; it seemed to be natural for them. For me it was difficult. I think it was Bob Bolt who said, in *A Man for All Seasons*, 'People move towards the light and they move away from the dark.' And anyone who has had a tragedy will know that people stay away, because they feel awkward, they can't do anything, and they don't want to feel fed up. I experienced all that. But what it did for me, in some ways, was excellent, because I was a sentimental southerner and it put steel in my soul. I got quite angry and it became a question of 'love me, love my Lalla'. Or else. I would deliberately take her out with me, even though she was incontinent, and when she wet the floor, I would just watch how people behaved. I became very anarchic in the popular sense of the word, because I couldn't hope to be middle-class or grown-up or intellectual, simply because I had this barmy kid. She took up a lot of my time, but it was wonderful.

If amniocentesis had been available, would you have taken the test?

Yes, I probably would have. And I would have aborted, yes.

You say religion helped, though you are not an orthodox Christian. Did you have a religious upbringing?

Intensely. I come from a town with a priory church which has been there for nine hundred years, and I went to the church school. My brothers were choirboys, so I heard oratorios and organ music throughout my childhood. The church and the music were unbelievably beautiful, but I could never quite work Christianity out. The Father and the Son, yes, but the Holy Ghost I never quite got.

I've read somewhere that you believe in reincarnation... is that a serious belief?

I think there's some evidence for it. I used not to believe in it, but now I have an open mind about it. I myself have also had many psychic experiences, including out-of-body experiences. After my son David was born, for example, I was in bed with flu and I suddenly found I was floating out of the window, and when I looked along I could see bright green grass growing in the gutter, and then suddenly I was back in my body. I said nothing for a week, and one day I mentioned to Keith that I thought the gutter might be blocked, and sure enough when he put a ladder up, the gutter was full of grass. I went up after him and it was exactly as I had seen it when I floated out of my body.

Are you afraid of death?

Sometimes I am surprised that I am not more afraid, and I think that has something to do with being a gardener. All this cyclic reduction from compost to flower to dying seems very natural to me. Of course, like everyone else, I fear illness and being put in a position where you can't behave with dignity.

Stanley Spencer is underrated and unpopular, you believe, because his icons are Christian, and you think that people are tired of Christian iconography – 'After the Holocaust, nobody believed in anything any more,' you say. The Christian God may be unfashionable but he does rather refuse to die, wouldn't you say?

I think that's true. People are generally post-Christian until there is a tragedy or a crisis. You know, it's like when you go through a ward of wounded soldiers – they're all crying for God or their mother. We can't throw God away because *in extremis* that's where we go for help. So there you are. But there is so much about orthodox Christianity that I don't care for. It's such a miserable religion, and so anti-sex. Catholicism is worst of all. Why be celibate? The idea of denying the body that God's given you, assuming you believe in God, simply doesn't make sense to me. The Hindu religion is far better. If we're going to enshrine our lack of knowledge about the Great Out There in some kind of formal belief, why not make it nice? What's wrong with hedonism?

Do you find it strange that we have elected, and apparently continue to admire, a prime minister who is an avowed and practising Christian?

No, I think it's a damned good thing. It makes him a good boy, makes him live by the rules. When I grew up you had the church and class structure which made for a stabilization in society which no longer exists. People nowadays are Macbethian; since there's no God they can do as they want, and the devil take the hindmost. Young people say to themselves, I've only got one life, so I'll get as much money as I can, and bugger everybody else.

You're a passionate defender of the family but see it as an endangered species. Why are you so worried? Is it not possible to redefine and reshape family units?

There are many groups who are like families but who aren't blood related, and they can be very successful, whether they are gay couples or sisterly communities – nuns, for example. But there is something very special about the blood relation; it's inimitable, and in times of real stress there's a bond that isn't the same if there isn't a blood relationship. I'm influenced by the fact that I come from the New Forest and in that area I had about forty relations – I miss that, very much. And I actually think it's the natural primate way of living, something we have to try and establish for the sake of our psychological health.

You accuse extreme feminists of having taken individualism too far and in so doing bringing about the destruction of the family. How could this have been prevented? Wasn't it made inevitable by easier divorce, equal education and vastly improved opportunities for women, including reliable birth control? You surely wouldn't want to deprive women of these freedoms...

No, and that's a very good question. You see, I think these are stages that we have to come through. Progress is always by the pendulum. Women started off trying to model themselves on men, but now it is becoming fashionable to have babies again, and settle for domesticity. It's all right to stay at home now, but not of course if we are just to put our brains to sleep for ever; we constantly have to find new ways.

When you were younger you spoke about the writer's desire to change the world. Is there any of that idealism left, would you say, or has something else taken its place?

I don't know how honest to be about that. To write at all you have to be very arrogant. In my *métier* you have to say to people, give me money, sit down, shut up and listen to me for two hours. You tend to justify it by saying, 'I want to change the world, I want to make it a better place,' but as I get older I realize it isn't true, because as a writer you always disappoint. Ibsen disappointed first the left and then the right, and I always disappoint the feminists who never get what they want from me.

What would you most like to be remembered for, first as a writer, and then as a person?

I particularly like several of my plays, and I would like to think they had an afterlife. As a person, I'm a fat lazy old thing but I would like people to remember me as always having an open door and a pot of tea. I can't ask for more.

INTERVIEW CONDUCTED DECEMBER 1999

VICTORIA GLENDINNING

VICTORIA GLENDINNING

Victoria Glendinning is a novelist, biographer and journalist. She was born in 1937 and educated at St Mary's Convent School in Wantage and Somerville College, Oxford, where she read Modern Languages. She became editorial assistant on the *Times Literary Supplement* in 1974 and published her first biography, *Elizabeth Bowen: Portrait of a Writer*, in 1977. This was followed by biographies of Edith Sitwell, Vita Sackville-West, Rebecca West, Anthony Trollope and Jonathan Swift. Her novel *Electricity* was published in 1995.

*You describe yourself as having been 'a thin, dark, difficult and secretive child'
who suffered pain and injury in silence – no running to parents or siblings, even
when your collar bone was broken. This is so very different from the behaviour
of most children as to be almost incomprehensible. What lay behind this attitude
of secretiveness and awkwardness, would you say?*

I would say that I wasn't very successful at being a child. It's a career like
any other, and most children understand quite early on that the job of
children is to please adults. I didn't try to please adults, so the adults
weren't very pleased with me. Also I had a cruel nanny, something only the
English could have, and she used to shut me up in a cellar. I sometimes
had trouble eating, and if I was sick, she would then put me with the sick
in the cellar and tell me I had to eat it before I got out. Small things like
that made me feel that grown-ups were not much to be trusted. And this
in the context of a very comfortable middle-class family – I cannot plead
deprivation.

Why do you think the nanny was so cruel to you?

How would one know? I think it was probably pathological. She covered
up all the mirrors, for example, because little girls should never look at
themselves in the mirror, so she said. Various things like that were
designed to bring me down, so it took me a little while to get confidence.
But it's very good having an unhappy childhood, because life gets better.

Did you report the nanny to your parents?

Children don't do that. They think it's normal, they think that's what
nannies do.

*Apart from the nanny, how else do you remember your childhood? What was
the relationship with your parents like, for example?*

My father was a very good man, a Quaker, a banker and a philanthropist.
He was always very busy so he wasn't home much, but when he was there
I really liked him. I don't know what love means in that context, but I liked

my father very much and I continued to like him in adult life too. What I admired about him was that he was always doing something. If he wasn't doing his professional work, he would be doing embroidery, *petit point*, or he would paint in watercolours or he would be planting his lettuces. He used his life very well.

What about your mother?

My mother was very pretty at a time when if you were pretty you didn't bother going to university, and her tragedy was that she was very clever, cleverer than my sister or me. She had read all the classics, she could do *The Times* crossword in ten minutes, but she never did anything with it, except wait for my father to come home. All her energy was wasted in a domestic setting, which made her slightly difficult. My sister's experience was perhaps different, but I probably wasn't the daughter my mother would have wished to have. I was thin and dark and she would have liked somebody much more bubbly and sociable, a little girl whom she could have dressed in little pink frocks.

Do you think that one ever really gets over the wounds inflicted in early childhood?

You do up to a point, but they remain little pinholes on the surface, and occasionally some event or some relationship can get into the pinhole and reactivate the anxiety or grief or uncertainty, whatever it is. But mostly it doesn't occur, because you are so grateful to love and be loved and to have a good time and do your work.

It is almost a clichéd observation that pain and unhappiness in childhood actually seem to inspire writers. Do you think that if you had had a carefree, happy time then your creative side might not have developed in the same way?

That's very hard to say. I have a lot of natural energy, so it would have had to go somewhere, but I think I might have done something different perhaps. Yes, I think there is an instinct to write down what you don't quite understand, in other people's lives and in your own.

Do you think that we inevitably repeat the pattern set by our parents, at least to some extent, or can the chain be broken if we set our minds to it?

The chain can be broken, absolutely. I think if your experience of childhood was strange enough, you almost go the other way completely. I relived my childhood with my children, that is to say I feel I had my real childhood in my children's childhood. What is terrifying every now and then is to find yourself making a gesture, or doing something, which is just like your mother or your father. I think there are genetic patterns and conditioning that you can't escape. When we were adolescent my mother used to go to bed before we did, and she used to annoy me by always plumping up the cushions in the drawing-room and saying, remember to turn the lights out. I have found myself doing exactly the same.

Your father was Lord Seebohm, a descendant of Frederic and Henry Seebohm, historian and ornithologist respectively, and both famous writers in their fields. I wonder why you did not use the family name professionally instead of taking the name of your first husband, particularly in view of your feminist feelings.

For a start you never think your own family is famous. Of course, I knew about grandfather and Uncle Henry and all that, but I didn't connect them with any advantage to myself whatsoever. They were simply the authors of books on the shelves. And when I got married and started having my children, I disconnected myself from my family quite a lot. I was Victoria Glendinning then, and having started as Victoria Glendinning, I felt I had to go on being Victoria Glendinning, even though I have been married not once, but twice again. It's like not being able to give a racehorse a different name once it has begun to win a few races, so Glendinning remains my work name. I have now had so many names – Seebohm, Glendinning, de Vere White, O'Sullivan – that I answer to almost anything. Victoria is what I regard as my name, and the last bit is a flag of convenience for whatever purpose.

The Seebohm family were Quakers and your mother was part Jewish, yet your education was in a High Anglican convent, complete with all the trappings of Catholicism: incense, veils, confession and communion. Whose idea was this and why was it thought suitable for a child from your background?

Two things. My parents thought the nuns would be kind to children, which of course they weren't, and they thought St Mary's Wantage was one of those OK girls' schools, the equivalent of an OK public school for a boy. They thought I would meet nice girls there, and that it would be a happy place.

At what point in your growing up did you reject all institutionalized religion and cease to believe in God as other than a metaphor?

When I discovered the opposite sex. When I was at the convent I used to have terrifically religious experiences. If you are surrounded by good religious art, or even bad religious art, and inspirational sermons from inspirational priests, and you say your prayers, and you're bursting with hormones and you are at the foot of the cross, religious experiences are very easy to bring about. Then I realized that with boys, after dances in the holidays, I was having experiences which produced much the same effect. I thought perhaps sexuality was another way of doing it, and somehow it seemed more interesting.

So you replaced God with sexuality?

Yes, with being in love, which is somehow transcendent; it is sexuality made golden or magic or somehow special. Now I think more and more that you must take any gate you can into any magic you can. There is something to be got from everywhere – I would certainly go to a Buddhist church if I was in a Buddhist country.

With the passage of time, are you leaning more towards religion?

Not in any sense of believing that Jesus Christ was God, or that God has any identity, or that God gives a damn about me if he is there. But sometimes one can harness the power to endure something, or to help something to happen. It's not exactly the power of prayer, but I do believe if you are thinking deeply or carefully about somebody it does make a difference to them too. It's the old *Hamlet* thing: 'There are more things in heaven and earth, Horatio,/ Than are dreamt of in your philosophy.'

In the second week of your first term at Oxford, you were invited out by your tutor, Nigel Glendinning, and began an affair – something for which you have said, 'in this politically correct age he would doubtless be accused of sexual harassment'. Did no one mind in the 1950s? Was it not frowned upon by Somerville College?

Somerville College were worried that I wouldn't finish my degree. Indeed they were not certain that I should be allowed to finish my degree if I married him – that was all they bothered about. But as for sexual harassment, that had not been invented.

Your father accused Glendinning of ruining your life. With the passage of time, and after you became a parent yourself, did you come to have any sympathy for your father's feelings?

I had sympathy for his feelings, but I think he went about things in a completely crazy way. He should have thrown us together, he should have invited Nigel Glendinning to every family party, to every theatre, every cinema, and then maybe I would have seen the light. But he went about it in the old-fashioned way of separating us, like Romeo and Juliet.

Did your parents' attitude or that of the college have any influence on your decision to marry?

I can't remember, but I think I wanted to marry Nigel. And my parents' displeasure naturally made me want to defend him. The college was not so important because in the end they let me complete my degree anyway.

In your novel Electricity *you end a chapter with an unforgettable sentence: 'And so I married, and fell off the edge of the known world.' Was that your own experience when you married Nigel Glendinning, I wonder?*

It is so funny that you should pick out that sentence, because after I wrote it in my house in Ireland I got a complete block and didn't know what happened to my heroine, didn't know what happened in her marriage. I wasn't able to write any more for about two months until suddenly a cinema reel started going in my head again and I saw exactly what happened. But whether that was anything to do with me getting married, I really don't know. What happened was that I had a baby at once, another baby, another baby, another baby... and for quite a long time I was very contented. I fell off the edge of the known world only in that it changed my life.

You had four children to whom you were both devoted, and many years of happiness, yet the marriage eventually ended, and you said once that it may have been this very preoccupation with the children, so much time spent with them rather than alone with each other, that brought about its erosion. This is perhaps an unwelcome idea to other devoted parents... do you still believe it to be true?

Yes, I do, because the relationship between two people can easily get eroded. Actually my mother, to whom I should give credit, was always saying, 'Why don't you and Nigel go off on holiday on your own?' and we always said that we preferred to be with the children. That was because when we were left alone we had nothing much to say; all the energy was going the way of the children. Couples should remember that the first relationship is between themselves. My mother also used to say that a woman is either for the children or for the husband, she can't be for both. In her own case she was for the husband in that during the war she went to be near him in his barracks, and we were left somewhere else. I think probably I was for the children. Every woman will know what you mean if you ask her if she is a woman for the husband or a woman for the children. And it is always a tricky one to have to decide.

In Sons and Mothers, *edited by you and your third son Matthew, he described his 'cracking up', which you call his depression, and you point to its connection with the long-drawn-out break-up of your marriage to his father. He has made a complete recovery, but if you could have foreseen this effect, would it have prevented the split?*

If you ask divorced people: 'Would you have embarked on that path if you had known there would be all that blood on the carpet, all the agony, all the hurt?' many would say no – even those who have made happy second marriages. When you hear about a 'compatible' divorce or a 'very amicable' divorce, don't you believe it. There is always pain, there is always grief, somebody is always the loser, and it doesn't stop. However happy and right the second relationship is, you are leaving behind a mess.

Do you think staying married for the sake of the children causes more problems than it solves?

I think it depends how you do it. If you can do it with a good will and make it work, that's fine, but not if it's all resentments and silences and nobody touching anybody. Two people living in the same house as if they were living in separate houses is a very bad example of lovelessness. A child does not like to see no love.

How important is love in your life?

Hugely. I have learned to be a whole person by loving other people; absolutely, without a doubt.

You were educated at expensive private schools, but your boys went to the local comprehensive. Was this a difficult decision? Did you ever have any doubts about it?

No, though I've had doubts about it since. At the time, I thought if I'd sent them to private schools, what we call public schools, I would have been sending them out into the world with a terrible impediment, in that they would only be able properly to relate to the people who had been at those same sort of schools. I wanted my children to be able to relate to all kinds of people, to be able to move in and out invisibly in all kinds of society. And I think they can.

I have read that your boys encountered what you describe as 'some of the usual problems' – which must have been testing for you as well as for them. It is often said by parents who send their children away to boarding school that the experience is character-forming and therefore worth any pain and suffering involved. Did you tell yourself something of the same vis-à-vis *the local state school?*

No, not at all. I was just very pleased they were able to come home for tea. Of course, there were some difficult things, like big boys in the playground waiting to get you, but that's part of life. At least they were coming home. I certainly didn't send them because it was going to be so bad it would build their character; I was sending them because I thought life would actually have a better unity if they had breakfast at home, tea at home, supper at home, and coped with life in between. There was no idea of hardening them up, no. I don't want to harden anybody up.

Would you have treated a daughter differently, do you think?

I don't know. I wouldn't know how to bring up a girl. I would love to have had a daughter, but I might have loved her too much. I'm very keen on my sons' girlfriends.

How do you feel about Tony Blair's choice of school for his sons?

I think he is completely within his rights, but it just makes it rather phoney that he is leading the Labour Party. I would have thought the first thing we ought to do is somehow make our education equal. I don't know how you would do it, but I don't like the argument which goes: I see there is privilege, I do not like privilege, but while there is privilege, I am going to avail myself of it. I think that's pretty weak, and I don't respect it.

You must have been delighted by Labour's overwhelming victory at the last election, but many supporters are now expressing disappointment in the government's performance. Do you share this feeling?

I'm terribly disappointed. It's partly because 'education, education, education' seems to have gone on the same, and housing doesn't seem to be any better either. And ethical foreign policy, don't make me laugh! Then little things come out in the papers like the fact that we are still manufacturing torture instruments in Birmingham for export to other countries. You see, as soon as people are in office they lose all their integrity, and attention is paid only to how to get in next time. Yes, I'm disappointed, but I suppose it was childish to think it would be different – though we all did.

You have described writing as being 'illicit like a lover, not a duty'. Can you elaborate on that?

I never have thought I am a writer in a kind of holy, special way. Writing is something I do in combination with many other things, and it is rather anti-social. When you are writing you remove your care and attention from the other people in your life, so it is rather like stealing the time, and I find it suits me that way. If I were given all the time in the world, and a blank sheet of paper, and all the day to write in, and a country cottage to do it in, I wouldn't be able to write a thing. I can only do it because I think I've only got two hours, and then my mind is wonderfully concentrated, and there is a kind of focus and excitement.

Is there suffering involved in the writing process, or does it come easy?

What doesn't come easy is sitting down to do it, so I would say I suffer in the beginning. I'm like a dog walking round and round its basket and not lying down. What I'm frightened of is this big concentration I can go into, which is quite exhausting when I come out of it. It's like a tunnel where I see nothing else but what I'm doing, but it's difficult approaching the tunnel, and it's also quite difficult emerging from the tunnel.

You've always maintained that life is more important than art, but your art has played a very important part in your life. Do you think there are dangers in elevating art too highly?

I think there's a danger in elevating second-rate art too highly. With the great emphasis on access to everybody of artistic endeavour, which is correct, there is a lot of bad art that gets treated as if it is good art, and I still think there is a difference between them. To praise everything equally is to treat everybody as small children doing their little cut-outs at school.

I think art will always find the place in society that society wants it to have.

You are celebrated for your biographies – Elizabeth Bowen, Swift, Trollope, Vita Sackville-West and others – so I am interested in your views on biography as an art form. Bernard Malamud famously said: 'The past exudes legend; one can't make pure clay of time's mud. There is no life that can be recaptured wholly; as it was. Which is to say that all biography is ultimately fiction.' How do you react to that?

I quite agree. I am completely off biography as a genre. Having worked on it for a quarter of a century, I now think it is an extremely dodgy exercise. The more you know about anything the more you see the mountains behind the mountains behind the mountains. I don't believe in it any more. The kind of authoritative tone that reckons to give you the whole picture of somebody's life is a complete cod. Equally, if you're going to say, well, I don't know but it might be like this, or it might be like that, then although it's not a complete cod, it's a piece of self-indulgence. A lot of it is quite pointless. I also think Americans who write huge collations of every single piece of information that could ever come into the world about an individual are wasting their time. Biography has had a very good run in the last thirty years, but it has done what it can do. Everybody in the field now has this feeling that the game is up, and you cannot say any more, this is how it was. You only have those bits of paper, those letters, diaries, documents that have been preserved, and of those you're trying to make a whole. How do you know that all the really interesting ones haven't quietly been torn up? How do you know that there isn't a box over there that you haven't seen?

Doris Lessing put it slightly differently in saying, 'There is no doubt that fiction makes a better job of truth than biography.' Do you think she is right?

I think they are different truths. There is something called fictional truth, which works in a novel. For example, if I were to put our encounter in a novel, it would be dead on the page if I put exactly what happened. I would have to give it some form, some slant, and then it would be true in a different way. But it would be fictional truth which is not the same as historical truth.

Your novel Electricity *was written while your second husband Terence de Vere White was dying of Parkinson's disease. One critic has said that the book read like 'a marathon of grief'... do you see it like that? I know your husband's death hit you very hard and both your parents died shortly before in a car crash...*

I didn't see it as a marathon of grief, it was more like an alternative world for me. I used to go into the world of the novel, which was very real to me, and though I didn't perhaps know it at the time, it was a sort of strategy for survival.

Did the experience of such anguish bring about any change in your attitude to religion... was there not a desperate need to believe that death was not the end?

There was no change in my attitude to organized religion. I think when somebody dies, you feel at the beginning that they have not quite got away; they are still around, and then after a bit you think, yes, they've got away now. You can of course talk to the dead and they will answer because you know what they would say if they were there, so in a way it's easy, and often places have the spirits of the people who used to be there. Life is more than it seems, but it's nothing to do with religion; it's a much wider, more diffuse, vaguer thing than a Church of England bishop would claim.

In Electricity, *after Charlotte's husband dies, she wonders where he is now and says: 'I believe, now, that he is in the hands of the Power that people glimpse and then diminish and distort into rival notions of God.' Does that reflect your own view to any extent?*

Almost exactly, yes. I don't know what the Power is; it's just that you go back to where you came from.

And we don't know where we came from?

Of course we don't. That's the mistake we make all the time. People keep saying, it's like this, and then others say, no, it's like this, and then they have a battle and people are killed. Nobody knows why it is.

The other constant refrain in Electricity *is: 'Nothing lasts, nothing is for ever.' Is that something of which you have been painfully aware in your life?*

It was one of Terence's phrases... nothing is for ever. And it's such a good motto for life because in good times it keeps your feet on the ground, and it also works in bad times because when you're very low you can think this is it, but it isn't. Everything moves along, nothing is for ever. I have it written up above the fireplace in Ireland.

Are you by nature an optimist?

I'm quite a happy person by nature... my glass of wine settles at a sort of cheerful contentment. Naturally, if there are genuine problems and life is horrible and difficult, then I am as shaken as the next person. But left to myself I'm not unhappy.

You have lived for long periods in Ireland and you have a house in Cork. We know from your biography of Trollope how involved he became with the country and the people, making them the setting and the characters of so many of his novels. Have you ever been tempted to follow Trollope's example?

No, because I think in Trollope's day the Irish were seen as a sort of tribe that you could use in that way. It would be rather like an English person writing American dialogue – you might get it wrong. And although I am fairly at home with and in the Irish psyche, I wouldn't presume to be able to write as an Irish person, certainly not from the inside. Cultural differences are very subtle.

Terence de Vere White's novel, The Distant and the Dark *(1973), is said to take the middle ground with respect to the Troubles, and it satirized the ignorance of so-called observers. Were you able to form your own opinion of the Irish Question and did you come to share your husband's views, or at least those expressed in his novel?*

Well, he was Dublin born and bred, so he would have had an endless amount of references and bits of information in his genes, in his bones, in his blood, which I wouldn't have, so I don't think I can compare. He was the sort of man who would have wished for a united Ireland while loathing everything the IRA did and stood for. Most Irish people would wish for a united Ireland; it's just the way you go about it that divides people. I've certainly gone through phases of being more lenient, if you like, to the Republicans, and phases of thinking they were untrustworthy, and I'm sure that happens to everybody else that has anything to do with the place. And I have very little patience with Unionist bigotry and Unionist bullish stubbornness which seem to me deeply unattractive. Only you have to keep hoping...

In Sons and Mothers, *Matthew tells us that although his stepfather was very much loved, his death came as a relief to everyone who had watched his suffering, not least to you. A man who loved to write and to talk was trapped inside a disintegrating body. If he had begged to have been allowed to die earlier, how would you have reacted?*

He didn't. He was a Catholic, raised a Catholic, and even though he had lost his proper faith, nobody who is raised a Catholic can believe in suicide, because it's so embedded in you that life is a gift from God. He did say to me once, 'I suppose I should kill myself, but I can't.' His morality wouldn't have let him.

But what would you have done if he had said to you, 'I want to go now...'?

Well, he did say, 'I wish I could die, I wish I could die...'

But would you ever have agreed to help him die?

No, I couldn't have, I couldn't have. With my mind, of course, I believe utterly in euthanasia in those circumstances. It's so easy to believe it in your head, yet when actually you're faced with it, with somebody you love, you can't do it. At least I couldn't.

Your son speaks with total admiration of how you behaved at that time. While mourning your parents and caring for your dying husband, you finished off the

Trollope biography and continued to write your novel, whilst remaining sane throughout, at least until after your husband died. Was it the writing that sustained you?

I don't think so. The writing was just one of various strategies. When you have something very difficult to do, you do it, and the elastic is stretched tighter and tighter and tighter, but you still do it because you have to. I was very lucky that I had the writing. I found it all very difficult, and I think I never really recovered from it. The elastic snapped back, but not quite all the way.

After your husband died, you experienced a period of solitude. When your sons were growing up and life was very busy and fraught, it was solitude that you longed for. When you got it, did it disappoint... in the way that something you want very much is sometimes a bit of a let-down when you get it?

Good question... but no, it was heaven. I went on my own to the Irish house, which is very remote, for quite a long time. At times I couldn't see people at all, I just couldn't, and then gradually that changed and I began to go back into the world quite happily. But I needed that solitude very much.

Your relationship with Matthew has not been easy. He says in the book that he put you through hell, but in your own contribution to the book you do not reproach him with this. 'There is no love without pain,' you say, and that is the message of the book. Is that an absolute truth, would you say? And if there is no pain does that mean that the love is not real?

I think it means it's not quite so intense and engaging. If there are no difficulties, no pain, and everything is smooth, then it's probably very sensible, rational, good behaviour, but if in fact you get quite close then you start sparking and the closeness can turn black on you. If you want to have a very serene, easy life you would never get very close to anybody; there are times of such happiness, but you have to pay for everything, there's no free lunch. I've got plenty of friends, close friends, that I've never fought with, because there is no need – we're not emotionally dependent on each other. But with lovers and husbands to whom one is very close there are always fights.

You once said in an interview that one consequence of your non-judgemental view of life is that you don't feel enough guilt. 'I feel remorse,' you said, 'I'm sometimes sorry I didn't do things better, but I don't feel guilt.' But in Sons and Mothers *you confess 'huge guilt' as the reason for not talking to your sons about the break-up of your first marriage. Were you 'in denial', as they say, when you made that first statement?*

I didn't deny it, I just probably forgot. You see, I don't feel that guilt all the time; it's only when I come to focus on the time when I was getting out of the first marriage, and I think, my God, that was terrible, yes. But I don't have it on me as a daily weight. I wouldn't even think about it from one year to the next.

In connection with that book you expressed the opinion: 'Mothers and daughters can seemingly rabbit on endlessly about one another without difficulty, however fraught the relationship.' Isn't that quite an odd remark from a feminist?

You seem to have a funny idea of feminism, as if everything about a woman has to be positive. It's like being a Communist and never being able to criticize policy, because you have a kind of totalitarian vision. Well, I don't have a totalitarian vision of women. I think there are as many bad women as there are bad men. I am a complete feminist in the sense of equality, and thinking that anything a man can do a woman can do, except lift a piano, but it doesn't mean they are let off all their sins and crimes, for God's sake.

At the end of his chapter in Sons and Mothers, *Matthew describes how his father, Nigel Glendinning, came to share Christmas dinner with the family for the first time in twenty years. It seemed to me that there was a note of hope there for some kind of reconciliation ... did you feel that too?*

It could have happened; it didn't happen.

It could have happened?

It didn't happen.

In an article you wrote for the Daily Telegraph *you described the older reader as someone forever bemoaning the decline in standards – 'the more distinguished the elder the more extreme his distaste'. And yet in the same article you say, 'I know people – women mainly – well over eighty, who have more fun and who are more open-minded than people a quarter their age.' How do you reconcile the two views? Are women somehow exempt from 'old-codger syndrome'?*

I don't think they're so bad at old-codger syndrome. If you do hear people complaining about the decline in standards, it tends to be blokes. Women are actually more anarchic at heart than men, and don't mind the rules being broken. They keep the rules when it suits them, but they don't make them; men do. And therefore when rules are broken and standards fall it's men who mind. Women are more adaptable, more flexible.

Coming back to religion, if I may, would you say that your Jewish blood has had any influence on your life?

My mother was half Jewish, something she dealt with by not telling us about it until we were adolescent. There was some family matter that she had to talk to us about, and she said, 'We don't need to make much of it, darlings, but you'd better know that grandfather was Jewish.' My sister and I were actually thrilled and went about being very Yiddish indeed for quite a long time. I was overawed when I heard that my grandfather and his brothers had carried cyanide pills in England in the 1940s in case there was an invasion. We had Jewish cousins, of course, and I knew that some of their families had experienced tragedy in the war, so it has made history closer to me than it might otherwise have been. But I think my attachment to my Jewish blood now, in the year 2000, is really more romantic than anything else.

You once said: 'My Jewish bits are my best bits.' What did you mean exactly?

Being a Quaker and English and a Protestant... while they may all be decent things, they are a little flat and too much in good taste. I like a little bit of flash, and being part Jewish just breaks up the pattern nicely.

I'm interested in your view that God is just another metaphor... presumably God is a metaphor for good as opposed to evil, an opposition universally recognized regardless of religious allegiance. Is that what you mean by metaphor?

I think probably God and the Devil are the same person. It is a wonderfully comforting construct of the human mind to split them apart, saying, this one is good, we like him, and this one is bad, we don't like him. But this sort of binary system of the universe is rather childish. It's a bit like electricity – very good if it's a nice heating system, very bad if it's lightning or a bare wire that's going to electrocute you.

One thing that puzzles me is your refusal to be judgemental 'about good and bad' – you say you simply can't handle it. I don't think when you said this you were referring only to books, but even if you were, is this a sustainable position?

I think I said originally I was not judgemental about the actions or behaviour of the subjects of biographies I've written, because I don't think that's the biographer's job. It's more interesting for the reader to think 'Wow!' or 'Good God!' or 'How could he *do* a thing like that?' without my underlining it or pre-empting it. It is my job, however, to explain if possible how the subject came to be the sort of person he or she was.

Are there any moral absolutes, would you say?

An awful lot of 'moral' absolutes are culturally determined. They would be different in the same society at different periods and in different societies at the same period. My own moral absolutes would be large and vague – to do with kindness, hospitality, truthfulness; in which, however morally absolute I may consider them, I naturally fail daily.

Terence de Vere White said of you that you lacked 'the tragic sense of life', which sounded like a reproach, but you think it is 'morally better to be contented when you can'. Are you sure you meant 'morally'?

Yes, I did and do mean 'morally', because discontent spills over on the people round you and poisons their air as well as your own. Also discontent is often connected with selfishness or greed or childish expectations of life. But I did say 'when you can'. Sometimes circumstances are intolerable and should not be tolerated. And clinical depression is another matter.

In Dante's Inferno *there is a circle of hell specially reserved for those who are wilfully sad... is that perhaps something you would go along with?*

I don't know if people are really 'wilfully sad', though sadness or melancholy or discontent can become a habit it's hard to renounce. And then the person feels 'happier' feeling sad, because it feels normal.

What might be called 'the tragic sense of life' has inspired men to great art, whether in painting, literature or music. This can't be morally wrong surely?

Of course that's not morally wrong. Creativity that comes out of being unhappy or having a tragic sense of life is turning dross into gold, a marvellous alchemy and a permanent gift to the world. Nevertheless, there's a price to pay, for other people. Living with a genius is notoriously difficult.

In 1996 you married Kevin O'Sullivan, and in March of this year you wrote to your husband's former wife, Shirley Conran, rebuking her for libelling him and threatening her with 'hell to pay' if she did it again. Am I right in saying that this was rather out of character for you?

It wasn't out of character to write the letter – I write all sorts of things when I am upset or enraged, to get it out of my system. And I would leap like a tiger to defend people I love. But maybe what was a bit uncharacteristic was actually posting the letter.

Do you regret the exchange of letters?

I don't regret writing the letter, or even posting it. I very much regret that Shirley Conran in her desire for personal publicity sent it to the newspapers, and then gave interviews about it. Mine to her was a personal letter.

In an interview you told Hunter Davies: 'Since childhood I've had an amazingly good life, which got better all the time. If I go soon, then fine. I always like to leave the party early.' At your present age, and in a new marriage, do you still think it would be fine to go soon?

No, I don't want to go just yet – there are too many things I want to do, like making another garden. I made a good garden in North London, which I left when Kevin and I got married. I have a garden in Ireland but it's much too far away to give daily attention, and Kevin has a small terraced garden in France. I think I should swap the Irish house for an English house, and have a green field site, like a paddock, in which I would make another garden. I probably wouldn't move out of London altogether, but from Thursday till Tuesday I would like to go and see to my lettuces.

INTERVIEW CONDUCTED NOVEMBER 1999

SIR NICHOLAS HENDERSON

SIR NICHOLAS HENDERSON

Nicholas Henderson was born in 1919 and educated at Stowe and Hertford College, Oxford. His diplomatic career took him to Athens, Vienna, Santiago and Madrid before he was appointed ambassador to Poland in 1969, where he remained for three years. From 1972 to 1975 he served as ambassador to Germany, from 1975 to 1979 as ambassador to France and finally as ambassador to Washington from 1979 to 1982. His publications include a volume of diaries, *Mandarin* (1994), and *Old Friends and Modern Instances* (2000).

You had what might be described as a Bloomsbury childhood, having been taught by Marjory Strachey, the youngest sister of Lytton. To what extent did you imbibe the Bloomsbury philosophy, their interest in ideas, their individualism?

I think I derived two things from my very young association with Bloomsbury. One was an interest in beautiful things, a love of being surrounded by them and not despising them or having what I would call a philistine attitude. The other was a readiness to discuss everything – ideas and behaviour and habits – without prejudice and without conventional reactions. Nobody was excluded from such discussions.

The Bloomsbury set had a remarkable lack of inhibition – as you say, they were able to discuss anything with complete freedom, no matter what its shock value. Did you admire these traits and did you adopt them into your own life?

At the age of ten I don't think one is able to admire something like unconventionality because one doesn't at that stage really know what's conventional and what's unconventional. I simply assumed that everything was discussible, without inhibition, and that people who dismissed subjects without being ready to analyse them were unthinking and in a sense inhuman. I think I did adopt these principles into my life. For example, I wasn't brought up in any religion or subjected to any sort of religious education. My parents were modern and didn't have me christened, and from my early days I heard things discussed around me and assumed that this was a reasonable thing to do. I have certainly never felt inhibited from talking about everything, expressing a view, not necessarily aggressively, but also showing a readiness to listen.

Would you say the Bloomsbury experience equipped you well for later life?

I don't think my Bloomsbury experience equipped me for the profession I later adopted, though in a sense it shaped the company I kept for pleasure, the world in which I lived privately. But I didn't lead at all an unconventional life, although I suppose you might say a free spirit helped me to analyse without prejudice the culture in the various countries in which I lived.

During the summer you went to school at Charleston, the house on the Sussex Downs where Vanessa and Clive Bell and Duncan Grant lived. You say you were influenced for the rest of your life by the beauty of Charleston. Can you elaborate?

I spent several summers there when I was very young, and I imbibed not only the beauty of the Downs and the landscape but the fact of having pretty plates, pictures on the walls, painted furniture and a wonderful garden. I somehow felt that these things became part of me, that I took them into my body and spirit from those early days.

Patrick O'Donovan described your background as being 'the sort of high-minded liberalism usually attributed to Hampstead'. Do you plead guilty? Do you see what he meant by that?

Patrick O'Donovan was of course the complete opposite. We knew each other as undergraduates at Oxford, but he was a very devout Catholic from Ampleforth, and in those days he was very conservative, very right-wing, whereas I was sort of left-wing. I think he regarded that as rather peculiar in someone, and he presumably attributed it to the world of Hampstead. But I must for the sake of accuracy and truthfulness point out that my father didn't at all share the Bloomsbury ethos. He was a professional economist, a very clever man, and he was very disapproving of Bloomsbury, and in fact he put a stop to my being educated by them and I was sent to boarding school. From then on I didn't have anything which could remotely be called a Bloomsbury upbringing.

What were the reasons for being left-wing at university?

In 1936, anyone who was at all sensitive and, say, between the ages of sixteen and twenty-five would have found it difficult not to be left-wing. There was terrific unemployment in this country, considerable social discontent, and there were already terrible threats from abroad – Mussolini in Italy, Franco in Spain and Hitler in Germany, all of whom you might say in rather crude terms were right-wing. It was very rare to find someone of what I call any understanding of the underdog spirit who was anything other than 'left-wing'.

In recollecting your time at Stowe you call yourself 'a boy of immaculate insignificance' – and this claim, you say, is made without false modesty. How did you arrive at such a judgement? Did you feel yourself to be inferior to the other boys?

I was inferior in several respects but by far and away the most important was that I had medical trouble. I got TB and I ceased to be able to use my left shoulder and arm. I had been very athletic and keen on games, and suddenly I was unable to play them, and for boys that matters. Because of my physical trouble I felt inadequate and odd and different, which I was. But I also had other limits. I wasn't particularly interested in books as a boy, in literature or poetry; I much preferred philistine things and so I was, you might say, backward.

You say that Stoics were encouraged to attach importance to the visual senses. How did this shape your life, would you say?

I think it's true that nearly all boys at Stowe take in the beauty of the park and also the monuments and statues. And my generation were influenced a great deal by the attitude of the headmaster, J. A. Roxburgh, who had a great influence on everybody of his time. He thought it was wrong for pupils to focus too much on the traditional things like games, and he encouraged interest instead in architecture, art and music.

You have said that the proper study of all diplomatic practice is man, the understanding of some of the deepest instincts of human nature. What skills and special qualities are asked of the diplomat, would you say?

I think you have to have quite a rigorous intellect to analyse where your country's interest lies in some particular problem, but I regard it as absolutely essential also to have some sensitivity about what really matters to the other side. This is a quality I think you are born with. I believe that in all great negotiations, not just diplomatic, but also business and even military, you have to have this. Some of the best diplomacy is carried out by people who have very much a quiet approach. Oliver Franks was extremely good; he never boasted, and he never revealed his hand until he'd found out what other people thought.

You write in the introduction to your book Mandarin *that ambassadors are apt 'to be subjected to alternating currents of awe and hostility, curiosity and contempt'. Is that something you accepted with equanimity, as being just part of the job?*

You have to accept in that particular profession that a great deal of work will be drudgery, where you have to do routine activities for which you may be despised, and that there are many moments which are totally inglorious. But that I do believe is an extremely important part of public service in the realm of international affairs.

Has diplomacy changed over the years?

You are raising one of the biggest subjects there is. The great change in diplomacy was the invention of the telegraph in the middle of the nineteenth century, and from then on of course things have continued to change. You might argue that the relevance of the role of the man on the spot has reduced, because prime ministers and foreign secretaries fly all over the world now. But you could equally say the opposite. If a prime minister has arrived somewhere, he often doesn't know where he is, who the hell anybody is, so he's got to be briefed, and the man on the spot is the only person who can do that. So in some respects the role of diplomat has become more important. I personally don't think it has diminished significantly, since all the problems that are going on in the world now – how to deal with Russia, what is to be done about the Middle East, the G8 meeting, what about the underdeveloped world – they are all in a sense diplomatic problems. Kissinger used diplomacy and foreign policy exactly interchangeably, and I think he's right. Diplomacy is the way of achieving your ends in foreign policy, but they are deeply interlocked.

Diplomats tend not to work in the limelight. Has that suited you, or would you have preferred a more public role?

That is the great difference between being a politician and a diplomat. A politician must be happy in the limelight, and I don't think a diplomat should want the limelight or seek it. I myself wasn't really equipped for a role in politics of which the limelight is the main ingredient. When I was young I thought I might have liked it, but I now believe it is a much more dreadful career than I thought when I was young. It's certainly very difficult to find a politician who reaches the age of sixty-five and feels he has had a happy time with his career.

Your book about your time in the Private Office at the Foreign Office makes clear the power and influence which a private secretary can have on foreign affairs. Did you relish that power?

Well, power is a loaded word, a very difficult word to start using. I liked to feel that one was wanted and what one contributed was of value. Having said that, I attach enormous importance to the Private Office, and to private secretaries in this country, who are different from those in any other country I know.

What would you say is the difference between influence and power?

Influence is a means of effecting a result, power is actually achieving a result. I think you could say that William Beveridge exercised power by bringing about the Health Service, but there were many people who were advising and influencing Beveridge on how to do it. The achievement of power is actually very rare. People talk about going into politics because they like power, but it's very rare that a politician actually does anything that wouldn't have been done otherwise, or is entirely due to him.

You were Assistant Private Secretary to Ernest Bevin, a man whom you greatly admired. Which qualities do you remember in particular?

His down-to-earthness, his sense of reality, his capacity to lead, his contempt for triviality and passing whims of fashion, and the fact that when he went abroad, or even when in London, he could say, 'When I speak, I speak for Britain,' and nobody could question it. He was marvellously unbiased, and he didn't have any inhibitions or hang-ups about people who had come from a different background. Even in those days, 1945, 1946, there were quite a lot of people who took the line that those who had been at public schools had no right, or certainly less of a right, to be in prominent positions. But I remember Bevin talking about his time as Minister of Labour throughout the Second World War and saying that when young men were needed to fight our battles in the air or at the front, the public-school boys were the first to come forward. I shall never forget that.

In 1994 you were rebuked for publishing your account of an ambassador's life in Warsaw, Bonn, Paris and Washington. The Foreign Office considered that the book portrayed Mrs Thatcher as being nervous during the Falklands War. Earlier, in 1989, you had sought and been refused permission to publish extracts from your diaries. Why did you later decide to go ahead?

I thought the banning of my book was outrageous and unjustified. I didn't believe that my book was in breach of the Radcliffe rules, and I thought the people in the Cabinet Office were wrong to reach that interpretation. I didn't like being accused of betraying the public interest, and so I wrote to them, telling them what I thought the Radcliffe rules really meant. And four or five years later, by which point I had complied with the stipulated length of time since ceasing to be a career official, I went ahead with publication.

You have suggested that Harold Wilson regarded all Foreign Office people in the same light, as sort of 'upper-class twits', a description from which you exempt yourself on account of your claim that your class and Harold Wilson's are essentially the same. What is the basis for that claim?

The basis is that my background is absolutely the same as Wilson's, and I feel rather indignant at your implied suggestion that it is not. My grandfather, my father's father, started life sweeping the floor of a small bank in Aberdeen, and he ended up as chief executive of the Clydesdale Bank in Scotland. My father won scholarships to school and then to Cambridge, and that is my background. I am very much against all this class talk, by the way.

What did you think of Harold Wilson?

It would be perfunctory of me to give a judgement on him or his career because I only saw him superficially. He was personally always extremely agreeable and amusing company, as long as you talked about all the things he was interested in, but I didn't admire him as a public figure. In my view he was the person who started this passion for spin-doctoring and thinking all the time about eye-catching initiatives. But he is much maligned and rather discredited now, and you very rarely hear anyone saying he was one of the great prime ministers. I don't myself think he was either, but he had some good human qualities.

You mention that Mrs Thatcher disliked the Foreign Office as an institution, but liked many of the people there. How did this dislike manifest itself?

She said that to seek to have good relations with a country in the abstract was pointless. What was needed was to pursue a particular objective, that there was no virtue in being on good terms unless it was directed to some particular issue. I disagree with that profoundly. I think having a basis of good relations is something on which you build up credit with a country and on which you can draw at some stage when you need help or understanding. I don't think she ever quite appreciated that. She was also fond of trumpeting something as a triumph, as she did with negotiations over the European Community. Nothing could be more likely to cause trouble; indeed scoring off people is the worst way of conducting diplomacy because they come back later and they won't trust you in the same way again.

You compare Ronald Reagan to Mrs Thatcher, suggesting that they had no sentimental or guilty feelings about underdogs. Did you come to this conclusion from private observation?

Yes. They may have recognized at some level that certain people needed help, but on the whole they thought it was up to people themselves to make the best of their lives.

In 1979 when you were ambassador in Paris you reached the age of sixty and retired from the foreign service. In the valedictory dispatch which it is customary to write on retirement, you strayed way beyond the normal bounds and chose to write about the decline of Britain and its reputation abroad. The dispatch was leaked and subsequently published in the Economist *which gave it a much wider audience than it might otherwise have had. First of all, why did you eschew the standard dispatch?*

Because I was so overcome by a sense of despair at the position my country and countrymen had reached. By 1979 there was a lack of self-confidence, a lack of dignity, and I felt that this affected and jeopardized all attempts to conduct a proper foreign policy. But the corollary of what I said was that part of our trouble was our failure to make up our minds about our relationship with the other countries of the European Community; and those two things went together in my mind.

Do you know who leaked the dispatch, and why?

No. All I know was that the *Economist* told me they had received many copies of it.

You said in your dispatch that Britain was 'in decline, poor and unproud'. Did you come to regret saying any of that; did you come to revise your views?

No. I am sure I was right to say what I did. It may have been a transgression of the conventional habits of ambassadors on retiring, but I felt that circumstances required something rather different. I never felt any regrets about what I had written at all or the fact that it had become public knowledge. In fact, I think I should have been more resolute. At the time I was a bit worried about having gone too far; I don't feel that now. Interestingly enough, I wrote something similar ten years later and published it in book form, but because that was published and not leaked, as it were, it received absolutely no attention whatever.

What is your view of Britain now, its standing in the world, its moral leadership?

I have no right to say. . . I'm not in a position to have a view on that.

But you don't hold office now…

No, but I can't judge what they think of us in Peru. I have only one view that is relevant or pertinent at all, and that is that I think we have made a terrific mistake in not defining our role in Europe more clearly and committing ourselves more wholeheartedly to taking part in what I regard as a very important international achievement: the creation of a strong and reunited and pacific Europe. I am rather ashamed that we haven't made that commitment.

Leaks are in the news once again, and clearly they are not new. They are usually designed to damage someone. Who was the target in the leak of your dispatch, do you think?

I don't think there was a target really. It was leaked because people felt that I had said something that should have been known beyond the narrow confines of the Foreign Office. This brings me to a point which is perhaps worth making. I always thought it was a great waste that one served all over the world and took a lot of trouble to come to a view about the country and one's own relations with it, and yet this information would simply be read by someone in the appropriate department and then put away. I felt it was a terrific waste of knowledge, information and wisdom, and I still think it to this day.

After Mrs Thatcher took up office you were brought out of retirement and appointed as ambassador to Washington. Did this appointment turn out to be the high point of your career?

When Peter Carrington rang me up and asked me to go to Washington he told me I should know that I wasn't the first choice. I guessed it was Ted Heath who was first choice, but obviously he felt he couldn't accept it. Yes, it certainly was the high point of my career because Washington is the most important place. It doesn't follow from that, by the way, that you can make all that much difference. I always felt the only place in which I made a difference was in Poland. My wife and I felt we were a lifeline for the Poles to the Western world, a world to which they aspired but couldn't join. Sometimes a small post can be extremely important and difficult, more important really than a great one.

There were rumours at the time that your appointment to Washington was a rather unpopular one. Was that difficult to deal with?

I don't know whether it was unpopular. Michael Palliser, who was at the time Permanent Secretary at the Foreign Office, told me not to believe any of the talk and assured me that everyone there at any rate was very pleased.

You greatly took to America and Americans … what was it that so appealed to you?

It is so difficult to generalize about America – it's a country of enormous differences and variety. But my job was perhaps made easier by the fact that there is much less inhibition and difficulty in conveying your government's views in America than anywhere else. I spent a lot of time in Congress, trying to persuade them of our position, and they never regarded it as an impertinence. In France, for example, you couldn't have done that sort of thing without being accused of interfering in their affairs, but Americans have no sense of that. They are so open and forthcoming and ready to listen.

You followed Peter Jay as ambassador. Was he a hard act to follow, would you say?

I don't know about that. He certainly had good contacts and made a lot of friends at a high level in Washington, there's no doubt about that.

Was he a help to you when you took over?

He wasn't a hindrance, but I don't think a retiring ambassador can ever particularly help a successor.

You obviously crossed swords with Mrs Thatcher over the conduct of the Falklands War. How serious was that disagreement?

It was a great problem. It was essential to have US support in arms and intelligence for our cause in the Falklands. We simply had to have America with us. America had all sorts of difficulties about supporting us – a lot of people, for example, believed we were looking after our colonial empire. Besides, South America was part of their hemisphere. They also wanted to be sure that we weren't being aggressive, that we would try, and continue to try in every way, to bring about a negotiated settlement; and that's where the principal difficulty arose. Haig, who was Secretary of State at the time, and Reagan were determined that before they could come out and support us we must show that we were ready for a satisfactory negotiated settlement, and Mrs Thatcher never thought it would be possible to have a negotiated settlement. She was perhaps right, but it was difficult to persuade her that one had to go through the motions of trying to reach a settlement of a negotiated kind in order to get the Americans to support us.

Referring to a crucial meeting at Chequers in 1982 you describe how 'the PM veered the whole time towards being uncompromising, so that the rest of us found ourselves under attack from her for being wet, ready to sell out, unsupportive of British interests, etc...' Which view do you think history will vindicate, yours or Mrs Thatcher's?

I don't know what history is going to say. It's quite difficult to put oneself back into the atmosphere of the time, an atmosphere which was very different in America from here. Pym, who was our Secretary of State at the time, flew over to Washington twice, and each time he was astonished by how different it was from the feeling in London. Trying to bridge that gulf was the problem, and to hold the Americans with us.

Professional diplomats are famed for sitting on the political fence. Now that you can risk a little indiscretion, what view of New Labour would you express, and how do you rate their performance so far?

I don't actually agree with the preliminary to that question. I never felt one was inhibited from having a view of one's own simply because one was a diplomat. One may have to be quiet and rather reticent or tactful in how a view is expressed, but one could always express a view. There is no doubt about it that Blair has achieved an incredible worldwide renown and admiration, but I am personally disappointed in what I regard as a somewhat hesitant policy towards Europe.

Can you recall a time when you felt uncomfortable in your diplomatic role?

Yes, Suez. I was serving in Chile at the time, as far away from the scene of the crime as it was possible to be. I asked my wife, Mary, 'Don't you think I ought to resign?' and she said to me, 'Have you lost your sense of humour? How could anybody take your resignation remotely seriously? How could you think it could make the slightest difference?' But though I couldn't do anything about it, I certainly was deeply ashamed of the Suez episode.

You were evidently a close friend of Donald Maclean at one time. How did that come about?

I met Donald Maclean in Washington, when I went there in 1947. He had already been for some years in the chancery there, and I got to know him very well. I saw him again from time to time in London until he disappeared behind the Iron Curtain.

Did he strike you as strange?

Only in retrospect, once I knew he was involved in a completely double life. I had had some suspicions of extreme left-wing leanings which certainly emerged over the Korean War. He was then head of the American department in the Foreign Office and he complained to me bitterly about a minute I had written in a file explaining why I thought we had to take up the cudgels on behalf of the UN over Korea. Later he came to a small dinner party I gave and again the subject of Korea came up. He was drunk and he became extremely aggressive and outspoken – you might say pro-North Korean, pro-Communist. So when he disappeared I wasn't as surprised as a lot of people, and I was also pretty sure where he would have gone. But as a man he was very agreeable, human, humorous and extremely cultured.

Did your association with Maclean involve a career setback?

No, although it emerged I had been a suspect for a number of years when they were still looking for the third man. I had been very ill again in 1955, and I was in London recuperating at the time, and it was then I was subject to a very long interrogation by Scarman of MI5. During the interrogation it was revealed that I had been under observation for some time and that they had been tracking me.

According to your daughter, you are not much given to shows of affection. Do you regard this as a personal strength or weakness?

I don't know what she's talking about. I can't imagine why she should say that since I spend all my time with my grandchildren. It's true I don't go in for a lot of kissing in public; I usually regard kissing and holding hands as a sign of deteriorating relations.

I could find no reference to religious faith amongst your writings. Are you religious at all?

No. I am not a believer. On the other hand, my wife is Greek Orthodox and I was married in the Greek church, and my daughter was christened not only in the Church of England but also in the Orthodox Church. So I am not against other people having faith.

What do you think happens when we die?

It's just death, like animals dying.

And we're gone...

Oh, yes.

So there is no hell, no heaven...

Goodness me, no. You don't believe that, do you?

I'm not sure ... aren't you afraid of death?

No, of course not. Death is a most natural phenomenon.

When you're in pain, when you have difficulties, do you pray?

No, never.

You were knighted in 1972. How important to you was this formal recognition of your service?

I don't regard it as a sign of anything except upholding the tradition of someone who is serving abroad as British ambassador being called Sir somebody rather than plain Mr. That's all – it doesn't make any difference otherwise.

But you must have been proud of your achievement ...

No, I don't think so. The only time you might say I made a difference, and I certainly don't want to make much of it, was over the Falklands, over keeping the Americans on our side. And I certainly got no form of recognition for that.

Are you dismayed when you look around the world today to find it a very far from peaceful place, that man is no nearer being able to get on with his fellow man than in the past? Will it always be so, do you think?

I'm a Hobbesian. I regard the life of man as nasty, brutish and short. I don't think human nature is going to change. There will always be conflict, rivalry, envy, pursuit of personal gain. It's not that I'm a pessimist, but nor am I complacent. There are lots of things about the modern world I hate, but I am not against the modern world. You simply have to pick the things you like, and avoid the things you don't like. I hate hearing it said that all the young are ghastly; I don't feel that. They are different, and of course they don't know about the past, but I like a great deal about them.

INTERVIEW CONDUCTED JULY 2000

MOST REVEREND RICHARD HOLLOWAY

MOST REVEREND RICHARD HOLLOWAY

Richard Holloway has been Primus of the Episcopal Church in Scotland since 1992. He was born in Glasgow in 1933 and began his theological studies at Kelham College in 1948. After a break for national service in the army 1952–3, he left Kelham in 1956 and served for two years as secretary to the Bishop of Accra before completing his studies in Edinburgh, London and New York. He was ordained deacon in 1959 and priest in 1960. He served parishes in Glasgow, Edinburgh and Oxford before becoming Bishop of Edinburgh in 1986. He is the author of many books, including *Beyond Belief* (1982), *Another Country, Another King* (1991), *Dancing on the Edge* (1997) and *Godless Morality* (1999).

You were born in Possilpark in Glasgow, an area synonymous with slums and extreme deprivation, but your background seems to have been more 'respectable working-class'. Would you agree with that?

It's quite complicated actually. It was certainly respectable in the sense that my parents tried to find work and they looked after us. But my mother had been orphaned at the age of eight and brought up in Quarrier's Homes, and that to some extent marked her. My father was unemployed a lot in the 1930s but he was a hard-working wee man. So yes, respectable poverty, certainly not chaotic poverty.

You seem to have been a child well loved by both parents... is that how you remember it?

Yes, I think I had unconditional love from my parents, particularly from my mother. She was a very expressive woman and even now I can remember some of her endearments. She was a large, emotional, combative, charismatic sort of person. My father was a quiet, kindly man, except when he had a drink in him, and then he could be quite voluble.

So there's no self-pity, no need to look back in anger...

Not for myself, but I do look back in a kind of anger at my mother's childhood in which the political and economic circumstances created a horrible rejection and poverty which scarred her. Although she was a fighter for her children, she was in a way quite a vulnerable woman.

You say she was the driving force behind your escape from very humble circumstances and that she was so fiercely protective that you never felt insecure. Yet as an adult you confess to feeling a bit of an outsider. When did this begin and why?

The archaeology of these things is actually quite complex. It must have started fairly early on in my adolescence. I started going to church only at the age of twelve, and coming from my kind of background I always felt that most of the people in church were probably more educated, more middle-class than I was, so I was perhaps a wee bit on edge. Then I was sent to England, to Kelham Theological College which is run by a religious order, and I suppose a kind of self-consciousness about my Scottish background crept in. I have come to believe that a lot of people feel themselves to be more outside than they imagine others to be. Even people at the heart of the establishment often feel strangely as if they are looking in on things. I don't know where this feeling comes from; all I can say in my own case is that although I've been loved and surrounded by friendship, I've always had a strange sense of not quite belonging.

You described your mother as intemperate, robust and reckless of speech, qualities which you say you have inherited. What has been your father's legacy to you? Can you tell me a little more about the 'small, quiet man' your mother married?

Whereas my mother could be quite opinionated and had angles on matters that punched into her own insecurities, my father was completely unjudgemental about people. He was a kindly accepting man and, though I know this is a cliché, I don't recall him saying harsh things about anyone. I would like to have inherited a bit of that. There was something about him that was quiet and steady and accepting, and I now see that he was a much stronger character than at the time I thought he was. I never disliked him, but as a wee boy I wanted a big romantic kind of father, a great soldier figure, and he was a typical wee Glasgow man, probably a foot shorter than me by the time I had stopped growing. Looking back I can see there was an extraordinary strength in the man, and unlike a lot of small men, he didn't have a chip on his shoulder.

You were born into the Scottish Episcopal Church. Was this not unusual among the Scottish working class? Wasn't it often called 'The Laird's Church' because of its association with the landed gentry?

I suppose it was more in the country that we were thought of as The Laird's Kirk, and yes, there has always been a wee bit of spiritual discomfort in that because I'm manifestly of a different background. The church I was born into and in which I was baptized, St Matthew's, was certainly a church for the poor, and indeed we have always had plenty to do in the cities. A more difficult thing to cope with was the sense of Englishness which attached to the Episcopal Church – we were often called 'The English Kirk'. In fact we were intrinsically and inherently Scottish, though I won't bore you with the details of the Reformation settlement. But the English tag was tough for a wee Scottish boy, and again led to this funny feeling of marginality.

On your first visit to church, aged twelve, you loved the High Anglican service and have claimed since, 'It was beauty that converted me.' Is that literally true, would you say?

I doubt I've ever really been converted in the deep and enduring sense some people are, the kind of twice-born types like Paul or Augustine, but I was undoubtedly grabbed by the beauty of the liturgy. It was a small church on the edge of an industrial town, Alexandria, in the west of Scotland, and Father Nigel McKay, who was the rector there, had elevated this little church to a kind of All Saints on the Clyde status almost, and I just fell for it. I didn't know what it was about, I had no clear understanding of any meaning behind it, but I was captivated by the transcendence that came through, by the mystery of it all. It must have been that, because I can't think of another reason for this twelve-year-old boy becoming interested in church and within two years wanting to be a priest.

Did a sense of vocation follow naturally from the beauty, do you think?

It was a combination of factors. I was certainly fascinated by Nigel McKay, probably to the point of hero worship. He was the first educated man I had met – an interesting, flawed man. Indeed this has been one of the themes of my theology: that grace has always been visited on me through broken people. I know Nigel McKay had a drink problem, and I suspect he was a celibate gay man who struggled with it; he was a broken man in a way and he ended up leaving the priesthood. But it was through that broken man that God's grace touched my heart enough for me to want to be a priest. That to me has always been a paradigm event, and it is one reason why I find perfectionist versions of Christianity not only personally discomforting, but somehow missing the point of the gospel. I didn't know what it was I was encountering, except a sense of unconditional glory coming through all this flawed humanity; and it was that which touched my boy's heart, I suppose.

You are quoted as saying, 'I loved the aesthetics before anything else. That and the liturgy.' But that falls rather short of what is understood by 'vocation', does it not? What else was driving that young boy?

There's no doubt at all that I was captured by a sense of the absolute, and I wanted to give myself to some great thing. I thought it would be easy but I found it very difficult because, as often happens, we give ourselves away and then we claw ourselves back. It was more than just aesthetics; I had a kind of longing to be surrendered to God, and in fact I assumed almost as soon as I went to Kelham that I would probably be a monk, because that was the absolute way to go. I became fascinated by the Cistercians, for instance. I wish I had known more about the reality of my own nature then.

You say you were 'marked for life' by the experience of being taught by monks. One hears this said quite often by Roman Catholics, but not usually by a Protestant, or at least what the Roman Catholics would call a Protestant. Are there many Anglican monasteries?

Not many, but some. The religious life revived in the Anglican communion in the nineteenth century, and the order that trained me, the Society of the Sacred Mission, was founded by a remarkable maverick genius called Herbert Kelly, also an outsider. This outsider theme is clearly important to me in all sorts of ways. Kelly believed that God wasn't calling only the Oxbridge-educated middle classes to the Anglican priesthood, and so he founded this order to train the poor. It was never respectable in Anglicanism, and his fairly radical theological ideas were elevated into the public conscience only in the 1960s, after he was dead. Kelham itself was a total institution; there were no servants, we all worked – cooking, scrubbing floors, looking after pigs – and there was not a single employee in the whole community. It made a colossal impact on a wee boy of fourteen. I went there in 1948, fifty years ago, and it still has profound resonances in my unconscious. It also built in real tensions because at fourteen you have these great ideas about absolute surrender, especially where sex is concerned, and you're not even sexual. I went there before I had reached puberty, before I really knew what sex was, and so there was always a kind of tension about the celibacy thing.

Would it have been very different if you had gone to a Roman Catholic monastery?

I imagine that the ethos probably wouldn't have been enormously different. I suspect that the atmosphere at Kelham was warmer and more liberal, though it was still very rigorous. I mean, we got up very early, and there was lots of prayer, and lots of manual work, but there was no heavy moralistic authoritarianism, which is the impression you sometimes get from reading the memoirs of people brought up in convent schools, for example. I don't recall any of that. There were certainly areas of questioning about human development that were not handled well, and it probably built into people certain blocks and inhibitions, but for its time it was a remarkably healthy institution and had a high level of eccentricity, which is always a good thing.

I'm quite puzzled by another statement. You say: 'If you are brought up in a monastery from fourteen, you buy into an official doctrine and it takes years to erode it.' What was the official doctrine – isn't it in part the doctrine that is now eroded, apparently without regret?

This is a highly complex subject. As a young man I was compelled by a fairly coherent packaged understanding of the truth, and the older I've got the more aware I've become of the mystery of the meaning of God, and the more certain that words never really fit the reality. Some people could very easily see this as an erosion of value, but there has always been a tendency in theological thought and in Christian understanding to make the words themselves almost as important as God. The words we use about God are not exact equivalents, however. Ultimately, perhaps, the only way to talk about God is in a wordless way, and that can be very difficult for people who want things neat and tidy and firm and packaged. I don't want to knock anyone else's theological development, but what has happened to me over the years as I've wrestled with these things is that I have become more certain about less. When I set out I was greatly certain about many things in the way that young people are, and also in the way that some religious systems inculcate, but now I have arrived at a stage where I think all systems are relative to the mystery of God. They more or less express the meaning of the mystery of God, but they are all provisional; they're all human constructs, and none of them pins down the mystery of God. We can afford to be relaxed and imaginative in the use we make of them and adventurous in finding new ways of expressing the mystery.

You became a novice monk and were sent to Ghana where you say you were 'radicalized' by what you experienced there. How great a change was this? Were you politically conservative before you went to Africa?

I was non-political when I went to Ghana in 1956. I was pious, I was interested in the spiritual life. At that time it was the Gold Coast and it became Ghana in 1957, so I lived through the tumult of the independence of the first African state. It was an enormously consciousness-raising experience, and it made me think about politics, about colonialism, about the meaning of liberation movements. I saw Nkrumah being shouldered in the great park on the day of independence and I remember feeling that this was a great moment in history. I also began to read newspapers for the first time; I can remember devouring the *New Statesman* and the overseas *Guardian*, and it was while I was there that Suez happened and the campaign for nuclear disarmament was started. So my time in Africa was a kind of growing up; there was no single event, more an accumulation, but clearly the encounter with political history was very important.

After that you threw yourself into campaigning for the poor, lobbied for better housing and organized rent strikes. Were you still a monk at this time?

No. I had a falling-out with the order, a kind of dispute with the novice master. He told me that either I had to go back to Kelham, or I had to leave the novitiate. I won't bore you with the details – it was a kind of stupid personal thing – but when I spoke to the bishop about it, he reckoned that I didn't have a vocation anyway. He thought I was probably a bit too turbulent, and he advised me to withdraw from the novitiate and stay on with him. At first I refused to do that, preferring as it were to be thrown out, but I was persuaded in the end and spent my second year in Africa as a layman. I came back to Edinburgh in 1958, finished my theological studies, was ordained in 1959 and then went to work in the Gorbals on the south side of Glasgow.

I asked that question because you go on to say that the decision to get married was a crisis for you, since you had 'more or less eschewed sex'. Does that mean you still felt yourself bound by a vow of chastity? Or does 'more or less' suggest your state of mind after you ceased to be a monk?

During my Kelham years I clearly absorbed and committed myself to what I now think is actually a magnificent aberration, namely the ancient Christian conviction that the really perfect Christian has to be celibate. That came into Christianity not from scripture but from fourth-century Gnosticism, but it became a very powerful root in Christianity, that the perfect Christian was the Virgin. I clearly struggled with that, as would any passionate young man, but I felt at the time that to be a perfect Christian one had to eschew sex. I'd tried the religious life, it hadn't worked out, but it still haunted me a bit. Part of me still had the feeling that if I were to get married, it would be a kind of giving in and opting for second best. That feeling hung around my consciousness for quite a long time. I used to ask myself, don't I have the courage and the heroism to be celibate? Well, I clearly didn't, but I'm not sure that it was the right question anyway.

When in fact did you become an ordained priest of the Scottish Episcopal Church?

I was made deacon in September 1959 and I was priested on St Barnabas's Day, 11 June 1960.

Shortly after your marriage to Jean Kennedy, an American girl and daughter of a Presbyterian minister, you quite suddenly lost all belief in the Christian faith. Were the two events in any way connected?

I don't think they were. It was a complicated period. It was during the early 1960s and I was working and living in one of the worst slums in Europe. My ministry was strongly socially activist, and I was reading voraciously at the same time, and only one particular kind of theology. I wasn't opening my pores, as it were, to poetry, art and music. Then I got a bad flu which seemed to lead to a post-viral depression, and I suddenly found myself no longer believing in God. That position maintained itself for about eighteen months. It was a terrible crisis for me, because I knew I couldn't sustain my lack of belief and be a priest. I had to ask myself if I was experiencing, as it were, the dark night of the intellect, or if it was something that was going to be finally defining for me. But the tide came back in a different way, gently, over the next eighteen months, and I found myself believing again, but in a different way, in a gentler, less propositional way.

'Torment' is how you described your experience of that time... you say you could find nothing at all to believe in, and yet presumably you had to conduct services. Did you ever consider resigning from the ministry? Did you ever feel that you ought to resign?

That of course was the big issue I wrestled with. I suppose it's a bit like a marriage; if you hit a really bad patch, you have to decide if you've reached the end of the road or if you can endure it and come through. It's a judgement call, and perhaps one of the saddest aspects of our culture is the way we tend to abandon these commitments too soon nowadays. But I can remember particularly the pain of preaching. At Eastertime, the midpoint of this experience, I discussed with my pal across the road, Church of Scotland minister John Harvey, what I could honestly preach about the Resurrection. Fortunately, you can use the great Christian narratives in all sorts of ways; they can sometimes be made to fit the human experience without requiring a transcendent reference. I wanted to preach honestly and not preach my doubts, and I managed, but only just.

Having lost your faith once, can you conceive of its happening again?

No, because I no longer think of faith as a thing that you can lose in quite that neat way, like a watch or an emotional commitment. I have come to think of faith as a continuum of responses to the mystery of life and the meaning of God and the reality of Jesus Christ. I have also learned what I don't think I knew then, that faith and doubt are coactive. The opposite of faith is certainty; you don't need faith if you're certain, only if you're uncertain. I've learned that faith is more a Zen experience than a kind of scientific certainty. I therefore don't think I can lose what I don't possess in that sense. Faith is always something that you receive but never own in that way; there's always a kind of grace-giftedness about it. The prevalence of the force of doubt as opposed to the sense of assurance varies, but I live with that and I see it as the experience of being faithful.

In the midst of the joy and relief you felt, was there no shadow of suspicion that wishful thinking might have been involved in the recovery of faith? That it could have been, just possibly, the easy way out of a painful situation...

That undoubtedly is a possibility and there is really no answer to that. I don't think, however, that the primary source of pain was professional – what do I do if I can't keep this job? It was deeper than that, it was an existential problem. I can remember watching a television programme at the time about a man who had run a theological college and was greatly loved by his students, and it felt as if I was someone looking in on an experience, at a love I had once had, like looking through a window at a happy family, and feeling enormous sorrow that I might one day no longer belong to it.

Do you think it follows that without God, without faith, life is indeed meaningless and purposeless?

No, I don't actually think that. Without God, it may be ultimately meaningless and purposeless, and I suppose intellectually, if you are an absolute atheist like Richard Dawkins, you have to believe that. But because it's true ultimately doesn't mean to say it's true penultimately; you can give meaning to it, you can believe that love is important, that truth and beauty are important. And in a strange kind of a way, if there is God then that experience must be part of the experience of God as well, so I think all the fragments get gathered up. I hate the kind of moralistic preaching that tries to blackmail people into believing, on the grounds that otherwise they will live lives of extreme anguish. I know lots of wonderfully committed ethical atheists whose lives are no more anguished than mine. They've chosen, as it were, not to believe in the way I have chosen to believe, but then to suggest that they are incapable of ethical vision, or love of their children, or enjoyment of the Monet exhibition is absurd. But I do think that the meaning of God is so extraordinary that even official atheism is somehow not safe from it.

Your wife was unaware of the extent of your suffering during your period of loss of faith, but she says that it changed you, and that you became less authoritarian, more open to changing ideas, less judgemental. Was it then that you started to air the unconventional views which have made you a figure of such controversy?

I suppose so, though I honestly don't think there has ever been a time when I've felt particularly constrained to give only official answers. And I was in one of the most congested slums in Europe, and it was impossible not to respond to that.

Do you sometimes court controversy for its own sake, just for the hell of it . . . it's difficult to believe you are trying to avoid the headlines when, for example, you call the opponents of women priests 'miserable buggers' and 'mean-minded sods' . . .

I genuinely don't know the answer to that question. But with regard to that particular incident, it was at a private meeting in support of the ordination of women and I was not aware that I was being recorded. Also, I know people don't believe this, but you've got to be a Glasgow man to know that you can use the word 'bugger' almost in an affectionate way; it's a term of endearment in Glasgow. The words out of context sound awful and I apologize for them – they were a lapse of judgement and of courtesy – but at the time I was talking about the experience in our church of having ordained women, and how most of us had found it a liberating joy, and I was saying that there were others whom it had rendered angry and hateful, and they couldn't share the joy, and it was in that sense that I said 'the poor miserable buggers'. The classic definition of envy is sorrow at another's good, and I always think that is the meanest of the sins; that you cannot enter the joy of an experience you cannot share. I don't honestly think I go out of my way to court controversy, although I clearly don't go out of my way to avoid it. But I do not wake up on a Monday morning and ask myself, how can I hit the headlines this week? The press is opportunistic; journalists want to catch you off guard, which is why so many bishops end up protecting themselves from these gaffes by saying nothing. You either choose to be more or less out of it, or you run the risk of occasionally making a fool of yourself, and I clearly opt for the second of these.

Your namesake, the Reverend David Holloway, has described your views on homosexuality as 'heretical and very serious for the Episcopal Church'. How would you answer this charge?

In two ways. The very use of the word heretical shows a mindset that I no longer regard as appropriate. It suggests that there is an absolutely defined and packaged truth and therefore that there is an absolutely defined and packaged untruth, namely heresy. If I'm certain of anything I'm certain of the fact that Christian theological and moral history is an evolutionary history. The ordination of women was heretical until we did it; the emancipation of the slaves was heretical until we did it; so the use of that kind of epithet is pretty meaningless. I'm much more interested in arguing the truth of the issue: whether, for example, it is appropriate for gay and lesbian people to have full Christian status and the freedom of loving in their way, I hope as responsibly and safely as the rest of us struggle to achieve – *that's* the issue, and not whether it has been traditional. Clearly it hasn't been traditional in the Church, but it has always been there, and I have known many wonderful and holy gay priests. I was brought up an Anglo-Catholic and the Anglo-Catholic tradition has undoubtedly had many gay priests. The real issue is the substantive one, about the moral status of gay and lesbian people, and not whether it's technically heretical. The Church is always evolving into another position, and these transitions are invariably painful. David Holloway is an intemperate kind of a person and he's always phoned up by the press for the standard quote whenever someone says something even mildly liberal; he's part of that pantomime cast of characters, just as I am, except I am phoned up for the opposite kind of quote.

At one time you spoke of retiring as bishop to stand as Labour candidate for the new Scottish Parliament, but have decided to stay in post to fight for gay rights within the Church. Are you still of the same mind?

Yes, but it's subtler than that. The Lambeth Conference last year had a profound effect on me. I've always associated Anglicanism with inclusiveness and tolerance of various angles on the truth, which is one reason why we're described as having a tendency to fudge. But I believe that liberal plural communities have to do that to maintain equilibrium. I myself have learned a great deal from other traditions, the Sufi tradition for example, and my life has been much enriched by otherness. The Anglican communion used to be good at affirming that; their catholicity was about universality, about liberalism and radicalism and conservatism, working together, sometimes painfully but creatively, struggling with the truth and mystery of God. Lambeth 1998 seemed to represent a declension from that particular way of being Anglican, almost in the direction of a unipolar fundamentalism about theology and morals, and it was profoundly depressing. Whatever you think of the gay and lesbian issue, the experience of sitting in that debate and hearing the hate was awful. I mean, my stuff about miserable buggers was Enid Blyton compared to the malevolence experienced there. I was overwhelmed by it. The underlying issue is how we interpret scripture, what we mean by authority, how we encounter evolving attitudes. For instance, we had an enormous struggle over women in the Anglican Church which your church [the Roman Catholic Church] is still just beginning. I've no doubt at all that it is appropriate to ordain women, and I have no doubt that the great Roman Catholic Church will eventually come to that – you move more slowly because you're a much bigger liner than we are. In some ways it's part of our prophetic vocation in Anglicanism to act as the tugboat in front of you, and that's one of the things that we have been quite good at doing. At Lambeth 1998 I felt that that way of being Anglican was being eroded. I tend to make decisions intuitively, I don't tend to agonize, and I found myself hardly able to wait to get back to Scotland, knowing that I wasn't going to go into the Parliament, that I would stay on as Bishop of Edinburgh for a bit longer and therefore as a player in the Anglican communion. I believe that this theological cleavage has to be tackled. So the issue is far bigger than the gay and lesbian thing, and in my letter to Donald Dewar I told him that there were trends in the Church that I wanted to stay around in order to challenge. The gay and lesbian thing is the symptom rather than the underlying cause.

How could you ordain a priest who practises sodomy... isn't that against everything you believe in?

Sodomy always comes up. I don't know the sexual repertoire of the average gay person, but I'm told in fact that the prevalence of sodomy is higher among heterosexual couples than among homosexual couples, and in fact it is sometimes used as a form of birth control. That is a separate issue, however. What you do with your sexual organs is not, I think, the moral question; it's the nature of the relationship and whether it is violent or abusive. Sodomy as such need not be either; it may be an unsafe physical practice, but there is no doubt that sexuality expresses itself in all sorts of extraordinary ways, including oral sex, fellatio and cunnilingus, and one might just as easily consider those to be unnatural. Homosexuals I know have a varied sexual repertoire, but I don't honestly think that's the issue. The issue is the quality of the relationship. For some reason there is a kind of fascination with other people's sexual practices. I get lots of letters in which SODOMY is written in block capitals. It's one of those words that set people off, though as far as we know the sin of Sodom was lack of hospitality and not anal intercourse. So the answer to your question is this: for a priest to be in an established relationship with another male seems to me not to contradict the possibility of a valid and fruitful priesthood. I know many examples where this is the case. What goes on in the bedroom is a matter of private choice, provided it's non-abusive and provided people are trying otherwise to follow the Christian ethic.

As someone who has considered standing as a Labour candidate, do you have any reservations about New Labour, about the emphasis on middle-class rather than working-class values, for example, and about their closeness to big business?

Yes. It would be dishonest to say that I don't, but I operate on two levels here because all political parties inevitably have to make compromises and alliances for the sake of power, and power is intrinsically corrupting. One of the ways of interpreting what has happened in the political culture in Britain is to talk about the triumph of the right in economic terms and the triumph of the left in cultural terms, and I am watching with interest to see if Tony Blair can pull this off. It seems to me that there is an interesting experiment going on here in trying to harness the economic modalities of conservatism which seem certainly to have been more efficient than some of the command modalities of socialism, but to use them to achieve social reform and an ethical vision of the left. I think it is a daring experiment and I hope it succeeds. There are inevitable losses, but there's no doubt at all that the old monolithic kind of opposition between absolute leftism and absolute rightism is a thing of the past. To that extent I am reasonably comfortable with it, but inevitably I get a bit anxious in case New Labour go too far and forget their historic commitment to the poor, who continue to suffer in our culture.

For the first time for many years we have a prime minister who openly acknowledges and practises his deeply held Christian faith. His enemies sometimes accuse him of parading it. What do you think about Tony Blair as a politician, and more importantly, as a human being and practising Christian?

I think it unfair to say that he parades it; he just doesn't hide it. I believe his faith is genuine and deep. He is clearly a man who needs the sacrament, and I don't think he flaunts it in the way that some American politicians do, for example. It's just part of the natural expression of his life. He's clearly a man both of rooted convictions and liberal sentiments. I find him intellectually a fascinating phenomenon. I'm impressed. He believes that the traditional political modalities are ethically bankrupt and there is a need to transcend them; hence his Third Way. There is almost something Hegelian in this, and I'm intrigued by it. The old conservative orthodoxies and the old socialist orthodoxies clearly on their own never worked in their pure form; they always influenced each other. The Tories inherited the health service and believed in it, and even though they might have eroded it, they were never going to cancel it. So I watch what is happening with a certain amount of intellectual excitement. Inevitably compromises are made, but I get the impression Tony Blair is trying to achieve a more inclusive Britain and I think that any person of goodwill would want to support that.

You have annoyed many people – again – by suggesting that there should be no prayers said and no blessing called down on the Scottish Parliament. What is your reasoning behind that? As an ordained priest, don't you believe in the power of prayer?

Let me put this in context. I did a *Thought for the Day*, a reasonably tranquil piece, not heavy, not attacking anyone, in which I addressed what seemed to me to be the two main issues. I think it is appropriate for the churches and all faith communities to be available to the parliament to offer spiritual sustenance. I also believe that the parliament itself should be studiously secular in its structure and its way of running, because Scotland is a plural country. There are probably as many unbelievers as believers in this country, and it's their parliament as well as ours, so why should we have, as it were, an official status which is denied them? Modern government in plural cultures should protect and allow freedom to all religious communities but privilege none, especially when you're setting out to create a brand new one. It's different in Westminster; there has been a connection between Church and State for centuries and they have a Speaker's chaplain who says antique prayers, and it's all part of the long-running costume drama that is the history of the British Parliament. We are starting something new here, we don't have to plug in to quite that tradition. Brussels doesn't do it, and I approve strongly of that kind of secular objectivity. I also believe in the separation of Church and State, because perilous collusions can happen if you privilege one group against the other. My second reason for suggesting that there be no official prayers is the difficulty of setting about doing it if you want to be truly representative. One MP who attacked my point of view said that there were eighteen religious groups in Scotland and he reckoned they should all get a shot at it, with the atheists getting two minutes silence once a year. Well, it then becomes almost a farcical thing, but it's not an opinion I hold with any great passion. I expressed a point of view, and it created a furore, but I fail to see why a minister of the Christian Church should not be allowed to have opinions on subjects like that.

Except perhaps that you are trying to spare the feelings of non-believers, but wouldn't even non-believers concede that prayer does no harm to anyone...

It's not a question of it doing any harm. It is very important to me in my understanding of the meaning and the mission of Jesus that we do not use spiritual power in an abusive way, that we do not assert it over people. There is a history of spiritual institutions doing what God doesn't do. God eschews power, empties himself of it, comes among us as a slave; but there is a history, particularly in Christianity, of lording it over people and operating dictatorially – in other spiritual traditions as well. That is inimical to the heart of the gospel, and the thing that moderately distresses me in Scotland is a sense that the Church is scrambling to get a bit of this power for itself, to assert its rights. Well, I don't think Christianity has any rights; it's about service, it's about receiving the grace of God. It's not about asserting your position over and against other groups. So, let all spiritualities be provided for, including Christian prayer, but let it not be officially stamped upon the parliament.

What is your concept of God? Who or what is God?

The old traditional way of positing a kind of super male figure, the Zeus God, Jehovah God, God of battles – all of that is clearly projection. And some philosophers reckon that all concepts of God are inevitably projections of our own longings. I believe that God is such a mystery that it seems to invade us with a sense of possibility; even the sense of the absence of God that is prevalent in our culture is strangely provocative, because how can you sense an absence if there had never been a presence?

You served on the Warnock Commission on Human Fertility and Embryo Research which produced results since denounced by the Roman Catholic Church. I refer, for example, to the commission's expressed view that research on human embryos up to fourteen days' development is permissible. Do you have any qualms about this?

I was not a member of the Warnock Commission, but a member of the Human Fertilization and Embryology Authority, which was set up as a result of the Warnock Commission. I was invited to join the authority which was formed in 1990, and since I knew nothing about the subject, I went on a fast-learning curve. The most contentious part of the debate was precisely about experiments on human embryos, but although it's morally problematic, I believe that it is morally justified. The Roman Catholic Church has a very clear and coherent point of view which I respect but do not share. They believe that from the point of conception the embryo has full moral status. This view certainly has the virtue of coherence, but I do not myself accept it. It was decided that it would be morally appropriate to allow embryo experiment for fourteen days since there are advantages in combating unexplained infertility and in investigating various kinds of genetic defects. It was one of those calculuses which have to be weighed up. It's like abortion. The Roman Catholic Church, the hierarchy at least, has a strong moral agenda on that, but one not necessarily shared by the rest of the population. On the whole, the Abortion Act is probably one of those problematic things that we need. I would describe myself as being anti-abortion, but pro-choice.

The ordination of women will never be granted in the Roman Catholic Church in the lifetime of the present Pope, nor will Anglican orders be recognized. If both these obstacles were removed, would you like to see reunion with Rome?

Yes. It would be with a changed Rome, but of course it is already a church that has changed dramatically since Vatican II. It is a magnificent, extraordinary institution and I have a kind of nostalgia for it. I've always had good Roman Catholic friends, and most of them are radical people, theologically and politically – monks, nuns, secular priests, and so on. If there is to be a united church I very much hope that it will be one that will diminish the tendency to authoritarianism within its structure, moderate the understanding of papal infallibility, and will allow a range of theologies to be expressed.

You say in your book Who needs Feminism? *that Christians are called to lead examined lives. Does that mean that beliefs have to be constantly inspected and modified and, if necessary, altered? And if so, what can it actually mean to say, 'I am a believer'?*

Christians should lead examined personal lives, that's fundamental. Plato said the unexamined life was not worth living, and indeed it is absolutely vital to know yourself. There's not much point in knowing everything about astrophysics if you don't know about your own reality. We should also understand the springs of our own prejudices, and listen to the challenges of others. That is fundamental. I think that where institutions are concerned it is more complicated. Obviously individuals can change their minds rapidly, they can leave one party and join another; but institutions take longer, and you need prophetic leaders who are out in front, because the mass of the centre ground, not to mention the people at the back, don't want any change. Cardinal Newman said that to live was to change and to be perfect will be to have changed often, and there's no doubt at all that the history of Christianity is a history of continuity and change. There are some things that abide. For example, the nature of God is unconditional love, and the Passion of Jesus is a symbol of God's love for the world, but how we express those concepts in words has varied. The Christian theological tradition has been one of dynamic change, but we are, as it were, committed to a living reality called Jesus Christ rather than to a permanent inalterable written text; that is what distinguishes it from Islam. We believe in a living presence, someone who walks with us through history, and is indeed ahead of us. We never ever get God down finally in any form of words, so there should be a certain kind of lightness of touch in the way we look at these things. Nevertheless, we have to be ready to say, this is the memory of the tradition, this is the way we expressed our relationship to this mystery then, how can we better express it today? We repudiate the years of persecution of the Jews, we repudiate our treatment of minorities, but we don't necessarily repudiate our credo statements. The same approach can be taken to institutions like the monarchy. A traditionalist defence of the monarchy would be to talk about the Divine Right of Kings, but a contemporary defence might argue that it's as good a way as any of expressing symbolic unity of the state, it's good for the tourist trade, it's good for exports, it's colourful, and so on. We maintain the tradition but we update it by offering contemporary justifications.

Apropos the persecution of the Jews, you have applauded Pope Paul VI's repudiation of the ancient accusation that the Jews had killed God, something which led to centuries of anti-Semitism. What worries me is this: before this act of public repentance, the view which we now accept as wrong was deemed to be right. If at any point in the future something which we regard as right can be declared wrong, doesn't this rather undermine all the views of the Church?

Yes, in one way. But one of the points that I'm constantly trying to make is that all our views have to be held with a certain lightness, a sense of their provisionality, their revisability. And this applies equally to doctrine and dogma. It's even truer of purely social and cultural and ethical ideas, which change dramatically. Just think, the Christian Church justified slavery for eighteen hundred years, and it's there in scripture, I Timothy 6, where the slaves are told to be good little slaves lest the Church be brought into disrepute. That to us is now obscene, and it's not enough to apologize for it; we have to identify it and say it was clearly a moral obscenity. OK, you can see historically how it came to be justified, because the early Christians didn't think they were going to be around for long, they thought that Jesus was going to come back, so what was the point in altering human arrangements in the short term. But the long reach of history succeeded that kind of apocalyptic expectation, and we went on justifying slavery, just as we went on justifying many other oppressive things. It is very important to be open to new knowledge, new ways of looking at things that might make us change and own that we've got some things wrong. We would not then be dug in so defensively that when a moral challenge is made to us we are incapable of responding. It would be marvellous if we had that kind of freedom and versatility. Behind your question lies an absolutely appropriate challenge, for when you look at our history, we have defended the indefensible.

Isn't one of the basic problems the fact that all the religions of the world lay claim to the truth? Even Mahatma Gandhi said that Hinduism was the religion of truth, and many other spiritual leaders would say the same of their own religion. Can there be such a thing as universal truth, do you think?

There probably is in the abstract, but I doubt if any single individual or institution gets a handle on it. A friend of mine who wrote a book on interfaith outlines an approach which he calls grounded openness, i.e. valuing the truth given to you by your own particular tradition, but at the same time being open to other truth systems. You don't become them but you're open to them, while being grounded, holy, good and compassionate within your own tradition. You respect the other tradition, you may learn from it, you may believe that you have something to teach it, but you remain in your tradition in a non-defensive way. I think it would be marvellous if we achieved that kind of maturity. In my own case, I've learned a great deal from Buddhism; I'm not going to become a Buddhist – that would be against my every instinct and culturally quite an odd thing to do – but I'm a Christian who is open to Buddhism. I'm also an Anglican who's open to Catholicism, and so on. If you have a certain kind of security in your relationship with yourself and with God then you're able to do this.

In your book Another Country, Another King, *you seem to dispose of hell and the Devil as first-century myths, but since the terms 'God' and 'Devil' are simply variations of good and evil, can we believe in one without the other — that God exists but the Devil does not?*

Yes. The history of the evolution of the Devil is fascinating, but if there is a Devil — and I don't believe there is in any objective sense — I think it's a metaphor for all sorts of experiences. The Devil has never had the same status as God because the Devil is a created reality, and God is an uncreated reality. Augustine said that an evil is essentially a deprivation of good; it's not, as it were, a substantive reality in its own right. So I do not think there is a contradiction in believing in God and not believing in the Devil. Ultimately Christianity is not a dualistic religion, which is what your question suggests. There have been many dualistic religions that posed God eternally against evil eternally, and in fact the Gnostics said that the Creation was the work of a fallen God, which is where a lot of Christianity's anxiety about sex came from, because in our wrestling with that we inherited their repudiation of the flesh. But Christianity is essentially a unitive vision; it believes that God will be all and all will be well, and all manner of things will be well, to quote Julian of Norwich. Hell can be used as a metaphor, as a projection of experiences that we have created. We saw a living hell in Kosovo, we saw it in the Holocaust. But I don't believe morally in the possibility of hell because I think there is something morally contradictory in a God of justice giving eternal punishments for temporal transgressions; I'm more likely to believe in purgatory than in hell because I recognize the importance of moral evolution. Whatever happens after death, I feel sure we will continue the journey, and that journey may involve pain, but not ultimate or everlasting rejection by God. This would be inconsistent with the understanding of God as made known in Jesus.

You seem to be saying hell is a state of mind. Is heaven also a state of mind?

You could say that. I certainly don't believe in a geographically locatable heaven. It is simply a convenient way of describing the closer presence of God. I don't know what heaven is except that if there is that mystery we call God, then there is a sense in which to be near God we will have to be in that state which we have in shorthand called heaven.

Unlike the Bishop of Durham you have not publicly cast doubt on the Virgin Birth or the Resurrection. Is this out of consideration for the simple beliefs of your flock; do you see them also as first-century myths?

I am genuinely committed to the plural approach to all of these things. If you can believe in the literalness of the Virgin Birth, if it works for you and brings you closer to God and your brothers and sisters, then I'm not going to undertake the project of disturbing that. If on the other hand you treat it as a Roman Catholic priest friend of mine treats it – as a theological symbol for the understanding that Jesus came from God in a spiritual sense – I can live with that as well. I am probably closer to the theological Virgin Birth understanding of it, but I don't have a problem with people who want to believe in miracles. The same goes for the empty tomb. For me, the important thing is what comes through these theological structures, and whether it enables you to be a better follower of Jesus. There are many fundamentalists who are lovely people, and to that extent I wouldn't even want to knock fundamentalism. If believing in the absolute literalness of scripture makes you a servant of humanity and a person of mercy and love, then praise God. It's when you try to universalize your own experience of these things that I get anxious. When people insist that there is only one way of understanding the Virgin Birth or the Resurrection, that's manifestly not true since lots of Christians use that material in a range of ways. But since it's beyond any kind of proof or historical recovery, I think a lot of it is very much beside the point.

Do you yourself believe in miracles?

I don't disbelieve in them. But I don't actually find much need to believe in them. I don't find it difficult to believe that Jesus performed works of healing. I think that the walking on the water is probably a metaphor for something else, but if he did walk on the water, so what? It doesn't bother me, and I don't have energy for it. It's like angels dancing on the head of a needle – if you like that kind of thing debated, fine. Jesus himself didn't seem particularly keen on the kind of faith which was the result of seeing miracles. So for me it's not a big deal, not a particular issue. The universe is weird and wonderful enough without miracles.

In your book Who Needs Feminism? *you say: 'All our language about God is oblique and provisional.' Since the language of faith is very imprecise, isn't it almost impossible to know what another man means by God, or salvation, or divine mercy?*

Yes. Apart from silence, all we have to talk about God is language, and language is always going to be imprecise. This is one reason why I increasingly prefer poetry, because poetry is about transcendent experience. Once you actually start defining these indefinable things you do violence both to your own intellect and to other people's hearts. In the book to which you refer, I was trying to promote the equal status of women in the church and to explore the possibility of using a more varied language to talk about God.

Is it possible to know the mind of God?

Certainly not in its totality. I'm always anxious when visionary, hectic figures tell me that they know the mind of God, because I know that someone is usually going to suffer for it. There are great dangers in making absolute claims; many people thought it was the mind of God to persecute the Jews. I would always like to have qualifying phrases, such as 'this is how it seems to us at the moment' or 'this is how we feel the mind of God is expressing itself through the community of faith, or through my own insights'.

You have talked compassionately about the pain and hurt caused to women over the centuries, in the way they have been treated in what has been a patriarchal church. Is it possible that God is a woman?

No, I don't think God is a woman. But it would be just as anachronistic or inappropriate to say that God is a man. It is possible to use both male and female metaphors and images to reach a certain understanding of God, just as you can talk about God as shepherd or as fountain. I think there is motherhood in God, and I feel it easy to pray to the Mother of God, by which I don't simply mean the Virgin Mary, but something even larger than that.

You once said: 'There are complexities in human sexuality that it behoves us to understand and not merely to condemn.' That is a compassionate position which a great many people would understand and sympathize with, Christian and non-Christian alike. Where does that leave you on the business of moral absolutes? Are there any moral absolutes nowadays?

I don't think there are many moral absolutes, and if there are any they are likely to be so general as to apply only in a very broad way. Sexual consent is an important principle, I would say almost an axiom, almost an absolute, which is why rape is always absolutely wrong. Obviously the young cannot give consent, and this makes pederasty and paedophilia tragically impossible. There can never be an allowable sexual relationship there, although it undoubtedly remains one of the mysteries of human sexuality. But given those overarching moral principles, there is still an enormous sexual repertoire which can be mutually fulfilling and consenting, and I think that we should mind our own business and not meddle with other people's lives. This should be the case even if we are personally repelled, as indeed I am by certain aspects of sado-masochism, for example. Mutually consenting sado-masochism, however, stops short of the heavier kind of wounding of people, and so I believe it is up to the people involved. I have no appetite at all for it myself, it's a mystery to me, but it does seem to be a part of some people's experience. I find it aesthetically displeasing, but that does not give me the right to try and outlaw it. There has been a lot of crucifying of people in the name of this kind of busy involvement in other people's sexualities. I would prefer to allow freedom within an understanding of constraint and appropriateness. Between consenting adults, I do not think that you can say confidently, 'You can do this, but you can't do that.' It is really up to the adults themselves.

What sort of society do you envisage if all the causes you have espoused come into being: if drugs and prostitution, same-sex marriages, even among the clergy, were legalized, and so on? Would it be a genuinely better society, do you think?

All I have said is that there are issues here that need to be debated and we should be able to look at all possibilities. I would decriminalize cannabis, for example, as would most sane people in this country. I would certainly allow its use for medical reasons, and it seems to me absolutely ludicrous that you can't even talk about that without having the tabloids on you. As regards prostitution, it is not called the oldest profession for nothing. It is always problematic when you involve the law in prohibiting something that most people seem to want, and prohibitionist cultures, as we witnessed in the States when they tried to ban alcohol, invariably don't work. But I don't know the answer to these things. I'm not in favour of prostitution, and the trouble with legalizing it is that you appear to give it a kind of favourable rating. On the other hand, it is a fact, and it will go on being a fact, and to criminalize the poor lassies that get into it – usually because they are poor – is a great mistake. But to go back to the substance of your question, I don't believe in Utopias. I do long for a society that takes care of the needy and the poor, that doesn't persecute, that allows as wide a set of freedoms as possible that are consistent with the public good. I want the maturity that recognizes that living in a plural culture, religiously, sexually, politically, requires great sophistication, tolerance and understanding. I prefer the risks of freedom to the risks of order. That's simply my own temperamental preference. At the same time I recognize that we have conservatives who prefer the risks of order to the risks of freedom. This thing that we call human flourishing is a descant between freedom and order; sometimes we overemphasize order, and sometimes we overemphasize freedom and things get a bit too loose. But it is never going to be perfect. There will always be losses, in discipline and restraint, for example, but there are also gains. I find that young people in our culture have a kindliness and tolerance about them that is very appealing.

Bertrand Russell once expressed the hope that the entire world one day would become one vast coffee-coloured republic. Do you have any sympathy with that view?

Oh, yes. One of the fascinating things about mixing of the races is that you get good results. You get more beautiful people, and also some fascinating genetic leaps, so yes, that kind of merging and human communion would be a wonderful thing. And I'm not much of a monarchist. Again, I wouldn't put energy into getting rid of the monarchy, but if I were given a blank sheet of paper, I would have some kind of republic, with a bit of fun and burlesque attached to it.

You have experienced 'the dark night of the soul', which you prefer to call ' the dark night of the intellect', when belief in God disappears. Have you experienced the opposite – the presence of God?

Oh, yes, I've had one or two moments of ecstasy. Oddly enough, I had one walking along Shaftesbury Avenue once. It was just a straightforward muddled streetscape, and then it's as though I went over a threshold and everything became a sort of a ballet. It was one of those oceanic moments and I just wandered down the street grinning at everyone I met. I had a similar experience in the Citizens' Theatre in Glasgow once. It was a Christmas pantomime when they did a tableau of the whole of Glasgow life, the women going to clean the offices, the shipyard workers on the Clyde, and I suddenly got a great sense of the human drama as a great ballet orchestrated by a loving mystery. There was another moment about eighteen months ago when I was driving back from North Berwick on a lovely June evening. I was listening to Radio 3 which was playing Holst's *The Planets*, and I was looking straight across to Fife, the evening was clear and still, and I suddenly felt that if I had only had that moment in time life would have been worth it. I saw that life is such an extraordinary gift, even for those who are experiencing tragedy and suffering. It gave me a great sense of thankfulness and reaffirmed my longing to be someone who said yes, rather than no.

You have three children, presumably brought up as Christians. Have they kept the faith?

They have all kept the faith in the sense that they are people who have values and a spiritual sensibility. I suppose they have an affectionate relationship with the church, they are still sympathetic to it, but for good moral and intellectual reasons they find themselves more on the edge than in the centre. So much of my own evolution has been in conversation with my children, so I'm very relaxed about where they are. We talk about these issues, we have a lot in common, but they are certainly not conventional members of the church.

Do you fear death?

No, but I am wistful about losing life and I hope that I'm spared a bit longer. Whether it's the end or whether it's a wakening to the new morning, it will be the last great risk and adventure.

Do you expect to be reunited after death with those you love?

I don't know. I do not have an opinion on that. I neither expect it, nor would it entirely surprise me.

INTERVIEW CONDUCTED JANUARY 1999

ANGELA HUTH

ANGELA HUTH

Angela Huth was born in 1938 and studied painting
in Paris, Florence and London. She worked in radio,
television and newspaper journalism before
publishing her first novel, *Nowhere Girl*, in 1970.
She is the author of several children's books, plays,
short stories and novels, which include *Invitation to
the Married Life* (1991), *Land Girls* (1994) and *Wives
of the Fishermen* (1998).

You have written fondly of your father, the actor and film producer Harold Huth, but you say little about your mother except that she went to live abroad in 1945. Was this a permanent arrangement, a marital separation?

It was a long separation but she came back when I was about twelve. She visited maybe once a year from the time I was three years old, so during the crucial bit of my childhood my mother was scarcely there. She is still alive, and there is really very little I can say about her in relation to my childhood. So it's better not to say anything really.

You weren't close to her?

We had just such completely different attitudes to life. It was my father who was my great hero because he gave me all that I needed in the way of encouragement and excitement and imagination. He was multi-talented: he could write, he could draw, he could play the piano, he could act, and this was my world from early childhood. My mother was a completely different sort of creature, a sparkling, party-loving, gregarious, energetic woman. She was very good at languages and I suppose the one thing she did teach me was that to be able to speak languages was a good idea. But I could learn far more from my father than I could from her.

You went to Paris to study art at the age of sixteen...was that a good experience?

I went to Paris because my mother didn't want me to go to university. This was in 1954 and she said that only blue stockings went to university. I didn't tell her that I wanted to write because it was a private thing, and since I was quite good at art I was accepted into the Beaux Arts, though I knew I wasn't an artist. The main object was to learn French, but I had a horrendous time living with the most disagreeable, mean-spirited, horrible people in Paris for a year. Apart from anything else I was so hungry, but every time I complained to my mother, she just said it was fine. Well, it wasn't fine. I spent the following year in Florence which was much better, one of the best times of my life. I learned Italian very quickly, and I went round the whole of Italy in the days when there were no tourists, so I saw everything you could ever hope to see. I used to sit by myself for hours and hours in front of Michelangelo's *David* and not another person came in. Nowadays you have to queue for four hours. I also did history of art, and I learned to paint with Annigoni, which I didn't much enjoy, but it was a wonderful experience. I went to a rather expensive school which my mother couldn't really afford, and I am forever grateful to her for that.

You were sent to boarding school at the age of eight, after your mother went to live abroad, and I suppose you also had to leave your sister behind. This sounds to me like multiple trauma ... was it?

Heavens no, it was perfectly all right. I didn't particularly like my boarding school, but I did have some wonderful teachers. There was one in particular who introduced me to the history of art. Every week she would bring along a postcard by a different artist and we would talk about the painting and learn about the artist. I absolutely adored that. Being in the country was also lovely, and although I wasn't exactly very happy I wasn't unhappy either. I didn't see my parents during the term, but it wasn't traumatizing at all.

Did you ever consider not sending your own daughters to boarding school?

I did consider it, but it would have been very difficult, simply because of circumstances. With Candida I was living in a remote part of Wiltshire, and Quentin, her father, was living far away. I was effectively a single mother, living in a small cottage, and I couldn't afford to employ someone else to take Candida to school every day. In any case there were no good schools anywhere in that remote part of Wiltshire, and so I had to send her to a boarding school. I don't think she was terribly happy at either of her boarding schools actually, and I regret that, but there wasn't much else I could do. In the case of my younger daughter Eugenie, she had a much happier and easier educational time, because I was living in Oxford and she went to the Dragon School which she loved. She then asked to go to Cheltenham Ladies' College, and although she wasn't terribly happy during her first two years, she's never regretted it. She had a marvellous education.

Were you conscious of trying to do things differently from your own mother once you had daughters of your own?

Yes, in accordance with most of my generation. When I was married to Quentin in the 1960s we did have a full-time nanny and a cook and so on – we were a little bit grander then, but all that for most of us is gone now. When I had Eugenie sixteen years after Candida, she was part of family life and I wouldn't have wanted it any other way. I did have a nanny who came in to look after her every morning so that I could write at home, but from lunchtime onwards I looked after her and I had her all the weekends. The pleasure of being near one's children growing up is just immeasurable. I remember when I was a child on my nanny's day out there was a nursery maid to look after me; my mother couldn't take me out even for an afternoon, it simply didn't occur to her. She never ever read me a story. And it was the same with all my friends. It was a different world, a lesser world really. What they missed and what we missed...

You have sometimes said that you feel inferior to most men who are generally better educated than you are. Do you regret not having gone to university?

Very much so. I've regretted it all my life. There is never another time in your life when you have the freedom to study whatever you want for three years, with no responsibilities, no dependants. Even now, after being a writer for thirty-five or forty years, I often wonder when I am writing a review, for example, if I might have approached it differently had I gone to university. As it is, I write instinctively, but I often feel that I have missed out. On the other hand, I would not have liked to have read English because I don't wholly approve of the analytical way they teach English. I'm tremendously unanalytical, both about reading and writing, so for me that would have been a bit of a difficulty.

You mentioned that although you were a pupil of Annigoni, you never kidded yourself you were a great artist. But I imagine these years must have had some influence on your later life...did they affect your perception of beauty, or form, or even your style of writing perhaps?

Though I regret not having gone to university I will never regret my three years at art schools in Paris, Florence and London. Looking at pictures, measuring space, thinking about colour, shape and form, going out and painting landscapes – all of these were invaluable. I always knew I wasn't an artist; I had a certain facility when I was about fourteen and it just hasn't developed much since.

Which writers do you admire?

My favourite writers are Jane Austen, Turgenev and Thomas Hardy. I used to love Dickens, but not quite so much now. Among contemporary writers the shining star for me is William Trevor. I simply don't understand why he's not world famous. He has had an enormous influence on me. I'd love to be able to match that combination of humour and blackness and romanticism, together with his love of landscape and incredible facility for evocation. I also admire Penelope Fitzgerald enormously.

Flaubert thought that great art was impersonal and claimed to have put none of his own feelings into Madame Bovary. *You have sometimes said that you don't want to write about what you know. Do you believe, as Flaubert maintained, that pure invention and complete objectivity are possible?*

I do to a certain extent. I've had a wonderful life, but in the grand scheme of things it's very tiny and narrow and probably not very interesting, and if I went on writing about the things I know about, it would be the same book over and over again. Before I wrote about land girls I'd never done any research for a book before. In the event I spent only one day at the Ministry of Agriculture reading up on the subject in a magazine called *Land Girls*. That gave me three or four facts, which is all you need, and then I just sat down and made it up. I've been congratulated many times on my war work, so I imagine it must have worked to a certain extent. After that I thought it was fun writing about what I didn't know about, so I decided to use as my subject the wives of Scottish fishermen, and spent some time travelling round the fishing villages in Fife. Apart from the fact that I got Inverness on the wrong side of Scotland because I didn't look at a map, I don't think I got too many things wrong. Obviously, my own thoughts are scattered among those subjects about which I know nothing, but I hope they're disguised well enough to prevent readers thinking, you know, this is Angela Huth speaking, instead of a fisherman's wife.

Just to continue this theme for a moment ... it used to be said of Flaubert that no one, after reading all of his works, could ever make out what manner of man he was in his private life. Is it the same with you, or would you say that your life can be explained in terms of your books?

This is a difficult question. I would think that certain things about me would be very obvious from reading my books – a love of the countryside, a sending-up of pretentiousness, an eagerness not to be earnest, a sense of *joie de vivre*; but I don't think you could begin to know what is in my innermost heart. I would never want to reveal that. I hope I am able to convey a sense of the importance and excitement of the ordinary. I'm certainly not a political writer – I have no messages to convey, nor am I a ranter. I want people to enjoy my books, and I'm rather scornful of the feeling prevalent today that everyone has to be able to relate to things. There is a whole educational theory which says you have to dumb down books so that children can identify with them. Well, if that were the case we would never have had *Alice in Wonderland* or Mervyn Peake. The point is always to exceed your grasp, to overreach yourself, to aspire to things, and I very much have that inclination. I always try to do better and in fact it gets harder and harder. After thirty or forty years of writing I can of course turn out a decent sentence, but that is only the half of it; there's an awful lot more to do, and I'm very conscious all the time of my own inadequacy as a writer.

Graham Greene once remarked that writers all tend to be governed by a ruling passion. Is this true in your case?

My ruling passion, if I have one, is the attempt to make the ordinary extraordinary. I love the idea of most moments of the day being intensely valuable. My husband and children are all great travellers, but I'm very happy to be in one tiny place. You can go anywhere in the world if you've got an imagination. I'm very happy to write on a small canvas. Jane Austen got the whole of life out of a few miles, and I'd like to be able to do that.

Graham Greene also said that a good writer, in observing the human condition, must have a splinter of ice always in his heart. Is that true in your experience?

I think that is absolutely true. If you are too kind, or sentimental, or generous in your opinions you are not so able to get to the truth. In France, where for some strange reason my books have taken off, I'm considered cruel; all my reviews say I have a kind of English cruelty. I wasn't aware that I was cruel, but I suppose I know what they mean. I'm a bit acid about appearances, taste, clothes, the way people speak. Sometimes truth is not very kind.

Are you sensitive to reviews of your books?

I've had lots of bad reviews in my life. I am absolutely prepared to take them on my head if they are by somebody whose opinion I respect, who has actually read the book, and who possibly offers up some sort of constructive criticism, something I always try to do myself when I'm writing book reviews. Unfortunately there are an awful lot of book reviewers who just read the blurb and a few pages, and I find that very annoying and rather insulting. If I am reviewed badly by a good critic whom I respect then, far from being offended, I am rather grateful, and I take note of what has been said.

Is your writing in any way a form of self-therapy?

No, absolutely not. It simply isn't a concept that appeals to me whatsoever. I'm not interested in relating to myself; I'm much more interested in something outside myself that is rather vague and amorphous. My principal philosophy is probably deflection. I believe tremendously in the old ways of the British stiff upper lip, and working things out for yourself. I have a sort of horror of the counsellor generation – the idea of going to a counsellor the moment something is wrong or if somebody dies. It works for a lot of people, I know, but to me it is just appalling.

Do you believe that writers have a moral responsibility towards their readers?

Yes, and in my case that means I never write a book in which evil wins. In real life evil wins over and over again, and while this fact should probably be recorded, I'm not the person to do it. Lots of disasters happen in my books, moral and otherwise, but I like to think that in the end good overcomes evil, and that effort and hope are in some way rewarded.

I was surprised to read that at social occasions in Oxford and Cambridge, dons never ask you what you do, but only what your husband does. Can this still be true? Do such dinosaurs really exist?

Oh yes, yes. Usually what happens when I sit next to a don is that I ask him about his subject, and he tells me brilliantly without stopping, and that's wonderful. I'm not against listening unless it is to someone who is not able to be very entertaining about what he does, but in fact I've learned an awful lot from sitting next to dons. The fact that they have learned absolutely nothing about me does not offend me. Why should they bother with me? I'm not half as interesting as they are, and they are not interested in asking. The only thing that puzzles me a little is that these very learned men are fairly low on human curiosity, so steeped are they in their subject. But that is generally why they are such great scholars. I'm married to an exception: my husband is enormously scholarly, but also completely intrigued by everything else in the world. There aren't many like that.

Do you enjoy these occasions? Or are they merely dutiful?

In Oxford these days wives aren't asked in very often, and you can understand why really. I've always attacked dons' wives – despite being one myself – because on the whole we're all married to men who are more brilliant than us, and on the whole it is more interesting to listen to the dons than it is to the wives. I mean, there is no doubt about that. It's obvious.

But do you think that is actually the reason? Is it not more likely that there are still men who don't take women very seriously?

I'm afraid to say that is the case, but then there are a lot of women who don't have to be taken very seriously sometimes. I'm not myself irritated by this because I think one should appreciate where one stands intellectually. I know perfectly well that I am no great intellectual, and not half as entertaining to talk to as people who have enormous knowledge and appreciation of the one or two subjects in which they are experts. On those occasions I don't want to talk about me – imagine all that boring stuff about whether or not I use a word processor. It's far more fascinating to be talking about how you work out the number of spots on a leopard's tail through mathematics.

It seems you find men more interesting than women. In a previous interview you called women 'a whingeing lot' and on another occasion you said 'there is a quality of greatness about some men that is not the same ever with a woman'. Can you elaborate on that?

This is probably a terrible confession, but I am biased towards men. I appreciate there are many wonderful and great women – I myself have many women friends whom I admire tremendously and of whom I am enormously fond. But I do think that when you have a man friend – a real friend, not a lover – it is a very extraordinary relationship. You know more or less instinctively that communication is not going to be so much on the domestic, gossipy level; you can rest assured that with an intelligent man friend you are going to have a stimulating time intellectually. There is a different timbre with men – they have an edgier approach which I rather love. Of course, there are lots of boring men with whom I don't want to be friends at all, but in general I feel easier with men. They are slightly less prone to asking prurient questions, the sort that less and less I find myself wanting to answer. I love the dignity of many men I know, that and their very British acerbic dry humour.

You describe your husband, James Howard-Johnston, as 'very English stiff upper lip', which you love, and you go on to say, 'I can't bear touchy-feely men who iron their own shirts'. Can you explain what the attraction of the stiff upper lip is, and why 'touchy-feely' types are so unbearable?

They just don't appeal. I can't bear married couples like Tony Blair and Cherie holding hands and swinging round. I prefer a sort of public distance. Whatever you do in private is an entirely different matter, but in public I prefer husbands and wives to act normally rather than being all over each other all the time. The stiff upper lip is more challenging, more entertaining, more amusing than having all the beans spilled at once. I've been married to James for twenty-one years and I'm still learning to read the stiff upper lip. He is the most wonderful company, and his erudition sits lightly upon him. I admire his enthusiasms, his encouragement, his humour, his dignity. I think Quentin had all these qualities too, so I obviously go for this kind of thing.

Your first husband, Quentin Crewe, wrote in his autobiography that to see you walking into a second marriage with a man you knew was an impossible choice was 'like seeing a stoat being mesmerized by a snake'. I know you prefer not to talk about that disastrous second marriage, but would you call that an accurate metaphor for your state of mind at the time?

I think Quentin quite enjoyed fashioning that sentence, and it is much quoted. I expect there was some truth in it. The fact is, I never think about those rather disastrous past days and I'm not going to think about them now. I shall write about them in my memoirs but I will never discuss the whole period, because it's past and it was a mistake. It was a nightmare, but there's no reason to describe a nightmare. I've learned from it, but some things are private.

What did you learn from it?

I learned more than anything the value of peace, and living without fear. I've never ever got over what happened twenty-five, twenty-six years ago, and still when I wake up in the morning it's good to realize that it's all right.

It is obvious from what you have said on a number of occasions that you came to regret your infidelity to Quentin; indeed you seem to have quite strict views on adultery. Do you see things expressly in terms of your own experience, or are there larger issues at stake? Is it strictly a question of sexual morality or is it the tangled web that follows?

I just think that infidelity is corrosive and it's not worth it. That's one of the things I've learned. I was young, I was foolish. Having said that, I can't actually think of anybody who hasn't been unfaithful, which is very sad. But unless you are very unhappily married and you find someone with whom you are obviously going to end up very happily, it's just not worth it. It's a very nasty world to get into – deception, lying, evading, having to leave out things. I've done it myself; I don't ever want to do it again.

Yet it can be very exciting at the time ...

But is the excitement worth all the guilt, the betrayal, the lying? I think maybe as you get older you don't want to be either that excited or that guilty. I'm very against the idea of betraying someone one loves just for the sake of a bit of excitement. Sex is such a private thing; I know it isn't so much these days, but in my world it is. And it should only really be afforded to the person you love.

Would you say that a measure of guilt is beneficial to people, or is guilt a totally unprofitable emotion?

None of us is going to get through life without experiencing it, but it is a vile emotion. Guilt, not only sexual guilt, but guilt about your children, about the way you may have behaved to someone, is a loathsome feeling. One tries to avoid things that engender guilt, but of course one is imperfect and one doesn't succeed.

Both you and Quentin came to regard the divorce as a mistake. Were the years that followed marked by regret, would you say?

I regret deeply the actual trauma of our divorce – trauma may be the wrong word, because it was all very easy and we were both very civil, but we were also both completely miserable at the time. I will never ever regret having been married to Quentin; it was a wonderful marriage in many respects, and I adored him, and continued to adore him until the end of his life. The strange thing is that although it was awful getting divorced, I'm not sure whether we would have lasted thirty or forty years. He was a unique character, and he was unbelievably forgiving. People in his life were always doing things which needed forgiveness, and he forgave and forgave and forgave. He forgave me totally, and I suppose I always tried to make it up to him by helping him when he was older and frailer.

The fact that you did divorce, however, led eventually to your long-lasting marriage to James Howard-Johnston, so perhaps as you have suggested, 'God knows best.' Was this just a turn of phrase, or do you have a strong belief in God?

I do have a strong belief in God, yes, absolutely. And God does know best, and I believe in destiny. I'm not a good Christian in that I don't go to church very much any more. I'm so appalled by the dear Church of England; I can't bear the language, and I loathe the new services, the whole dumbing-down process. But I pray to God and I think about God. My old headmistress in school used to talk to us about God every Sunday night and some of what she said seeped in. She used to tell us not just to ask for things when we prayed, but to walk and talk with God. I've always remembered that from years ago, because I think it is quite a good way of keeping him in your life, as it were.

But does your belief stretch as far as thinking that God takes a special interest in you to the extent of arranging marriages and divorces?

Well, I think God wouldn't have created the whole thing if he wasn't going to take a special interest. How he does this, nobody in the world can begin to understand, but I've met so many people who feel that something has happened in their lives which has nothing to do with them. And also, how can you not believe in God if you look at the changing seasons, or if you think about Beethoven, or great art? It seems to me there is evidence everywhere. I think that for all the horrors in the world it is ultimately benevolent. I'm a bit of a coward when it comes to thinking about these huge issues, but I do think that God tests us and is ultimately concerned with each one of us.

In describing East Burnham House where you lived until you were twelve you mention a guest suite which was allegedly haunted. Do you believe in ghosts and the supernatural generally?

I am aware of odd feelings in certain places, and in that house as a child there was one end of it that I really didn't like, and entering it gave me goose pimples. I sometimes get very strange sensations, from walking in a wood at dusk, for example. Nature is quite ghostly, and I believe there are ghosts around, certainly.

Do you think that the dead still exist somewhere in some form?

I believe that the dead whom you've known and loved remain for ever within you; that's their form of life. For instance, my father died nearly thirty years ago, but not a single day goes by when I don't hear his voice in my head and remember something of him, either his face or an event or something he said. The same would apply to Quentin. I will never stop thinking of Quentin; I will always hear his voice. There is a very narrow divide between life and death, narrower than we think.

INTERVIEW CONDUCTED JANUARY 2000

SIR LUDOVIC KENNEDY

SIR LUDOVIC KENNEDY

Born in Edinburgh in 1919, Ludovic Kennedy was educated at Eton and Christ Church, Oxford. He served in the Royal Navy (1939–46) before becoming a librarian, lecturer and, in 1953, editor of the BBC's *First Reading*. He was an ITN newscaster from 1956 to 1958 and contributed to BBC's *Panorama*. He contested the Rochdale by-election as a Liberal in 1958 and the general election of 1959. He has investigated many alleged miscarriages of justice and published accounts of his researches, notably *Ten Rillington Place* (1961), *The Trial of Stephen Ward* (1964) and *A Presumption of Innocence: The Amazing Case of Patrick Meehan* (1975). His autobiography, *On My Way to the Club*, was published in 1989 and his most recent book is *All in the Mind: A Farewell to God* (1999).

You have written a best-selling autobiography and given many interviews, so it is easy to think that one already knows a great deal about you. What I wonder is this: is it all there for anyone to read or is there another Kennedy behind the public persona, one that I have little hope of reaching?

No. I've always been very open, sometimes perhaps too open in what I say to people about myself, so there's no hidden agenda anywhere. What you read is what there is.

Going back to your roots, we all know you adored your father, but you seem actually to have disliked your mother and blame her for the self-doubt and anxiety which have marked your life. In retrospect do you think you have given a fair picture of her?

Fair to me, though it may not appear to be so to other people. My relationship with my mother was never a happy one for the simple reason that she never showed me any affection at all. As far as I can remember she never gave me a cuddle when I was small, and when I grew up and greeted her or parted from her she never kissed me; she merely offered her cheek for me to kiss, and I resented that. But I was powerless to do anything about it and I thought, as people do in those circumstances, that the fault was mine. But later I came to attribute some of the anxieties I had as a young man and beyond to those early days when I lacked that affection.

But with your own experience of being a parent, do you ever think that you have perhaps judged your mother harshly?

No. My mother concentrated on my faults the whole time. She was forever saying: ' I think we ought to sit down and thrash the whole thing out.' Well, thrashing the whole thing out just meant my sitting listening to her going on and on about my faults. Did I judge her too harshly? I don't think so.

You were the first child and the only boy in a family of three with an often absent father...one would expect the usual scenario of intense mutual love between mother and son...

You are wrong in supposing that my father was often absent. I was born in 1919 and he retired from the navy in 1922, so for all my young years he was at home and I got to know him pretty well, though he was not an easy man to know. I suppose my love for him was in a way exaggerated because of the lack of love between me and my mother. He never got angry with me, even though I did some silly things when I was young. My mother always called me feckless, but my father never did; I appreciated that.

Did your sisters find their mother equally difficult?

My elder sister, Maura, suffered in the way that I did. My young sister, Catherine, did not, for the simple reason that she was adored. Nothing was too good for her, and my mother gave to her all the affection which she had denied to my elder sister and myself. Why, I don't know.

Both your parents were Scots by birth, and you were named after your maternal grandfather, Sir Ludovic Grant, a distinguished professor of law at Edinburgh University. Yet you were sent to an English prep school and then to Eton. Why was that?

Although I was born in Edinburgh I didn't live there. I went to an English prep school because we lived in England at the time, and then a trust fund set up by my grandfather – this was before the old boy went bust through speculating on the stock exchange – enabled me to go to Eton. I adored my grandparents and used to go to Scotland for holidays to visit them. When I got up there on my own without my parents I had the happiest of times. I used to play golf with my grandfather on equal terms when I was twelve and he was seventy. He had been a former captain of the Royal and Ancient at St Andrews and was a very good golfer. He would go a hundred and twenty yards straight down the fairway and I would go about two hundred yards either to left or right. That was great fun and we had a very close relationship.

You have talked about the inferiority complex inflicted by the English on the Scots, but to a neutral observer might it not seem that Scots who choose an English education for their children are perhaps contributing to this sense of inferiority?

I don't know about that. What I would say is that the English have always regarded Scotland as an extension of England; they simply don't realize it's a quite different place, with its own culture, its own laws, its own education system, its own tradition of literature, music and painting. The English simply don't appreciate this, and they feel rather aggrieved. Indeed, the latest attempts by Scotland to regain its own parliament and even to go for independence is something that many English people feel rather offended by. They would prefer us to stay with them and forget all about our own parliament. But we can't. We're an older kingdom than England and we are very proud of it.

The argument in your book In Bed with an Elephant *is that Scotland should be content with a devolved parliament at first, but gradually move towards total independence 'in the spirit of love and friendship with England, not with rancour'. Given the rise of the Scottish National Party under Alex Salmond, are you still of the same opinion?*

Yes, I am. Isaiah Berlin wrote rather well about this and quotes the German philosopher Herder: 'No minority that has preserved its own cultural tradition or religious or racial characteristics can indefinitely tolerate the prospect of remaining a minority for ever, governed by a majority with a different outlook or habits.' In other words, there is a limited time for which any nation can remain subservient to another nation. The Scots as a nation have always wanted to run their own show. In the Treaty of Union in 1707 they entered into partnership with England because they were bust and they couldn't go on as they were. They did this because it was expedient, and then having joined with England they became the British and they helped build the British Empire. That was a wonderful time for Scotland, and it made them prosperous for the first time in their lives. If you ask any Scot how he would describe himself, he would always say he was Scots first and British second. It's also a psychological thing. Maurice Lindsay, a very good Scottish poet, wrote a lovely poem the last line of which is: 'Scotland is an attitude of mind.'

In the past you have stood as a Liberal candidate for Parliament. Did you become more nationalistic in your views as the years passed?

I suppose I did. I went back to live in Scotland in 1966 and stayed there till 1984, first of all in the Border country and then in Edinburgh. Living in Scotland gave me a sharper sense of what it meant to be Scottish, and so it did grow, this feeling.

Did you ever consider joining the Scottish National Party?

I considered it, and in the end I rejected it. I spoke for the SNP on one or two occasions. In fact, I spoke for Winifred Ewing when she got in at Hamilton in the famous by-election and I was glad to do so because there was no Liberal candidate standing. Actually the Scottish Liberal Party hardly ever spoke about self-government, and that's why I gravitated towards the SNP, but I never wanted to commit myself wholly to them.

Your book All in the Mind: A Farewell to God *is one you say you have been wanting to publish all your life. You have always been at odds with the Christian religion and say it has done you good to write it. Is that reason enough, would you say?*

Yes, I think so. All writers want in the first instance to find something out for themselves. My reactions against religion in the early part of my life were spontaneous and emotional and I wanted to discover whether I could justify them by reason; that is why I researched the book, wrote it, and then finally published it. I am now certain in my mind that what I wrote was the truth. It may not be the truth for you, it may not be the truth for the Archbishop of Canterbury, but it was the truth for me.

On the final page of your book you seem to admit the possibility of a God of creation when you write: 'Whether it [the world] came about by a purposeful act, a physical evolvement, or something accidental, must remain a mystery beyond human comprehension.' Whose 'purposeful act' could it have been?

I don't know, I think it is a mystery. A lot of people think there was a purposeful act, but I can't go along with that because I don't know. I also said that it is not in my view the distant past which should exercise us now, but the future. We are now profoundly influenced by such things as global warming, pollution, nuclear bombs, the possibility of terrorist attacks with anthrax, the possibility of a new plague spreading across the world, and so on. There are numerous threats to human life on this planet, and we should really concentrate our minds on them instead of wondering how we got here.

Since you admit you don't know certain things, wouldn't it be more accurate to describe yourself as an agnostic rather than an a-theist?

Yes, except that all religions believe that their god is the real one. I say I am 'a-theist' – against gods; I simply don't go along with the whole idea of gods. I don't want any truck with gods, they don't mean anything to me.

You fear that you may have left it too late to attack religion, since you claim it is dying already. Yet seventy-five per cent of Americans are churchgoers and eighty per cent of the Irish still attend mass; to say nothing of the seventy per cent of non-churchgoing people in Britain who nevertheless profess belief in God. Might it not be said that reports of God's death have been somewhat exaggerated?

First of all, the Americans are a law unto themselves. America was founded on the Puritan ethic by people who came from Europe where life was nasty, brutish and short. They crossed the seas and left everything behind except their faith, and their faith sustained them to set up dwellings and to cross the prairies and cope with Indians who might be lurking under every bush. It's a very primitive kind of faith. The Irish are a different matter. It seems to me that the Catholic influence has profoundly lessened. It used to be the great thing to have a priest in the family in Ireland; it isn't so now, partly because there have been terrible stories about child abuse by Irish priests. As for non-churchgoers still professing to believe in God, that is easily explained. If someone knocks on the door and asks, 'Do you believe in God?', people who haven't got much education or self-confidence are very unlikely to say no. It's a kind of insurance against being struck by a thunderbolt. Remember that poem of Hilaire Belloc's: 'Better to hang on to nurse for fear of finding something worse.'

Your recounting of all the torture and killings and the wars of religion and of the Inquisition are horrifying to read, but of course they are not news nor have they anything to do with what Christ preached. Does the fact that people have committed atrocities in the name of religion amount to a good argument against religion?

I was really trying to explain why it all came about. The appalling atrocities which the Church in the Middle Ages inflicted on people came about simply because the Church was a tremendous force for social cohesion. Today we don't get that feeling of social cohesion from the Church; we get it from sport, from television, from football. The great binding force in all countries is the World Cup. It's not a religion, but it is a substitute for the cohesion which the Church used to offer.

Both Catholics and Protestants in Northern Ireland have been taught from an early age to love God and love their neighbour, but this has not stopped them killing one another. What do you say to G.K. Chesterton's claim: 'Christianity has not been tried and found wanting; it has been found hard and not tried.'

I suppose that's true, but again I just don't go along with the idea that Christianity is the be-all and end-all of human relationships. What I believe in is human altruism, but the Church has hijacked human altruism and called it Christian values. I would answer Chesterton by urging him to think more in terms of the brotherhood of man and the love they show for each other in all sorts of ways in the course of their lives. In my view, Christianity doesn't really add to it. I just don't think that Christianity is all that valuable or important. It's an artificial thing. I remember at Eton we had to turn to the altar and say, 'Almighty and most merciful God, we have erred and strayed from thy ways like lost sheep and there is no health in us, we have followed the devices and desires of our own hearts...' and so on. It was all grovel, grovel, and all the wonderful things that people do and feel for each other were neglected entirely.

But is it not the case that even if you set religion aside, the human capacity for the infliction of evil and pain is ever with us? I mean, religion was dead in Russia and in China when Stalin and Mao Tse-tung outdid the Nazis in torture and killing...

Yes, that is so, but you are making a political point. What I'm saying is that you can have a democratic society such as ours in which the people have abandoned the Christian religion on the grounds that it has outlived its usefulness. That doesn't make them any the less good people. The Scottish philosopher David Hume said we should do things that are right and good, but not because the chaplain or Jesus Christ or God said so. I agree with David Hume.

But in the absence of religious guidelines how are we to differentiate between good and bad?

It is possible to put something in the place of religion. For example, I mention in my book the Victorian poet Walter Savage Landor who wrote a famous poem before he died: 'I strove with none; for none was worth my strife./ Nature I loved and, next to Nature, art;/ I warmed both hands before the fire of life./ It sinks, and I am ready to depart.' Well, that's my philosophy too. He didn't mention religion, only his love of nature and of art, and that is what I myself feel very much too. When I go to Scotland and walk in the mountains there, I think about the line from the Psalms, 'I will lift up mine eyes unto the hills from whence cometh my strength.' I'm tremendously moved by music and poetry and particularly religious poetry which I find inspirational. You don't have to be a Christian to enjoy religiously inspired lines.

In your final chapter, 'Touching the Transcendental', you describe your own experience of the spiritual, especially when on night-watch at sea. This is what you say: 'Stars, billions of miles distant, seemed a watchful presence above my head...for me it was both a glimpse of eternity and the peace that passeth all understanding.' You use the language of religion to express what you felt. Has it ever occurred to you that you might have been having a religious experience?

No, I can't say it did. It was a spiritual experience. Only a Christian would say I was experiencing God, but I don't recognize God. I love the experience, but I don't want to specify it in any particular way. The experience is very personal and very profound, but I keep God out of it.

When you say 'spiritual', do you mean something beyond the body? And if so, is it something which might survive death?

Good heavens, no. I'm not saying it's beyond the body, I'm saying it's part of the body, part of the mind. And when I die I will be cremated and my body will be gone; in its place will be a small bowl of yellow ashes. Don't get the idea that there's something else called spirit which is unconnected with the body because I simply don't believe it. If you talk about a spirit outside the body, let me ask you this: can this spirit see, comprehend, judge, observe, have a relationship? Can it do all those things or any of them?

I don't know. But the fact that I don't know doesn't mean that it doesn't exist.

But why postulate? There are a lot of batty ideas floating about but you don't have to pay any great attention to them.

Let me take this a bit further. In the same passage you write that 'sky and sea and I were one, concordant and indivisible'. Other sailors have described similar experiences and offered them as the basis of their religious beliefs. What separates you from others in this respect?

Nothing except that others want to put labels to their experience and claim that God is in their minds and in their presence, and so on. I just don't want to use this word God; I don't know what is meant by it. Let me remind you that the Church has shifted its goalposts in recent times because people can't believe any more as literal historical fact such absurdities as the Virgin Birth, although right up almost to the present day they were happy to go along with them. I remember doing a television interview in about 1955 with Michael Ramsey, the Archbishop of Canterbury, a darling old duck of a man who looked a hundred and two but was younger than Cary Grant. He told me then that the Resurrection as a historical fact was the heart and core of Christianity. So right up to that time people were being asked to believe that events in the New Testament, and in the Old Testament as well, were historically true. Well, they weren't. There is no evidence of Christ leaving any record of what he said himself; the things he is supposed to have said were put into his mouth by the evangelists, and if you did that sort of thing in a non-fiction book or a documentary film today you'd quite rightly be taken to task by the critics. But now the Church has moved its position and is saying the Virgin Birth and the Resurrection can be regarded as myth and metaphor.

Your daughter Fiona describes how, when the family were involved in a serious road accident, you travelled to Scotland, still unaware of the details, not knowing if they were all alive, and you prayed and prayed and even sang hymns. Is this true?

No, I didn't pray. What happened was this: I was putting on a television programme that night and the editor suddenly told me he had received a call from the police at Hawick in Scotland about a very bad road accident involving my wife and children. He arranged for a car to take me to Victoria for the train to Gatwick to get the last flight to Edinburgh. Half way between London and Gatwick the train suddenly stopped and the lights all went out. I was terribly shaken and I found myself, not praying, but singing, rather out of tune as I always do, *Abide with Me*. It was an absolute spontaneous outpouring of sorrow and grief and hope mixed together, and afterwards I wondered if this meant that I had found something beyond myself which was going to be a permanent part of my life. But it wasn't; it was simply a thing that occurred at that moment, although as an experience it was perfectly true and perfectly valid. It also helped me understand that many people do get comfort from such a feeling, and not just when there is some dramatic event, but as a permanent part of their lives. That's why I say in my book that I'm not in any way criticizing people who get inspiration and comfort and faith from Christianity; indeed I wish them well.

When you were on the train you must have envisaged the possible death of the people you loved most dearly. Could you do so without the hope of an afterlife, of some way of being reunited?

The so-called afterlife is one thing I've never ever subscribed to. It seems to me such wishful thinking as not to be worthy of consideration.

Does your wife share your atheistic views?

Yes, she was not brought up in a Christian household, and was never given any instruction at all in Christianity. She was quite free of any influence of that kind in her life, and I don't believe she's any the worse for it.

Does it disturb you to find intelligent people, including some distinguished scientists, usually physicists, still believing in God?

It doesn't disturb me but it does surprise me.

For the first time in many years we have an avowedly Christian prime minister, Church of England himself, but with a Catholic wife and children who attend Catholic schools. Clearly he has swallowed the whole bag of what you call Judaeo-Christian mythology. Do you think the less of him for this?

[laughter] Slightly, yes, slightly. I think he's quite a good prime minister, but I don't give him any brownie points for his beliefs.

Will Blair's Christian beliefs prevent him from being a great or even a good prime minister?

I don't think so – it hasn't done in the past. But I am fascinated by this incredible gulf between, on the one hand, highly intelligent, educated people who believe and, on the other hand, highly intelligent, educated people who don't believe. To me it is a total mystery and I've often wished that somebody would make a study of it.

Several of your books refer to your being plagued by self-doubt and anxiety. Given that you had these feelings, how did you find the courage and confidence to take on the establishment over the many cases you considered miscarriages of justice, for example?

I don't know. All I knew was that I had a burning sense of injustice within me. I have always believed that to be condemned and tried and punished for something you haven't done is about the worst thing that can happen to you, and if you're executed for it, as poor Timothy Evans was, it is the final dreadfulness. When I was a teenager I spent a lot of time in my grandfather's house in Edinburgh going through William Hodge's *Famous British Trials* on the top shelf of his library. What fascinated me at that time was the immaculacy, the majesty, the accuracy of the law, and I had the most profound admiration for it, because I've always been a bit of a romantic. I never thought for a moment then that witnesses could lie, policemen could perjure themselves, judges could be biased. After the war when I started to look into some of these cases and found this was exactly what was happening, I was profoundly shocked, so that's why I started to write about it.

What would the late Sir Ludovic Grant, professor of law and captain of the Royal and Ancient, have thought of your tangles with the legal establishment and your being blackballed by Muirfield Golf Club?

The blackballing came about when I helped to clear a man called Patrick Meehan who had been sentenced to life imprisonment for a murder which I knew he hadn't committed. Muirfield Golf Club was full of lawyers who didn't want this upstart outsider criticizing the Scottish law. I attacked the judge, a dreadful man called Lord Robertson, and you can quote me on that – Robertson's either dead or he ought to be.

Your campaigning must have made you very unpopular. The Birmingham Six for example were not a very attractive cause at that time, I seem to remember...

There are still many people today who will tell you that they were guilty. I remember the last time I saw Woodrow Wyatt, he was being very provocative about something or other, and I said, 'Woodrow, you'll be telling me next that the Birmingham Six were guilty,' and he replied, 'Well, they *were* guilty.'

You stood up for people like poor, simple-minded Timothy Evans, and for Derek Bentley who had a mental age of eleven, and for ill-educated Irishmen, apparently guilty of atrocious murder. There must have been a lot of social pressure on you . . . Were you ever tempted to give up the struggle because of that?

No, never. I wouldn't have allowed that to happen, though I was often criticized. The last case I became involved in was that of the two Scots guardsmen who were found guilty of murdering a youth in Belfast six or seven years ago. I believed that their trial was a travesty of justice, because the presiding judge had chosen to believe the words of witnesses who were local residents and sympathetic to the IRA rather than the soldiers on patrol who had no blemish on their records. I think the judge believed that if he acquitted the two men there would be rioting and looting and burnings in Belfast, and that was something he couldn't face. At the time I got rather unpopular with a journalist called Roy Greenslade who accused me of supporting the establishment in trying to clear these men, and that this besmirched my honour. It didn't particularly worry me since he didn't know what he was talking about.

In all of these cases and in others you were proved right, and judges were forced to admit that innocent men had been condemned to years in prison, or to death. Your book Ten Rillington Place *set in motion the long campaign to clear the name of Timothy Evans. Would you say that this is the achievement of which you are most proud?*

I suppose so, because there was a real and positive conclusion to the case. But it did take a long time, thirteen years. There were two enquiries and finally Roy Jenkins, whom I have always known as a man of principle and courage, advised that the Queen should grant a posthumous free pardon, which she did.

Lord Denning thought it better that an innocent man be found guilty than that the police should be thought to have lied. Do you think he ought to have been made publicly to recant that statement?

Yes, I do. It was an absolutely disgraceful thing to say. He's applauded today as a judge who was an amusing and eccentric character and very ready to speak on behalf of the poor widow, but in some ways he was a racist of appalling judgement. He would not allow the Birmingham Six to sue the police for the injuries they had inflicted on them on the grounds that the police might be found to have been corrupt, and as a result these men who were imprisoned might have to be set free and apologies made. He said we couldn't entertain that idea. Awful, awful man.

When I interviewed Lord Donaldson he said that judges and barristers enjoy immunity for a very good reason, namely, that if they could be challenged there could never be any finality in litigation, and the process would go on for ever... do you accept that?

There's a certain amount of truth in that. As far as judges are concerned, there's no great worry because the appeal courts exist for cases where judgement may be in question, and the ultimate appeal court is the House of Lords. Barristers are a little bit different and in my view should be called to account. There are many examples in the courts of poor barristers who don't bother to see their clients until ten minutes before they go to court. That's wrong.

Another case you have espoused is voluntary euthanasia. Do you think it is likely to become legal in your lifetime?

No, but I do think it will be legalized within the next twenty years or so. In Holland it has been permitted with certain safeguards since 1980 and increasingly it is being allowed in other countries. I became a supporter of voluntary euthanasia because of my mother. When she was eighty-two I visited her in a nursing home and she told me she had had a wonderful life, but that she felt exhausted and now she wished to be 'gathered' – a lovely Scottish expression. I soon discovered there were literally thousands and thousands of other people in terminal illness who were not only in pain, which can to a certain degree be controlled, but were suffering the disintegration of personality that comes with advanced stages of cancer. This is why I accepted the post of president of the Voluntary Euthanasia Society. Thirty years from now more than half the population of Europe will be over sixty, sustained by an ever diminishing workforce, so the legislation will come. It is fraught with difficulties because we shall get abuse and neglect of the elderly, but in fact that is happening already. Read the paper any day and you will find elderly people in residential homes are being abused and neglected all the time.

In her review of your Farewell to God, *Jane Gardam asked if you can say farewell to something you have not only never known but believed never to have existed...*

That's a charming way of putting it, I suppose. The fact is that in my early days I did feel that I ought to try and believe in God because it was the common thing to do. When I was a young man just before the war, the force of conformity was terrific; people just didn't question the existence of God, and I was never told at school that some people had other ideas. So it was a struggle, and I felt that it was my fault that I couldn't believe.

I couldn't help noticing in some of the reviews the implication that because you lack faith you are to be pitied. This is not an uncommon response from those who have faith to those who don't. Do you mind that attitude? Do you mind being patronized by Paul Johnson?

I've had it for so long, I'm used to it now. Ever since the publication of my book I've had scores of tracts and little booklets sent to me with letters from people saying that Jesus loves me and that God is waiting for me and that they will pray for me. I just put them straight into the wastepaper basket.

But aren't you touched by the fact that people are praying for you?

No. [laughter] It won't do them any good, or me any good.

Paul Johnson ends his review by saying: 'Faith in God is a divine gift, and those who possess it, even if precariously, are much to be envied by those who dwell in doubt.' How do you respond to that?

Paul Johnson is the most brainwashed Roman Catholic I know. He was taught at infant school by holy sisters, then at prep school by holy brothers, and he went from there to Stoneyhurst where he was taught by the Jesuits. Paul Johnson is the most perfect example of a highly intelligent man who on this one subject is totally brainwashed.

But he does make the point which a great many people would endorse – that we live by hope, and that hope and faith are closely related. I think you yourself do not deny that there is this predisposition in mankind to believe in something, however nebulous.

I believe in hope too, but I quite disagree when you say that hope and faith are closely connected. I've always been hopeful; for example, I always hope each book I write is going to be a bestseller and it very seldom is, and I am always hopeful that my children will be happy and make happy marriages and they don't always succeed. So you're not looking at a man who doesn't believe in hope. Faith is a different matter. I mention in my book that when European seamen were exploring the world in the seventeenth century they discovered many different peoples in various countries, especially in Siam, China and Japan, who had no belief in a God at all, no belief in the immortality of the soul and the life everlasting. The English philosopher John Locke made the point that not all human beings have found the necessity to create a God, and indeed all gods are created by human beings.

Let me take a slightly different approach. No doubt you would agree that there are many individuals who hold sincere religious beliefs and lead what we might call good and decent lives, and the fact that they live good and decent lives may be connected (at least in their own minds) to their religious beliefs. Is there anything wrong with that?

Nothing wrong with it at all, and I wish them joy and success. What you say is true, but there are also many Christians who are uncharitable, not compassionate, bigoted and so on. The conservative Christian is really a very undesirable character, and there are many about who are emphatically not good people at all.

What about those in religious orders who devote their lives to God and to prayer? Are they to be disapproved of? Are they to be pitied? Or are you happy to leave them alone?

If they are getting satisfaction from what they do, I'm delighted for them. I think they are misguided, but that's not the point. If they have found something that gives them a rich life, then good luck to them. Many of them are unselfish and courageous people and I know what good works they do.

So you do admire them...

I admire people who are committed to some path in life which they feel is taking them somewhere. Yes, I do admire them, but not specifically more than many other people.

You reject the idea of an afterlife, and dismiss it as mere wishful thinking. What exactly is wrong with wishful thinking? If there is only oblivion, it will hardly matter, surely?

I quite agree. There is nothing wrong with wishful thinking. If you want to believe in rubbish, by all means believe in rubbish.

INTERVIEW CONDUCTED MARCH 1999

ALAN ROSS

ALAN ROSS

Alan Ross was born in India in 1922, and after spending his early childhood in Bengal, he went to Haileybury and St John's College, Oxford. He served in the Royal Navy from 1942 to 1947 after which he worked for the British Council. From 1953 to 1972 he was cricket correspondent for the *Observer* and he has been editor of the *London Magazine* since 1961. He is the author of several books including *Death Valley* (1980), which was a Poetry Book Society Choice, *Colours of War* (1983) and two volumes of autobiography, *Blindfold Games* (1986) and *Coastwise Lights* (1988).

You were born in Calcutta and lived in India until you were seven years old. The first seven years are said to be the most important and to set the pattern for life. Did India do that to you, would you say?

Yes, certainly. I went back after the war in around 1960 and when I got off the aeroplane, I felt as though I was coming home. The smell of it and the look of it were absolutely enchanting to me. I used to think up every kind of excuse for going back, because it called me in some curious way. And it still does.

You were sent to school in England, aged seven – the first step, you say, in 'an alienation from all family life'. This rather suggests an estrangement which has lasted throughout your life. Is that what happened?

When I was sent to England I was farmed out on various people who were very kind to me, first of all a farmer in Cornwall and then a clergyman in Sussex. I spent the whole of my adolescence with these people, so that when my family came back after the war, they seemed to me strangers. It wasn't so much an estrangement, but I felt very shy with them, and they had a different outlook on everything. My father had been a soldier, and then he went on to be a very successful businessman and politician in India, but we had nothing in common, except the three things which I inherited from him – a love of cigars, whisky and racehorses.

Was your own son sent away to school or were you anxious to save him from that experience?

We did save him from that experience. He went to a prep school as a day boy and he was at home all the time, but then he wanted to go away to school when he was older. Curiously enough, the same happened with my stepdaughter also, but she wanted to go at an even earlier age. I think if you give children a happy time at home they quite like the adventure of going away.

Do you think that the alienation you experienced at a young age was to have an adverse effect on your marriages?

No, I think marriage is quite difficult anyway. One turns one's wives into friends, which I think is good in one way, but perhaps not in another way.

Would you say that you are a difficult man to live with as far as women are concerned?

No, very kind and gentle.

Then why do you think the marriages failed?

I've only had one proper marriage, and it went on for thirty years. I had other relationships at the time and they didn't seem to conflict with the feeling I had for my wife, but of course in the end people want to have something different, and so they change.

Have women been important in your life?

Very important. They have given me great pleasure. Of course, they can give one a hard time, but I do love their company.

Your father's Indian bearer cut his throat soon after you left for England. Was there any connection between these two events?

Not that I know of. He was an eccentric fellow who used to cover his lips with that red stuff which made it look as though he was bleeding all the time. He wasn't a very pretty sight, and he was slightly mad – what they call *puggle-wallah* in India.

You say that during your time at boarding school it was the brown hands that you craved, not the alternately distant and crowding affection of your parents. Why did you feel so close to the Indian servants? Did they give you something your parents could not provide?

Yes. Most British children in India were brought up by Indian servants.

The father would be away all day long, and the mother was possibly in England, so the rewarding thing in children's lives would always be Indian hands, those of the ayah or the bearer who looked after you and treated you as an important person. They were always very kind, and you never forget that.

You describe yourself in the poem 'A Wartime Present' as 'an exile, without family, without family feeling'. Do you still feel like that?

Well, my parents are both dead now, so I have to think of my own family and children, and we are all very separate. I see my wife sometimes, I see my son more, and my stepdaughter a bit, but we're not a family in the normal sense. Of course, at the beginning of one's life, one hoped to be close.

At one point you write with near contempt about Calcutta society in the 1920s 'with its ignorance of almost everything to do with Indian history, religion, architecture and art'. Your mother's family had been in India since 1790... were your grandmother and the aunts equally philistine, or was this a twentieth-century phenomenon?

Reluctantly I would have to say that the British were pretty philistine. I mean, they were mostly in trade or in the army, the exception being those who were in the Indian civil service who were extremely well read and aware of what was going on in India. But the generality of the British in India were not very cultivated people. They worked quite hard, they played a lot of games, they drank and they played bridge, but they never opened a book. This is a delicate point, and indeed the only row I ever had with my father in my whole life was when he was vice-consul in St Malo and I called in on him on my way back from Paris. We had an amusing evening but somehow – perhaps after too many drinks – I said in a most tactless way, 'Of course, the only reason people went to India was never on behalf of the Indians; it was only on behalf of themselves.' And this to a man who had spent his whole life in India, who'd been a minister in the government and head of the Bengal assembly for many years. He became absolutely furious, till I thought he was going to kill me. It struck at the root of everything he had done. At the back of his mind he must have believed that it was all for the Indians, which of course it wasn't.

Did your parents live to see the end of British rule in India?

My father left India very suddenly in 1946. He has been offered a job by Mountbatten, who was Viceroy at the time, but he suddenly lost his nerve when two close friends with whom he'd spent his whole life in India died in the same week of amoebic dysentery. Within the space of forty-eight hours he had sold everything and left. I suppose he was a rich man, but the Indians allowed people to take only one third of their capital and so he instantly became rather a poor man. He then announced to my mother that he would travel the world once before settling down. So he set off on his travels, and halfway round the world he wrote to my mother to tell her he had fallen in love with another woman and would not be coming back. 'I hope you'll forgive me,' he wrote.

And he never came back?

He did, because this woman, who thought he was a very rich man, suddenly realized he wasn't, so she wasn't so keen on the idea and their affair lasted only three or four weeks. My father then wrote to my mother saying he was sorry, he'd made a bad mistake, and would she allow him to come back. Which she did. He never strayed again after that.

At Haileybury you became interested in the French romantic poets, but found them disastrous as an influence on the writing of poetry. Has any modern poet influenced you?

I was influenced by Louis MacNeice more than anybody. He was my kind of person, interested in sport, and fond of writing about women, and having affairs all over the place. Whereas there was a homosexual, austere background to Eliot and Auden and Spender, and so on, MacNeice was a jolly fellow who could see that modern poetry could be interesting about ordinary things.

You seem slightly defensive about your belief that sport is poetry in action. You were delighted, for example, to discover Auden's 'Odes to School Footballers', as if these somehow legitimized your belief...

Yes, I think that is true. When I was at Oxford first of all I thought of nothing but sport; indeed the idea of poetry had hardly entered my head. I was obsessed by playing different games and trying to get a blue, and there was a slight feeling – not exactly of shame – but the feeling that sport was not quite right for a serious literary figure.

Is it because sport is often perceived as frivolous, whereas poetry is to do with serious matters like the soul?

It is to do with that. I don't think about the soul too much if I can avoid it, but poetry in the end is about all sorts of things. When I was very young, however, poetry seemed to me a rather solemn, slightly effete activity which I couldn't quite relate to my own life, and then gradually I found that the war gave me a subject to write about. Then I began to see that it could transform one's whole life, just in the way music or painting can.

Do you think that the self-discipline you acquired in learning to play cricket well was any help to you in your wartime experiences? Was Wellington talking nonsense when he said that the Battle of Waterloo was won on the playing fields of Eton, or is there something in it?

When I was in the Fleet Air Arm we had to do sentry work when we were not learning to fly. This meant standing in a box with a rifle and guarding the aerodrome. On one occasion I was on sentry duty before going for a weekend leave to see a girlfriend of mine acting in a play up in Liverpool. I stood in this box till four o'clock, half-past four, quarter to five, and still no one came to relieve me. My train was going at quarter-past five, so I went across the road to a call-box and rang up the main gate and told them my relief hadn't come. In the meantime, the commander had arrived in a car, and when he saw there was nobody in the box, and moreover that my rifle was just lying there, he was furious and had me put under arrest. I had to appear before him the following Monday – this was called jankers – and he said to me that I had deserted my post in the face of the enemy, whereupon I replied that there wasn't any enemy. He got very angry and told me I would go to prison, which would have been the end of my naval career. In fact, the next day a signal came from Lords saying I had been chosen to play cricket for the navy, and since the commander-in-chief of the whole shoot at Portsmouth was an old naval cricketer, he immediately took me off arrest, although I still had to do fourteen days running around with a rifle as a kind of punishment.

You say of Haileybury as you knew it in the 1930s that no anti-élitist could have taken exception to it, the boys being the sons of clergymen or army or naval officers. It was also philistine in that it gave little encouragement to art and literature, and you think this was probably true of most public schools. What is your impression now? Do you think they give value for money?

I suppose they do, but the number of people in society who are interested in music, painting or poetry is pretty small, and unless you have one or two masters who are exceptional, there won't be much encouragement in any school. But most of the boys don't give a bugger one way or the other.

The Oxford University Press closed its poetry list, presumably for reasons not unconnected with profit. Is there just no market for poetry in this country?

The market in general is very small, although what the Oxford University Press did was a disgrace. During the thirty-five years or so I was a publisher I suppose I brought out thirty or forty books of poetry, but none of them made money. On the other hand, they didn't lose much and you would have to be a very miserable figure to feel you couldn't go on with such an enterprise.

What's the future of poetry in this country? Do you think people are becoming more aware of poetry?

They have never been much aware of it. There are always some people who will take it very seriously and feel passionately about it, and we have produced great poets in this country and continue to do so. But none of this affects the generality of people at all. It's actually quite hard to read poetry.

I have read that you have a dislike of literary criticism...

Well, I don't think literary criticism has done much for literature. It seems to me a rather dead hand on it, and I don't like reading it very much.

You have edited the London Magazine *for over thirty years, and it has been entirely shaped and nurtured by you in form and content. It is perhaps the last literary magazine in the old style... do you feel very much as if you're swimming against the tide?*

I don't know what you mean by the tide. I consider the *London Magazine* to be absolutely a magazine of the time. It's the best magazine in the world of its kind, and the only thing that we've never managed to do because of lack of money is promote it properly, and I'm very sad about that. If one had a patron of some kind, then instead of having two or three thousand subscribers we could have ten thousand, and then we could pay people better. At the moment we pay them appallingly; my partner gets only two thousand pounds a year for a full-time job, and I get nothing at all. Well, this is disgraceful, and one can't go on like that really, although we have gone on like that. But even if we had a million pounds given to us the actual contents wouldn't change – the quality would remain the same.

Kathleen Raine believes that poetry is irreconcilable with tranquil, stable love relationships. She says that very few poets have been happily married... do you have a view on that?

Their relationships may not last all their lives, but I don't think one can read into that more than you would read into anybody else's experience. I mean, do lawyers have happy marriages, or sportsmen, or dentists? Sometimes they do, sometimes they don't.

I suppose we think of poets leading tortured lives...

That's a romantic idea. Eliot wanted poets to be like bank clerks, and I think the better poets are nearer to bank clerks than rough and ready scoundrels who get drunk every night. The romantic figure – always drunk, dying at twenty-five – is not really relevant. A poet's life does not need to be dishevelled. A good writer is a good writer.

In your account of service with the occupying forces in Germany after the Allied victory, I was struck by your compassion for the defeated enemy. This, of course, was a truly Christian attitude. Would you call yourself a Christian?

I have no great belief, but I believe in justice more than anything. Any kind of injustice upsets me a great deal, and in Germany you saw a great many people suffering appallingly through no great fault of their own, and that was very moving. The dispossessed people of the 1940s, moving with their carts through Europe, that was a heartbreaking sight.

Has religion played an important part in your life?

No, although I was brought up by a country clergyman and I used to enjoy going to his church. He was so boring he used to fall asleep in his own sermons, but when he actually dropped off his little dog would rush up to him and wake him up. Having said that, he was a very good priest for all the people in his parish, and it was all very nice and calm; but exciting it wasn't.

But do you find yourself turning to God when things go badly?

Yes, I do. I've had two very bad illnesses in my life, and the last one was a very severe depressive illness lasting five or six years, and I was on my knees practically every night. Out of weakness one flies to God – not a very noble thing, but one does. The trouble is, I can't believe it's really true, although I would like to. And I'd prefer to die a Catholic because it's so much more romantic to have incense all round you, but until that moment comes...

After the war you could hardly bear to look at old school photographs, so many of your friends were dead, as are so many friends of later years. Has this caused you to reflect on death a great deal?

As you say, in the wartime days a lot of people died, and then twenty or thirty years seemed to go by with very few people dying, and now suddenly they all seem to be dying all over the place. You begin to ask yourself how many years you've got left. Death is this tiny little moment between living and dying – you're there one minute and gone the next. One hopes it happens very quickly. Of course, I would be rather annoyed not to have a little bit more life left. There are a lot of things I like doing and I don't relish the idea of them coming to an end. For example, I would like to know what Tottenham Hotspur are going to do next year.

As well as your lack of rancour towards the Germans, I notice that there was none towards the people who featured in your memoirs, with the exception perhaps of the boy who bullied you at school. Is your nature exceptionally benign, would you say, or have you been fortunate in your life?

I've been fortunate except for two appalling nervous breakdowns. As a young man on a ship on the Arctic convoys when we were set on fire and people were being killed, I thought that was about as bad as it was ever going to get, and nothing would ever be as bad again. But in fact my breakdowns were far worse than anything I experienced in the war. I'm sure everybody who has had a bad depression would agree with me.

Would you like to be remembered chiefly as a poet?

I'm rather uncomfortable with the word 'poet' since it is hard to think of oneself in those terms. I would rather be remembered as somebody who made his friends happy and wrote reasonably well about different things, and for forty years kept a magazine going which did a great deal for a lot of writers.

INTERVIEW CONDUCTED FEBRUARY 1999

BRIAN SEWELL

BRIAN SEWELL

Brian Sewell was born in 1931 and educated at Haberdashers and the Courtauld Institute where he was taught by Anthony Blunt. He spent several years working for galleries, then ten years as a valuer at Christie's, including a short time as an art dealer. For three years he was art critic with *Tatler* before going to the *Evening Standard* in 1984. He has been named Critic of the Year several times in the British Press Awards.

You are a distinguished art historian, but it is as an art critic that you have earned yourself a reputation – indeed you might easily be called the doyen *of art criticism. Assuming that you didn't set out to achieve this designation, is it nevertheless one from which you derive satisfaction?*

Oh dear, I think I have to argue with several of those statements. I have absolutely no distinction as an art historian. I've never written the book I want to write, and I've never been involved in a major exhibition, at least not since I was a mere boy. When I first left the Courtauld I had a very promising career. I was regarded as quite a bright boy and it all looked as though it was set fair. Then I was offered a job at Christie's and I spent the next ten years of my life there being diverted from serious scholarship. Working at Christie's is a game of swift judgement and even swifter identification, or sometimes mis-identification. I became a critic by accident, and the fact that I did so seemed to me clear evidence of my river having run into sand, the end rather than the beginning. I had spent my whole life up to that point looking at pictures, going to exhibitions and experiencing the *frisson* of excitement as things changed in the contemporary art world. As a student of art history, I was very much aware of what David Hockney and his contemporaries tried to do, and I had considerable sympathy with them. But I now find myself very detached from those revolutionaries of the 1960s and 1970s, having grown old with them, as it were. I have come to realize how trivial and idiotic much of post-war art is; I am therefore disdainful and dismissive of it. And this has given me a certain notoriety; that's all.

Critics are of course creatures much reviled – the artistic equivalent of traffic wardens, one might say. To what extent does this bother you?

The abuse doesn't bother me because although it applies to an enormous number of critics working in this country, also in France, Germany and America, I don't think it applies to me. There are very few people who are prepared to speak out and tell the truth as they see it. Most critics are ill-informed; they have no practice either as painters or as art historians, so they come to the business of looking at pictures almost like strangers. There are other critics who can only be described as Vicars of Bray, in that whatever is stuck under their noses they feel bound to praise it. Richard Cork [art critic on *The Times*] is a very good example; it really doesn't matter what it is, as long as it has been vouched for, as long as it has a certificate of quality from the Tate Gallery or the Hayward or the Arts Council, he is prepared to say it is wonderful. There is yet another kind of critic who, thank God, is now in the decline – I'm thinking of people like Marina Vaizey. She believes in signposting; that it is her duty to say that something is there, and that that is enough. Well, it isn't enough. A critic should have some kind of bite on the subject with which his readers are not expected to agree. What he should be doing is providing an intellectual peg on which readers can hang their own arguments and their own judgements.

Flaubert said: 'A man is a critic when he cannot be an artist, in the same way that a man becomes an informer when he cannot be a soldier.' Do you think there is an uncomfortable truth in that view?

No. I don't think there is any truth in that at all. Edward Lucie-Smith, for example, did not become a critic because he couldn't paint. Edward came to criticism from poetry, from being a writer, from an interest in acquiring things, which led him naturally to the intellectual pursuit of what lies behind the things we acquire; it has absolutely nothing to do with his inability to draw or paint. The curious thing is that when you do get critics who can to some extent paint, and they are rash enough to put themselves on view, they are appalling. One simply cannot understand why they have not exercised the first principle of the critic, which is to examine what he himself does, whether as a painter or as a writer.

Oscar Wilde had a different perspective from Flaubert, believing that it is precisely because a man cannot do a thing that he is the proper judge of it. Are you any more inclined to the Wildean view of things?

I'm not, but the last Conservative government was, and this New Labour regime quite certainly is. There is a belief amongst those who have the power to make important appointments that the amateur is best. This applies particularly in the area of visual arts. There is a very good example now in the invention of this New Labour organization called MLAG. It has to do with museums, libraries, galleries and archives, and yet it is headed by somebody who cheerfully admits that he is not interested in any of those, and his right-hand man is that celebrated cook and entertainer Loyd Grossman, a man who looks through keyholes for a living. It is the devil of the art gallery and the museum in this country that their trustees are amateurs, and it is the devil of organizations like the Museums and Galleries Commission that their commissioners are people who know absolutely nothing about the history and purpose of galleries and museums. So don't blame the critic; blame the government, because in one shape or form government is always the institution through which appointments are made. They seem to have a sense of mischief for putting the cat among the pigeons. But pigeons can get on with their business perfectly well without pussy upsetting it.

The few facts that I was able to glean about your early life suggest a not very auspicious start. Your father committed suicide before you were born and your mother by all accounts was stiflingly possessive. How does a child survive such a childhood?

That's an exceedingly difficult question to answer. I think I survived my childhood because my mother treated me from my very earliest consciousness as an adult. The consequence was that when I eventually went to school, very soon after my eleventh birthday, my abilities were absurd for a child of my age. I had a considerable command of things like Greek mythology, Roman history, and opera and I read the novels that my mother read instead of baby books. This was rather unbalanced in one way, but it gave me a head start in terms of general culture. I was taken to the National Gallery every week as a child so small that I can remember looking at the undersides of frames as they projected from the wall. I don't know what I would have done had my mother not brought me up in such a one-sided way, but her one side opened windows all the time. That is why I didn't stifle.

You have said – touchingly – of your father's suicide that he put the cat out before he gassed himself. How important was it for you to be made aware of that gentle and humane gesture before an act of such self-destructiveness?

In so far as I have any folk memory, as it were, of my father, it is the thing that means most to me. I share my father's melancholy nature and there are moments when depression becomes unbearable, but what prevents me from committing suicide is that I have dogs. And I care more for them than I do for myself.

There was presumably a temptation to romanticize the father you had never known... did you find that you could turn him into almost anyone you wanted?

No. In the very early days his absence was really not important. My life was very full with the entertainments provided by my mother. And by the age of eleven I had acquired a stepfather who was interested in music and religion, and also in the observances of the Church of England, as opposed to the Roman Catholic Church in which I had been christened. So there were plenty of things to excite and divert me from worrying or wondering about my own father.

For the first eleven years of your life you did not mix with other children... did you accept this as part of the natural order of things?

Yes. I had no idea of what I was missing, none whatsoever.

Do you subscribe to the Larkin view of things: 'They fuck you up, your Mum and Dad'?

If you had asked me that question thirty years ago I would have said, yes, I am well and truly fucked up. But now I look at the married couples who are my friends, I look at their children, and I realize that the happy marriage, the untroubled family, is a great rarity. It is the nature of parenthood to fuck up children, and that's that. We shouldn't expect anything more.

Did you consciously decide against having children of your own, and if so, was this related to your own experience as a child?

I went through a period in my early thirties when I thought that it would be wonderful if one could settle down and lead the absolutely conventional life, marriage and children, and so on. But I knew deep down that this was an impossibility – I had been solitary for so long. I also had to confront the irredeemable nature of my homosexuality, which at an early stage had come into extreme conflict with my religious life. This wasn't exactly straightforward because I had been born a Roman Catholic, and though I had been diverted into the Church of England by my stepfather, I had always wanted to go back to being a Roman. But what disturbed me was the hostility of both branches of the Christian Church to what was my essential nature. It was something with which I was born – I am convinced of that; it could not be trained or educated out of me, yet it was a barrier that all my priests demanded I should deal with. It seemed to me that the only solution the Church offers a homosexual is to be a eunuch, and that, I believe, is simply not possible. Like all men I am a sexual being; it need not be very fruitfully applied, but it cannot be denied.

You have described your mother's possessiveness as 'utterly destructive'. Is that something you have found hard to forgive?

Oh, I don't think I have found anything really hard to forgive. She had a fairly tough time and she did the best she could. I sometimes joke and say I am the victim of a deprived childhood, and in many ways I am, but there were many compensations. When I started school at the age of eleven, we were required to give a little talk for five minutes to the class. The other boys talked about their pets and their school holidays, but I stood up and talked about Wagner. I rejoice that I had a mother who brought me up to be able to do that.

You were packed off to school at the insistence of your stepfather. Were you dragged screaming and kicking, so to speak, or was it in some ways a relief to get away?

I had no idea what school was, so I didn't know what to expect. My mother didn't want me to go to boarding school, so my stepfather lugged me round all the possibilities in London, the City of London School, St Paul's, University College, but none of them would have me because I didn't know anything that fitted the school curriculum. I couldn't add two and two, and my English was completely instinctive, not soundly based on grammar. This was a huge problem, but eventually I was taken in at Haberdashers, and then only because they were desperate. Haberdashers was just about as low as you could go. It was exceedingly unpleasant and would have been a disaster had it not been for my innate ability to run, not only quickly but over very long distances. Cross–country running and rugby saved me, otherwise I would have been teased to death.

You say somewhere that your stepfather was treated extremely badly by your mother and also by you. Was this something you recognized only with hindsight, or were you aware of it at the time?

I recognized it when I did my national service in the army, an extraordinary experience for me. It was then for the first time I realized what a decent man my stepfather was.

Is there a feeling of self-reproach when you recall the way you treated your stepfather?

Not particularly. [laughter] My stepfather got his own back in the end because he left all his money – not that there was much of it – to his first wife and his daughter, not to my mother and me, though he had been with us much longer.

Do you believe in self-improvement, that people can recognize their faults and do something about them?

There are probably episodes in people's lives that cause change of some kind. In my own case, it happened suddenly when I found I had a fairly useless heart. I had been wonderfully fit until I had a heart attack and its consequences have been disastrous. I have looked over the edge a couple of times, and the business of looking over the edge does make one feel slightly more generous perhaps.

You spent two years in the army . . . was that a tough time for you?

It was tough in all the conventional ways, but it wasn't intellectually tough. It was just something one had to do. The real problem for me was whether or not I should take my violin with me. I was quite good in those days, and I didn't want to stop being good, but somehow a kind of common sense intervened and told me, no, no, you do not go to Aldershot with a violin, you do not. Of course, it was the end of serious violin playing, but it did help remove any kind of lingering vanity that one might really be a brilliant violinist.

Is that a major regret?

No. Quite frankly I don't think I would ever have been good enough, and even if I had been good enough I would have been far too emotional, because music gets to the heart of me, and I can't really control my emotional reactions to it.

You turned down a place at Oxford in favour of the Courtauld Institute. Did you ever regret not going to Oxford? Do you think things might have turned out very differently if you had?

I don't think Oxford would have been the place for me. I'm unclubbable, and Oxford is a very clubbable place – it is where people go to network as much as to learn. The Courtauld as it then was suited me very well. It's a very large body of exceedingly good teachers and a very small student body. Some of us were fortunate to be taught one to one by people like Blunt, which was wonderful. No, I don't regret it at all.

You have sometimes said that your time at the Courtauld taught you how to look properly at a picture. Do you think this is something which has to be learned, that one cannot know instinctively how to look properly?

One can look at pictures in so many different ways. You can look at a picture like a clerk: how big is it, what is it made of, what is the medium, to whom did it belong, where has it been, who has written about it? And you accumulate all that information and you never ask yourself whether it is good or great or whether it excites you; it is simply documented. There are an awful lot of art historians like that who are incapable of responding to a picture as they would to a piece of music – they have absolutely no idea. And then there are other people who just look at a picture and say, isn't it wonderful? They are sent witless in front of abstracts by Mark Rothko, trying to induce some trance-like state as a result of sitting in front of a sea of colour. That's also pretty uninformed. One definitely needs a bit more than that. For myself, I need to respond not only to the dry documentation of a picture (which nevertheless can sometimes illuminate); I want to respond to the working of the painter's hand and brush, I want to see the lifting-off point, that little tail of paint when you take a brush away, I want to see when something is in pastel, when something is in glaze, I want to involve myself in the act of painting in exactly the same way as when playing a musical instrument one is somehow involved in the mind of the composer. There's a wonderful little picture by Mantegna which is always called *The Entombment of Christ*, but I think it's the Resurrection and I think it's the Resurrection because the usual paraphernalia of the entombment are not there. Christ is being propped up on the narrow end of a sarcophagus by two angels, both of whom have one leg in the sarcophagus, and they seem to me to be heaving him out of it rather than laying him in it. His lower limbs are over the edge to the fore of the picture and the face is full of pain; it's the most agonized face you could hope to find in the whole history of art. The body is pallid and the face is ruddy, and you sense that after being three days dead the blood is flowing again – think of the excruciating pain that you experience when you've been sleeping on your arm, and the blood begins to flood into it again. This is what Christ is experiencing over his whole body. If you can look at a picture like this and see those things, then I think you are seeing everything that you can. To take a different example, if you look at *The Resurrection* by Piero della Francesca, you see a wonderful triumphant Christ. There's no Mantegnesque examination of the how, but there is everything in the why and the consequence of it in that really magnificent body triumphant as it comes out of the sarcophagus; there is no pain, just victory. It's another way of looking at it, another way of informing us.

How does this fit with your view that good art should be accessible to all and that there is something in a Donatello or a Michelangelo that can be understood by every man?

I cannot imagine that even the humblest Florentine peasant on seeing Donatello's *Habakkuk* would not immediately recognize it for what it was. Similarly, a French peasant coming into contact with Rodin's *Burghers of Calais* would immediately understand, perhaps not the historical story, but from the expressions, from the body language of those figures, he would know exactly what was happening, who was being compliant, who was being heroic – all the information is there. But you look at contemporary art now, what is to be divined from ninety-nine per cent of it? Absolutely nothing. And when lecturers in galleries like the Tate are asked, 'What does this picture mean?', the answer is invariably, 'Oh, it means what you want it to mean.' This just isn't good enough.

One of your principal complaints about modern art is that there is no place for beauty, and that beauty has become almost an irrelevance. Can we talk a little about your concept of beauty... can beauty still be found in the depiction of something ugly, for example?

It depends on the ugliness. In the Metropolitan there's a piece of sculpture by Kiki Smith of a woman emptying her bowels. I don't see anything beautiful in that, just as I don't see anything beautiful in the very late Picasso of a woman emptying her bladder. But these are graceless works, disturbing only in the sense that they are distasteful. There are, however, ugly subjects that are perfectly acceptable. Goya's *Cannibals*, for example, where a human leg is waved about, is a painting so exquisite that it lifts the subject and takes the horror out of it. Again, you have Géricault painting heads that have been sliced off by the guillotine; they aren't very beautiful, but they are beautifully recorded, the beauty being in the facture of the paint. I could live with those; I might not put them in my dining-room, but I could certainly live with them.

Do you find the works of Lucian Freud or Francis Bacon beautiful?

I have problems with both. I think that Bacon was a mannerist in the sense that his way of doing things was more important than the subject itself. The easiest evidence of that is when he used to load his brush with white paint and flick it at a picture which was nearing completion. This stream of white paint tells us absolutely nothing. However, there are aspects of his work which are very beautiful in terms of subtlety of handling and modelling, for example. With Lucian Freud, I think that in some ways he is such a bad painter, such a lazy painter, someone who cannot be consistent and who gets bored with what he is doing. He is also obsessive, and there is a tremendous irregularity between the various parts of his pictures.

You deplore the breed of artist who urinates in the snow and makes bronze casts of the result, and there are many people who agree with you. Do you believe that there are objective standards by which we can judge what we might call real works of art as opposed to fashionable, gimmicky pieces?

The short answer to that is no, because if you apply objective standards you will get no advance. You might condemn new ways of doing things as nineteenth-century academic painters condemned the Impressionists. Having said that, I do have very serious problems with so-called artists like Helen Chadwick, because it seems to me that neither her *Piss Flowers*, as these snow pieces were called, nor her *Chocolate Fountain*, which was a pure reference to the emptying of the bowels, nor throwing furniture out of a first floor could possibly constitute works of art. If they are works of performance, then perhaps their place is in the theatre, but not in the art gallery.

One of the central difficulties for art historians and indeed anyone who is interested in art is what might be called the matter of taste. Can taste ever be a reliable yardstick?

No, we should never have an intellectual argument based on the stomach's response to things, though I do think you can trust your stomach, since it is often a very reliable guide as to whether something is good. I know that sounds absurd, but it's that same kind of visceral clench that you get when wonderful music is being played. It should do the same when you're looking at something.

Is it possible to say, for example, that David Hockney is not to my liking, not my taste, but I recognize that he is an important artist?

I could demonstrate to anyone who would care to listen to me that David Hockney is a rotten painter. In the late 1960s and the first half of the 1970s, he became, fairly briefly, a brilliant draughtsman, and that is all I would give him. David is somebody who does not understand the paint; he has absolutely no feeling for it other than as colour between lines, absolutely none. He talks a great deal about perspective, but he has no sense of aerial perspective, nor does he know anything about varying colour, nothing at all.

To what then do you attribute his rise to fame?

Entirely to his homosexuality. He came in as a flamboyant homosexual at just the right moment in the 1960s, when everyone for the first time ever was determined to be liberal about it. People who were not themselves homosexual would buy David's work and hang it in the drawing-room as a demonstration of their own liberal attitudes, and it's just gone on from there. And once you entrench a painter in the public mind as the great painter of the day, he goes on as such. We are now turning him into a guru, a wise old man, but he's no wiser than the street cleaner, if as wise.

One problem, I suppose, is that we know that when people saw the pictures of Manet or Cézanne over a century ago, they seemed outrageously modern and people were shocked and dismayed and felt that everything that they had known and loved about art hitherto was under threat. We are traditionally very bad at dealing with the shock of the new, are we not?

No. You just have to consider the history of collecting to dispute that. I mean, Degas had an agent in Manchester, for God's sake. That doesn't suggest to me that there was no appreciation. Or if you look at the great Scottish collections, there were some far-sighted Scottish dealers selling wonderful pictures to people who built ships. Then there's that old foolishness about all the Impressionists dying in poverty. They didn't. It cost Monet just ten pictures to buy Giverny, that's all. He was turning out a picture a day, and he was a rich man. Degas was rich, and Renoir was also rich. Gauguin and Van Gogh were the odd men out; you can't apply their level of penury to all the others. I simply do not understand how this myth survives. Of course, there have always been opponents, but right across Europe there have been collectors and dealers who have supported the painters at the time – you only have to look at how early their work was being bought by major institutions. In the Neue Pinakothek in Munich there is a wonderful picture by Manet, a kind of breakfast picture – I can't remember what it is called – but it went there pretty well at once. It didn't have to hang around a studio. There were great German dealers in places like Düsseldorf – Düsseldorf, for heaven's sake, the Manchester of Germany!

Setting aside your specific objection to modern conceptual art, would you concede that art, like music or architecture or literature, does not stand still; it moves (as it has always done), and this is in itself not a bad thing, but just something that happens?

It's something that *must* happen, otherwise there is no change. If it didn't happen then the whole of Western art would be exactly like the wretched icon painting in Cyprus, produced for holidaymakers and resembling things that were painted a thousand years ago. You must allow change, and the wonderful thing about the history of art is that change is so evident. How do you get from Giotto to Donatello? How do you get from Donatello to Michelangelo, from Michelangelo to Bernini? It isn't a single line, it's a cat's cradle of a line of development, looping backwards and going up and down in terms of quality.

Conceptual art leaves you cold – there is nothing, you say, that lifts the spirit. Can you be sure, however, that there is nothing that lifts the spirit of others?

That isn't quite my view. Let's take something which is possibly a familiar example: the first set of cage pieces by Damien Hirst. These are glass containers with steel frames and when they were exhibited in the ICA some years ago, I was deeply moved by them. They were very disturbing. They were not beautiful, but they did what beauty does, which is affect the spirit. Which is why I am very defensive of Damien, because he has gone through phases which are not just flamboyant things with sharks and sheep; he has also touched on things that are essential to the darker side of human nature, and no one can take that away from him. My esteem for his work is very high.

A few years ago you said: 'It is terribly disturbing to find oneself literally loathed by people. I hardly go out at all now, except to go to galleries.' Has that situation changed at all, or are you still disturbed by the strength of people's reactions to you?

I am disturbed, yes. I have become something of a recluse, and I now very largely no longer go to the press views of exhibitions in case those who most dislike me are there. My presence seems to disturb them even more than their reaction disturbs me. There was one woman critic, for example, who had a fit of hysterics at the Royal Academy and said she couldn't bear to be in the same room. She just screamed to the company at large, 'There's that terrible man!' She tried to go to another room but found she couldn't get out because she was at the end of the sequence of rooms. So I just said, 'Oh, sod the bloody woman. I'll leave and come back when she gets herself out of the gallery.' And I left.

But isn't there a very real sense in which by holding such strong views you invite strong reactions? I mean, your writing style is, to say the least, provocative, and some would also argue that it is gratuitously insulting and also sometimes designed to hurt. My point is this: if you feel wounded and distressed by people's loathing of you, aren't you also engaged in dishing out hatred and venom to others, who presumably feel pain and distress just as you do?

I only ever write about people and exhibitions which are there as targets. I am in awe of no institution, so if an exhibition is put on at the Royal Academy or the National Gallery and it seems to me to be shoddily done, then I will say so. If there is an exhibition of, let's say, the early works of Gainsborough at the National Gallery, and they are so foolish that they can't see they've got the order wrong or they have simply not understood the material, then they deserve to be slaughtered for it, because they of all people should know how to do it. If they do it badly or foolishly, then they must put up with the criticism. I very rarely tackle a young painter. I will tackle an old one who is well established, like Lucian Freud or John Wonnacott, a British representational artist. I would normally never think about writing about him, except that he is suddenly thrust under my nose as one of the great figurative painters of the late twentieth century. Well, he is nothing of the kind. I feel challenged, so I respond. But at the same time I write quite a lot of letters to painters who are virtually unknown. I am invited to their exhibitions and if I go, then I think they deserve some comment. That way they are not exposed in the *Evening Standard*, no damage is done, and I haven't been beastly to them in public, which is what I am always accused of. If they tear the letter up in a rage and stick pins in a wax image as a consequence, so be it, but I have done my duty as a critic, albeit privately.

But do you ever worry about the effect that your attack might have on the person who is under attack?

I think it's fair game. If a man has put himself forward, or is put forward by his dealer for gain, then he must take what comes. It's absurd that he should ask for praise and then be angry if he gets something other than praise. One of the most disagreeable things that ever happened to me was going to an exhibition and bumping into Lawrence Gowing, who at one point had been my tutor. He put his arm round me and told me that he hoped I would give the painter unalloyed praise. If you knew how much Lawrence spat when he said the consonant p, you would have some idea of how unpleasant this was. But the real unpleasantness lay in his expectation of unalloyed praise for a boy who was a pupil of his, just because he was his pupil and because Gowing thought he ought to be pushed. This is not good enough. Art is much more important than the people who make it.

A few years ago the American painter R. B. Kitaj left this country after his wife's death, which he felt was connected with the savage reviews of his work. Allowing for the fact that he was clearly disturbed by his wife's sudden death, the fact remains that you called him 'a vain painter, puffed with amour propre, *unworthy of a footnote in the history of figurative art'. Did you feel any measure of regret about writing that?*

None whatever, absolutely none. It's completely true. Nothing has ever been published that I have felt the need to retract, although I have occasionally written a review and wondered about it afterwards, returned to the exhibition, pondered the problem, and then rewritten the review. So I do sometimes reconsider.

Putting it another way, even if you stand by your judgement of Kitaj's work, did you have second thoughts about how it was expressed?

No.

Your Evening Standard *articles are widely read and enjoyed, but the articles clearly offend a number of readers. Indeed a few years ago a group of thirty-five prominent members of the art establishment wrote to the then editor demanding your resignation. How did you feel about that at the time?*

I was given warning of the letter by young Waddington [of Waddington galleries]. He rang me and said that it had been sent to him for his signature and he thought it was a disgrace, and he wished to read it to me so that I should know what was coming. What he read was a letter which I really wish had been published in that form, because I could have sued every one of the signatories. As it was, they had clearly been told to take a bit of legal advice, and so it was rephrased, which is a pity, because I was looking forward to a fight. It made me feel physically sick, because there were names on that list of people whom I respected, whom I did not think of as enemies. I now know that many of the signatories got there by chance. Marina Warner, for example, had not read the letter or sent it – she was just told by those who organized it that I was violently misogynist and I ought to be taken down a peg or two. She is a feminist and so her name got on to it, but I know she regretted it.

You were accused of virulent homophobia and misogyny ...

[laughter] I plead guilty to one or the other, not both. Some of my best friends are women. I own pictures painted by women.

You have sometimes also been accused of being anti-Semitic...

I am not anti-Semitic, I owe an enormous debt to my Jewish mentors, particularly at the Courtauld Institute. I am also indebted to the Jewish boys at school, whom I am sure I called 'bloody Jews' just as everybody else did, though I regret it. They brought a level of maturity to the school that would otherwise not have been there. A twelve-year-old Jewish boy is older than a twelve-year-old Christian boy, and I benefited from that.

In your article on Clause 28 in the Standard *you wrote that a man's sexuality is deeply determined, and that we all know what we are well before the onset of puberty. Do you think that those who appear to remain confused about their sexuality in adulthood are really homosexuals trying to come to terms with their homosexuality, or perhaps trying to fit into the heterosexual mould?*

I don't believe that everybody who is opposed to homosexuality is simply covering up some kind of homosexual drive of his own; that's just a comforting myth. 'He's kicking me because he's really queer' does seem to me to be a silly argument. I don't know what the answer is. There is a deep-seated homophobia in the English psyche, and I don't know why it's there or why it persists.

The bill to repeal Clause 28 was defeated by a sizeable majority in the House of Lords. What do you think about this and the concerns of Baroness Young that standards of decency and morality are at risk if Clause 28 is repealed?

I don't think that any boy – I can't speak for girls, I know so little about them – is ever diverted from his sexual path by the alternative. He always knows what it is. About twenty years after I left school one of the few boys I had kept in touch with decided to give a dinner party for our contemporaries. There were about forty people there, men and their wives, with me the only unmarried one there. The wives seemed to me to be largely vain and silly women who were talking boastfully about their aspirations for their children and so on. At some point homosexuality came into the general discussion and during one of those crystal moments of silence, I suddenly heard myself say, 'I think I've had enough of this debate. There isn't a single man here with whom I have not had sex. And on that note I shall bid you all farewell.' The point of that story is that I had had sex with every one of those boys, and they had all married and had children. I was the queer one. They were all normal. So whatever we did together – and they were perfectly happy to have sex with me at the time – our sexual drives were established well before we were involved in any way with each other. I am convinced that we are what we are at a very early stage.

In your article about Clause 28, you refer to the 'righteous' Cardinal Winning and his 'hysterical bigotry'. Without wishing to defend Cardinal Winning, isn't he in a sense merely expressing the traditional view of the Church based on scripture and theology?

Yes. It's precisely what confronted me when I was in my late teens and early twenties, trying to reconcile what I believed to be my faith, with what I knew was my sexuality. That was a long time ago, and the Church is still unchanged in its attitude to the problem.

Cardinal Winning is deeply conservative – he does not want the Church to move with the times on issues such as homosexuality and abortion, and there is little reason to doubt that his views are sincerely held. When it comes to art, many people would argue that you too are deeply conservative and resist any attempt to accommodate modern practices. What distinguishes your own approach from that of Cardinal Winning?

[laughter] I think you are too clever by half. But it's actually quite an easy question to answer in the sense that there hasn't been enough time for the dross to fall away. In the art world we make various assumptions, one of which is that it is enough for an artist to declare himself to be an artist for him to be regarded as such. Since the artist is a creature of great instinctive wisdom, it follows that everything he does and says must be taken very seriously, which is what happened with David Hockney. But with the passage of time, when most of these works of art have fallen to pieces and can't be reconstructed, people will begin to sort the wheat from the chaff. The advantage of being a critic is that one can begin that sorting process very much earlier than an institution like the Tate can. The Tate is a museum as well as a gallery and as such it has a different duty from the National Gallery. The National Gallery is small, and it has no hope of covering the whole history of art. It can therefore choose the most exquisite, the most moving, the most exciting, the best examples. The duty of the Tate Gallery, certainly as a museum of British art, is to be complete; therefore it should have eighteenth-century rubbish in it, it should have nineteenth-century rubbish in it, and by the same token I expect it to have twentieth- and twenty-first-century rubbish in it. That's what it's there for.

The point I was trying to make is that sexual mores have undoubtedly changed over the last twenty or thirty years. Things that would have once caused outrage are now widely accepted in society, if not by the Church. Could it not be said that the art world is similarly resistant to change?

No, I think the art world does accept everything; it's not a bit like the Church. The art world would benefit from the odd bit of discipline, somebody of some standing to say, 'This is not art – whatever it is, it isn't art.' Take so-called video art, for example. If you were to put it in the cinema, it would be seen as crap; it wouldn't have a hope of surviving because it's professionally inept. The average video artist is simply incompetent and would not be employed by any advertising agency. So I would prefer to scrap the lot of it, for it illuminates nothing, it adds nothing to the sum of beautiful things that move the soul. But going back to your basic point, to me being the Cardinal Winning of the art world, I don't think that's true. There are things that excite me, there are things which from time to time get through what may seem to be my carapace of prejudice.

Would you argue, as many people do, that there is moral equivalence between straight and homosexual sex?

I think that in a fair society there probably could be, but I go no further than that.

Do you think ideally sex ought to take place in the context of love, or are the two quite separate in your view?

Oh, for heaven's sake, that's a terribly old-fashioned thing. Sex, like food, works at all sorts of levels. You could go to a restaurant and have something that is exquisitely titillating to the palate, or something that simply stokes the boiler. Sex exists as a kind of constant in men's lives: it's there all the time. It varies between extremes of affection and extremes of activity, which are simply purgative.

I notice you say in men's minds. Do you think women are different?

I imagine an enormous number of women, once they've had a baby or two, would say they'd rather sex went away, that they really don't want any more.

You say somewhere of your mother: 'For the first part of her life, she was a flapper and easily bedded.' What is your feeling about that? Is it pride, or dismay, or perhaps incredulity?

I think of it as a possible explanation for my own inclination to be at her age as promiscuous as I was. I'm sure that anybody who remembers me at school will remember me as the school whore.

You say in the same article that children inherit their parents' sexual problems. Would it be too literal an interpretation to infer from that comment that you are also a flapper and easily bedded?

I was. I am now something of a monk. I can no longer believe that young men with whom I would like to go to bed would like to go to bed with me.

What place does love have in your life? Do you fall in love easily, or are you circumspect when it comes to love?

I have been deeply in love with the same man for almost thirty years. He's married, he's on his second marriage in fact, but the love isn't quite unrequited. Occasionally I leave a message on my answering machine which says, 'I am busy committing adultery. Please leave your number and I will return your call when I stop for coffee.' And it's true, because although I am not married in any sense other than to him, he is committing adultery, so I share it.

Some people have suggested that you might suffer from loneliness. Is there any truth in that?

Probably. I am a melancholy soul. I have absolutely no control over it. The melancholy comes and goes without any obvious explanation; the only consolation about it is that it goes, it always goes.

Where are you on the political spectrum, would you say? You described William Hague in an article as 'ludicrous' and 'repellent'. Are you more enamoured of Tony Blair?

No. He is ludicrous and repellent too. I hate that grin, that ready grin. It's even worse than John Major's.

But do you think Blair is a good prime minister?

No, he's all wind and waffle. What I deplore about Tony Blair is that he is prepared to run with the Thatcher legacy; it suits him because it will get him re-elected. I had great hopes when John Prescott said before the election that there was a strong possibility that they would renationalize the railways, that they would not be run for profit, that we would get our money back. If he had stuck to that, I would have voted Labour but by the time the election came it was already perfectly clear that wind and waffle were all that they had to offer, and that is all we've had since. There's only one serious politician in the Labour camp, and that's Gordon Brown.

In an article entitled 'Me and My God', I couldn't help noticing that you have a slightly tortured attitude to religion. Would that be a fair comment?

Yes. [laughter]

You started off as a Roman Catholic and then had Anglicanism imposed on you by your stepfather, but gradually you began to have more and more doubts about what might be called the core beliefs of Christianity, though you also seemed to be troubled by guilt...

The guilt is entirely associated with my homosexuality. It is the feeling of exclusion and rejection. If one could change that, I might feel differently.

Would you say perhaps that it is almost as difficult not to believe as to believe?

I think it depends entirely on your background. If I had had no background in the Church, then I don't think I would have any longing to join it. It would be enormously comforting to be able to return to a belief, but I don't think I shall. My lack of faith is supported everywhere I look – Rwanda, Kosovo, Bosnia. Where is God?

From what I read you are obviously troubled by what might be called the problem of evil and suffering in a world created by a benevolent God. You say, 'I have some sympathy if he cares not a damn for the human race; it is pretty ghastly. But that he should inflict harm on the animal kingdom seems beyond acceptance.' Is that your sincere belief, or is it intended to be slightly rhetorical?

It is my sincere belief. Christ preaches about the importance of the lilies in the field, the sparrows in the air, but look at what has happened to the lilies in the field and we now have no sparrows. What is the answer? The answer is that he isn't there, because if he were, he of all people would do something about it. Every time, for example, I read about the Siberian tiger or the Pyrenean bear becoming extinct, it makes me so angry.

Your love of animals is well known. What is it about animals? Do you feel they are safer than people perhaps, more loyal, more loveable?

The care I give to a bird with a broken wing is not conditional on being rewarded with loyalty and love. But the wonderful thing about owning dogs, and to a lesser extent cats, is that you do get a response which is human in some degree, or recognizably of the same nature as a human response, but that's a bonus. If I had the opportunity to live my life again knowing what I know now, I would not be an art historian, I would be a vet.

Your stand against religion seemed to waver when you had your heart attack and then a heart-bypass operation. Indeed you told the staff that if anything went wrong they were to send for a priest. Was this a version of Pascal's wager?

[laughter] No, it was an entirely unconscious reaction. The nursing sister had challenged me with her brisk bright businesslike approach, and with her clipboard in hand she told me there were one or two details which had to be settled, one being that I was down as an atheist. Although one feels more dead than alive in such a situation, I said, 'No, no, I'm not an atheist. I am an agnostic, but if anything goes wrong, call a priest.' It was purely instinctive. Besides, I see absolutely nothing wrong with going through the motions of the Roman Catholic preparations for death, which can be very beautiful and moving.

Are you afraid of death?

I don't think so. It will be the nature of its coming that really gives the answer. I think I can put up with pain or physical disablement, but if my brain should become addled … of course I shall not be aware, and that is the comfort. My mother in the last year or two of her life had no idea at all that her brain was not functioning. I used to go and visit her as a regular discipline, and one particular day when I went into her room she was lying with her eyes shut and her hands doing quick finger movements, as though playing the piano. I sat there and she took no notice of me – she didn't even know I was there. Eventually I got down on the floor and touched her knee. She opened her eyes, went on making her hand movements, and just said, 'Don't interrupt! I've told you before not to interrupt me when I'm practising.' And it just went straight back to my childhood. I found it terribly disturbing because it was quite clear that she had no idea how old she was, she had no idea of the circumstances, her sense of reality had gone. But I think she was perfectly happy.

Are you resigned to oblivion when you die, or would you like to think that there might be an afterlife?

Of course I'm resigned to oblivion. The great book on Michelangelo is not written. It won't be on anybody's shelf. That is the only afterlife I should have liked, to have written that book, and I now know I shan't. I suspect I shall die in harness with the *Evening Standard*, scribbling ephemera. And the book won't be there.

Interview conducted February 2000

MILTON SHULMAN

MILTON SHULMAN

Milton Shulman was born in Canada in 1913 and educated at the University of Toronto. He served with the Armoured Corps and Intelligence in the Canadian Army 1940–6 and was mentioned in dispatches in 1945. His long career in journalism began at the *Evening Standard* and *Sunday Express* in 1948 when he was engaged as film critic. He was theatre critic for the *Evening Standard* from 1953 to 1991, winning the IPC award for Critic of the Year in 1966. He has also been a commercial television executive and a BBC radio broadcaster. His memoirs, *Marilyn, Hitler and Me*, were published in 1998.

In your memoirs, Marilyn, Hitler and Me, *you say: 'I have no deep curiosity about who I am.' You are not keen either to analyse yourself or have others try to analyse you. Is this maybe because you are afraid of what you might discover?*

All my analyst friends tell me that I have something deep down that I want to hide. Well, maybe I do, but it doesn't bother me. My father died when I was six so I was brought up by my mother and an unattractive stepfather – that might account for my indifference to discovering who I am, but I don't know. What I do know is that today I am nothing like what I was at twenty-one. It seems as if I've had about three or four different lives and each one has come to me by accident.

Have you ever wondered what your alternative history might have been if, for example, your parents had not emigrated to Canada?

If they had not emigrated to Canada I would have gone to Auschwitz or Belsen. My parents lived in the Ukraine and most Ukrainian Jews were eventually either murdered during the Russian war or put in the gas chambers. I always think of myself as having escaped that fate by the accident of my parents having been frightened by the pogroms under the tsars in 1909 and 1910 – that's essentially why they came to Canada.

Your lack of curiosity seems to extend to your father who died aged only twenty-six in the post-World War I flu epidemic. Naturally you have hardly any recollections of him, but you seem not to have asked your mother what he was like. Haven't you wondered, for example, what qualities of character he might have passed on to you or might have bequeathed to your children?

That's a question I've often asked myself. You have to understand that my mother didn't read or write English until she began taking English lessons when she was about fifty. So communication with her on the things that mattered was practically nil. I used to ask about my father, and why, for instance, I was given the name Milton. I asked if my father read a lot, and if he knew who Milton was. But my mother had no idea, and after a while I realized that there really wasn't much point in pursuing the secret of my early life. She was not obstructive in any way; she just didn't think these things mattered very much.

Do you actually feel Canadian? Or after all these years in England, do you think of yourself as British?

I don't think of myself as Canadian, but everybody else does. In this country you're always a foreigner. I've been here for over forty years and people still refer to me as the Canadian this and the Canadian that, even though I've been back to Canada only once about twenty years ago.

One of your earliest memories is being ill in bed with flu and listening to your mother cry because your father had just died. The nurse looking after you complained: 'Why do these Jews have to wail so loud?' – which was your first recollected experience of anti-Semitism. Were there to be many more throughout your life?

Oh, my whole early life was dominated by anti-Semitism, but as a Jew in those days one accepted it – it was quite natural. I imagine it was like blacks today taking it for granted that there will be prejudice against them. In my youth the Jews in Toronto ran their own tennis clubs, their own golf clubs, their own university fraternities; you set up a community within the community, and you never expected anybody in Toronto to give you a job in the big industries, the banks or insurance companies. I tried to get into these jobs after I left university in 1934 but they wouldn't even answer the letters. Before long we had fascist parades and riots in Toronto, pro-Mosleyites parading up and down the streets, and so when I was about nineteen, I became involved in what was called the Anti-Defamation League which was very strong on defending Jewish interests. Anti-Semitism to me is normal – I don't resent it any more. I just assume everybody is anti-Semitic at some stage.

What causes people to be anti-Semitic? Is it part of the Western culture, do you think?

Yes, I think it is. The Christian ethic has so permeated the West, and even though the Pope has now forgiven the Jews, the majority of Catholics don't want to forgive the Jews. In America and elsewhere neo-Nazi groups are on the rise. It seems everybody has to have a bogey, somebody who is inferior. And it's always possible to make a Jew inferior, no matter how rich, how prosperous, how important – Rothschild himself is less important than the dustman's feet because he is a Jew. Anti-Semitism is everywhere. There's a very well-known editor who was at the Garrick the other day – I don't want to give you his name – and someone asked him, where do you rank Jews? And he said, 'I rank Jews somewhere between blacks and homosexuals.' This man is a so-called liberal journalist, someone who writes columns all over the place and who is recognized as a very important liberal figure. He knew I was there, and I'm sure he didn't mean to hurt me – it was just a sort of glib remark.

You say early on in your book that for some inscrutable reason Canadians are regarded as a bit of a joke... have you perhaps also suffered from anti-Canadian prejudice to some extent?

I don't want to sound paranoiac, but being a Canadian Jew is about the worst background for achievement you can have in our society. For some unknown reason Canadians are counted a bore in this country. It's not so much that people are anti-Canadian; they're just indifferent to Canadians. They regard them as even less important than Belgians.

You rose from your bed one morning with the firm conviction that Jehovah did not exist. How complete has this been, this 'obliteration' as you put it?

Total, total. I was brought up in a very Orthodox Jewish home. My grandfather lived with us and he used to go to the synagogue every day and my mother used to keep all the things necessary for Jewish practice. We even had a little boy who came in on Fridays to turn the lights on, because Jews aren't meant to turn the lights on. I'm told that in some parts of the East End today there are still boys who come in to turn on the television set. In my view, making a little Gentile boy take on the sin because Jews want to watch television is about as hypocritical as you can get. Up to about the age of fifteen, I was so frightened of Jehovah that it ruled my life – everything I did, everything I ate, whether I rode a bicycle on a Saturday, and so on. But then I began to read and gradually I became paralysed by doubt and eventually it began to seem that there was no Jehovah. First of all, the Jews have no image of him; you don't see him, he's just a voice up there, thundering down. He's never kind to you, he's always threatening you, and after a great deal of thinking about it, I woke up one day and decided, he doesn't exist. I was no longer frightened. From then on I shed my feelings of sin and guilt, and I don't believe in an afterlife; I see death as going to sleep; it just comes, and you won't wake up in the morning, that's all. Logically it is very strange for anybody to be very religious.

But do you feel relaxed about it?

I don't feel relaxed about it in a way, because when I think of all the great minds who even today believe in the fundamental tenets of some religion or other, I think there must be something wrong with me, that I somehow lack the capacity for religion.

You say that you have never been seriously troubled by any anxieties about sin or guilt since that time. Does that mean that there is no non-religious context for the idea of sin or guilt? Doesn't an atheist feel guilty?

I might feel guilty about personal things, but I don't feel guilty before God, no. Also, I don't press people one way or the other. My wife is religious, and my children have been brought up to be religious. I always told them when they were young that I would leave it up to them, and indeed they went their own ways. My second daughter, Nicola, for example, has had all her children baptized, and I attended all the baptisms.

So you're not hostile to religion as such?

I'm hostile to religion when it moves into the spheres of ultra-fundamentalism, whether Jewish, Arab or whatever.

I was interested to read that in moments of great sorrow, such as the death of your mother, you find yourself whispering the words of a Hebrew prayer. Doesn't this rather suggest that you want the comforts of religion without the challenge?

Well, you make me sound like I'm a hypocrite. And I suppose it is sitting on the fence to some extent, the fact that I do say a small Hebrew prayer almost every night. But if there is a God, then he will forgive me for saying I'm not religious, otherwise he would be pretty mean. A proper judgement would be to look at the whole measure of my life.

Very often the children of those who have abandoned their faith and 'married out' return to their Jewish roots and are reconverted. How would you feel if this happened?

My children seem to be set on not being Jewish as far as I can gather. Nicola is married into the aristocracy and is now a marchioness, but although she's had the opportunity of divesting herself of her maiden name, she writes literary reviews under the name of Shulman. Her sister Alexandra has done the same.

You describe as the most important decision of your life the moment you volunteered for the Armoured Corps during the war. What were the feelings which informed that decision — was it duty, was it 'King and Country' patriotism, or what?

As a Jew I knew that as soon as we got to war with Hitler I'd have to join up. Even before the war I took night courses in artillery and infantry, and I became qualified as an officer before I signed up for the army. When I first tried to sign up, nobody wanted me because the Canadians had no equipment to form any kind of unit. My mother was terrified of my going in, so I was under her influence to some extent, but in the end it was something I just had to do. I was a Jew and it was imperative that I took part in the struggle against Hitler.

You had a 'good war', as they say, and your memories of it form a fascinating part of your autobiography, especially the chapter on your dealings with Hitler's generals. Is it not the case, however, that von Rundstedt's claim of being forbidden by Hitler himself to attack the British at Dunkirk is only half true? According to official reports, Hitler eventually left it up to him, and it was in von Rundstedt's delay of forty-eight hours that the war can be said to have been lost?

I saw these generals before anybody else did after the war since I was one of the official interrogators. I was a major at that time, and I was doing it for the historical department of Canada. The main concern of these generals at that time was to blame Hitler for their defeat, because Hitler had dominated them all their lives, and the whole Wehrmacht had been turned into a sort of organization which carried out orders. In this particular case von Rundstedt told me that Hitler was afraid of the dikes and the canals in that area, and he thought his tanks wouldn't be able to get through them to attack the British who were waiting to get off the shore. Von Rundstedt told him there would be no difficulty, but Hitler wanted to have enough resources to attack Paris. That was his main goal, and he figured that if France fell Britain would obviously fall next, so for that reason he wanted to keep his resources. Hitler was all for peace with Britain, because the British Empire and the Catholic Church were the two institutions which were going to make his conquest of Europe total. So it's a question of whom you believe, but I myself think that von Rundstedt would have wanted to wipe out the British troops if he had been given the authority, and for whatever complicated reasons he was not.

Even more fascinating is your account of Operation James Bond in which Martin Bormann was allegedly extricated from Berlin and brought to England in return for his signature on documents that would release millions of German Nazi assets held in Swiss banks. Do you still believe this to be true?

I believe it even more now, because of the lengths to which MI5 and the intelligence services have gone to kill this story since the revelations. They have taken fantastic trouble to make it a laughing stock, and they've succeeded brilliantly, because to mention the word Bond is a music-hall joke now. They have planted Bormanns all over the world – in Venezuela, in South Africa, everywhere. A man called Peter Hartley, for example, was brought out of prison, given this persona, and masqueraded as Bormann. Another device was to bring out a book just before ours, written as a spoiling operation, entirely designed to rubbish our book. A television outfit then came to interview us to try and expose us as charlatans and spent at least ten thousand pounds on a fifteen-minute programme. Now anyone who knows anything about TV finances knows that that kind of money could not have been spent unless the company involved was financed by somebody with an agenda. About six months go I received a death threat telling me that if I didn't stop investigating this business, I would be killed. I couldn't go to the press about it because they would regard it as a publicity stunt to plug my book. But I telephoned Scotland Yard and they took it seriously and spoke to the German police about it, but again something happened to make them decide to take no action. OK, so it's an outlandish story and it's terribly difficult to believe, but the more I read and the more I discover, the more I believe it's true.

Why do you think Bormann had such a great influence on Hitler?

People like Schellenberg and Goering always said that Bormann was the most important man. Hitler trusted only Bormann. If you look at a book called *The Rape of Europa*, a fantastically detailed account of all the pictures and works of art taken out of all the European countries, it shows that Bormann had inspected every one of these pictures before he went to Hitler and told him which ones to keep and which ones to sell. Bormann was also Hitler's sole executive – he was there at his wedding, he signed the marriage certificate, and he was supposed to have been there when Hitler committed suicide. Everything about Bormann indicates that his relationship with Hitler was closer than those of Himmler, Goering, Goebbels put together.

I know that investigations into the role played by the Swiss bankers are still going on. How hopeful are you that the truth as you see it will eventually emerge?

We've done everything we can, I think. We've sent letters to the Jewish World Organization, who are investigating the story, and I wrote my book partly to alert people to the possibility of what happened. In the papers I was called a dupe and reviewers wondered why I had fallen for this incredible story. But the truth is that not one of the historians or journalists who reviewed it ever produced a single fact showing that what I said was untrue. For instance, none of the biographers of Ian Fleming – there are two or three of them – is able to say what he was doing from January 1945 to April/May 1945. All they say is that he was on intelligence duties; in effect he disappeared for those four or five months. As regards the Swiss banks, I believe that they have had to reveal what they have had to reveal only very reluctantly. If it were found that they were in cahoots with the British and Americans for cheating posterity of all these millions, particularly the Jewish victims, there would be a tremendous row. So I think the Swiss banks are keeping their heads down over this.

Just two months before you left Canada for England you married for the first time, but in fact you parted for good and you never saw your wife again. Did you suffer feelings of regret about this episode in your life, or were such things regarded as casualties of war?

We're talking about a separation of almost four years during the war, and that is a long time for people to be apart. When I came here I had to decide whether or not to stay here and be a journalist, or go back to Canada and be a lawyer. If I had gone back it would have been to a domestic life with a wife, and my prospects of being a writer would have been killed. So I more or less stalled. I was having an affair with somebody here with whom I was very much in love – it had gone on for about a year and I didn't want to leave her. My wife, I think, was already involved with somebody else, and so it was just a natural progression. We had never lived together, we had never even unwrapped our wedding gifts – it was a non-marriage.

In those days adultery was the only acceptable cause for divorce, something which seems absurd now. Did it seem absurd then also?

Of course. My girlfriend and I went to Brighton, the Grand Hotel I think it was, and we had to make sure – by giving huge tips – that the waiter and the housekeeper would remember seeing us in bed together. That was the only way you could get a divorce, by independent witnesses saying they had seen you in an adulterous situation.

You say in your book that you have every sympathy with Sir John Betjeman who said towards the end of his life that his greatest regret was not having had enough sex. How exactly would you define enough?

That's a terrible question. Enough, I suppose, is the level at which you feel that you don't need it, that you can go to bed at night without having the urge, that your equipment doesn't respond any more. I've never yet reached that situation, so it could perhaps be said that I've never been totally satisfied in terms of quantity, though I'm very satisfied in terms of quality.

I was also intrigued by your remark: 'I have never been sure, whenever I have bedded a woman, whether I was the victor or the vanquished.' Can you elaborate?

Very early on I became a well-known figure in England. After about two years as a film critic in 1946–7, I was spread all over the *Evening Standard* and Beaverbrook warned me when I got the job that I would have to be careful. He said they would try to bribe me with liquor, money and women, and I thought to myself that it sounded the best job I could possibly be offered. There were actresses and other girls for short periods of time – I never allowed myself to get into a situation where they could ever believe that it might be a permanent relationship, but of course women tend to boast about the men they sleep with. Nowadays the *Daily Mail* gives women fifty thousand pounds if they reveal that they've gone to bed with somebody important, but in those days nothing like that happened, and everybody was very discreet. The only other thing I can say is that in those days it was quite a victory to get a girl into bed, and it usually took a long campaign of taking them out to dinner two or three times, flowers, chocolates, the lot. But girls found my personality attractive and I didn't seem to have a problem.

You have been married to Drusilla Beyfuss for over forty years... is that attributable to good luck or good judgement, would you say?

No, it's a tribute to tolerance on the part of Drusilla. The fact that she has put up with my vagaries for forty years is quite something. I haven't been a perfect father, in the sense that I hardly saw my children when they were young because of the work I had to do. I was a theatre critic for thirty-eight years, and almost every night I went to the theatre from six o'clock to ten o'clock and then I wrote my notice till one o'clock, so there was no chance in that period to see any of the family. I used to take the children out on Saturdays and give them Coca Cola, but that was about as far as my fatherly efforts went. Drusilla had to do it all, and even though she was a journalist too, she managed to raise the children and keep a job and make a contribution to the household resources, and the fact that she tolerated me all these years is something that I very much cherish.

You became a socialist at around the same time as you became an atheist. Were the two connected in your own mind?

There was a vague connection, but my socialism sprang more from anti-Semitism and Hitler. At that stage the only people who were seriously attacking Hitler were Communists and Socialists; indeed far too many people on the right wing in Britain and Canada had vague sympathies with Hitler, and thought he wasn't too bad. I could have joined the Communist Party, but I was always frightened of Communism, so I became the representative of the Canadian Socialist Party, and I represented them for three years in this country after the war, taking over from Robert Mackenzie of swingometer fame. I took up with Barbara Castle and Healey and Michael Foot – in fact Michael became my best friend and was best man at my wedding. Everything was fine until Hungary and Czechoslovakia and then I realized that socialism was a road to tyranny and inefficiency. I slowly moved away from my deep socialist convictions to become a neutral for a short time and then eventually became seriously anti-socialist. I still am anti-socialist, just like Tony Blair and the whole Labour Party, except for a few die-hards.

Your journey from socialist idealism in impoverished youth to right-wing prosperity in middle age has a familiar ring to it. What finally seemed to turn you off was 'the winter of discontent' after which the Labour government was deservedly rejected. Surely, however, you would agree that socialism has come a long way since then?

I don't think it has come a long way. A lot of people believe that underneath it all Tony Blair is probably the most radical prime minister we've had for decades. He is breaking up Britain, and there is no doubt that if the Scots vote for independence and the Welsh vote for a kind of independence and we get an English parliament, then Canada will go, Australia will go, New Zealand will go, there won't be even a remnant of the empire left. The Queen will have nobody to rule over, and we will become the Bulgaria of the North Sea. Some surveys show that something like fifteen or twenty per cent of people are mentally unbalanced, and they form a significant part of our electorate. We are in the ludicrous position of electing a government on about forty per cent of the vote, with the result that the rest of the people are under some kind of democratic dictatorship. Tony Blair now is as much a dictator as Hitler was; he can do anything he wants, he can even get rid of the Queen.

But don't you have sympathy with the idea of creating a fairer society?

A fairer society, as you call it, is what is generally known as egalitarian, and egalitarianism is probably one of the worst philosophies that has ever bothered mankind. The idea that everybody is equal has come to mean not that everybody is responsible, but that everybody has the right to everything. We're into a kind of nutty thinking that believes every dustman should get as much money as newspaper editors and people running companies of sixty thousand people. Egalitarianism as a basis of socialism is vicious. And political correctness is an even more horrendous thing. I have a children's book which is about a pigeon in Trafalgar Square – it's sold about a hundred thousand copies and I want to get it reprinted, but the children's editor at Collins tells me we can't because pigeons are a nuisance and the book is not politically correct any more.

I actually meant a fairer society in the sense that people are given equal opportunities, not equal pay...

You can't give equal opportunity, because people haven't got the ability to take advantage of equal opportunity.

You chose to educate your children in the private sector, but you seem to feel the need to justify doing so. Why? Is it because you accept it is divisive?

I don't think I ever attempt to justify it. I've always spent a good deal of my income on education, and also on private medicine, believing, as Bernard Shaw believed, that I was contributing to the upkeep of socialism by doing so. I was helping to maintain the public sector in nursing and education by paying twice over, by paying normal taxes on my earnings and by paying a vast sum of money to keep the private sector going. I've therefore never understood this claim that we are parasites; we are actually the opposite. My children went to St Paul's, which is the best school in England, and the idea that I should have deprived them and sent them off to a comprehensive school because of some egalitarian idea that even Tony Blair doesn't subscribe to is absurd.

As a journalist you have waged many campaigns – one of the most interesting on behalf of war criminals who, in your view, should not be pursued so many years after the events. They are old men now, you say, and proof positive is impossible to obtain. Is there not a problem, however, about the idea of justice being contingent upon the passage of time?

The cases I campaigned for were very specific. They involved two minor people, one who was pursued till he died at eighty-odd, and the other, an old man who is still being pursued. They were both tiny figures, both corporals or sergeants in Belorussia. Britain spent fourteen million pounds on the first trial and they will probably spend another ten or fifteen million on the second, trying two minor individuals. Most of the other countries who have tried war criminals had real villains, concentration-camp people who were responsible for the deaths of millions. We on the other hand have been working on these trials for I don't know how many years now, and wasting the country's money in what I regard as an amoral way, in the sense that the whole concept of British justice is being abandoned to bring about these trials. It is the same sort of philosophy which has led to the Pinochet business. We passed a law enabling us to prosecute people who were not British, who killed people who were not British, in a country that was not British; because of some vague idea about humanity we granted ourselves the right to prosecute them. Pinochet committed the crimes in Chile, against Chileans, in a country that has nothing to do with us, but because of the legislation over war crimes we are entitled to try anybody in the world who commits crimes anywhere in the world against people we know nothing about. To me that is such a weird concept in philosophical and judicial terms that I simply can't take it.

The Nuremberg trials, in which the plea of 'only obeying orders' was ruled out,
came as a surprise to the Nazi leaders. At the time, or in retrospect, do you
think that justice was done?

Justice was done against those people, yes. You must remember that in the
First World War we didn't have a war-crimes tribunal. The Kaiser and his
men were not brought before a jury and indeed they were honoured
figures in their country even though they had committed crimes,
slaughtered Belgian babies, and so on. When it came to the Second World
War, Bormann and people like that never thought they were going to be
tried, or if they did, they thought that they might get three or four years
after which they would live comfortably for the rest of their lives.

You were astonished to discover how ordinary and 'just like anybody else' were
the German military – far removed from the Hollywood stereotype. The things
that they did, however, were extraordinary in the extreme and not at all 'just
like us'. During your interrogation of them, did you conclude that, given their
history, we might have behaved in the same way?

Yes, I'm sure we would. If Hitler had won the war and had taken over
Britain, he would have done away with trial by jury, the right to defend
oneself in certain circumstances, the right of *habeas corpus*, and so on. And
I'm sure we would have gone along with it – the vast majority of people
would have been happy. There would have been an underground
movement, probably financed from Canada where the Queen would have
been sent after the war, but you can't have an underground movement
against tyranny unless you have hope of victory. When the French had no
hope of victory, the Maquis didn't exist, or hardly existed; they started to
take an active part only in 1943 after the Americans came in. By then they
could see that the Germans were going to lose the war, but before that very
few of them stuck their necks out.

Another notable campaign of yours has been against violence on television.
Your arguments are very persuasive, but I wonder why you distance yourself so
completely from the argument that sexual permissiveness on television also has
an effect on society. In fact the greatest rise in crime figures is in the area of
sexual assaults...

The sexual argument is entirely the result of the violence argument. Television has a pollutant effect and it has been shown that from the age of six or seven to fourteen or fifteen, violence comes to be regarded as normal. Once that happens, it's only natural that sex crimes become part of the picture. Stamp out violence on television and you'll stamp out some of the concomitants of which sexual violence is one.

Back in the 1970s you fought a campaign against what you saw as LWT's failure to live up to its promises. Frank Muir said to you at the time: 'You're like a man who is worried about the population explosion so he goes out and shoots a couple of his friends.' What was your reaction to that remark?

I still say that the quality of television is dire. Now even the BBC has followed the trend and is dumbing down. Nobody is interested in quality any more. This interview is a refreshing experience because it is on a level which is unheard of in normal newspapers now. Nowadays everything has to be geared to an ill-educated society which can just bear to read the *Star* or the *Sun* or the *Mirror*. At one stage I had great hopes for television; I thought that if you changed television it would somehow have an effect. It's too late now.

In your years as drama critic at the Standard *you have seen everything and everybody worth seeing in English theatrical life. And yet you seem very hard to please...*

There are so very few great talents, so very few people with genius in any field of activity, be it music, theatre, art, or anything else. I suppose I have come to recognize that the theatre is an entertainment and that people go to the theatre as they might go to a restaurant, or go to a circus – to be amused, to have a moment of fun. Perhaps I was too hard on a lot of the plays, and didn't sufficiently take account of people's need to be amused in that way.

You seem very reluctant to apply the word 'great', far less 'masterpiece', to any performance or production. Do you think these words of praise are too often squandered?

They are squandered all the time. Frankly, my colleagues are simply keeping their jobs. If they really adopted high standards there would be no need for critics, you know, because there wouldn't be much to write about. Even very good critics find two or three masterpieces a year. They have been encouraged to be lenient by their editors who don't want too much criticism of the arts in their newspapers.

Is there a play or a performance which nevertheless stands out as the greatest in your experience?

The greatest play undoubtedly is *Hamlet*. I am overwhelmed every time I see it, and I could see it every day of the week. Olivier as Hamlet was a performance I will never forget and it is a standard for acting in a great play that is very difficult to match.

One of the chapters in your book is entitled: 'No Statue Has Ever Been Put Up for a Critic', and indeed critics as a species are much reviled. Has that aspect of things ever seriously bothered you?

No, it's never bothered me. I didn't want to hurt people, and I always looked with regret at actors taking their bow at the end of a performance when I knew there was a chance they would lose their jobs the next day. That was an ugly responsibility, but I always thought to myself that there were about eight or ten critics in the country, and I was just one. Another critic would probably take a different view, so I stopped feeling guilty.

Is there a review that you seriously regret, or that you know was unjust?

I don't think so, although my judgement may occasionally have been wrong. For instance, *Waiting for Godot* may indeed be a great play. I have rather changed my mind about it and realize that not only did I underestimate it, but I didn't understand it when I first saw it. But *Look Back in Anger* I regarded as a second-rate play when I first saw it, and I still think it's a second-rate play.

Are you yourself sensitive to criticism? Sheridan Morley's review of your autobiography must surely have hurt...

Of course it hurt, particularly because it was Sheridan Morley and he was supposed to be a friend of mine. I don't believe he read it all. I think he read only my chapter on the theatre and he based his entire review on that tiny segment. I was very upset because it was the first review, and it was in the *Sunday Times* which is after all a very important paper.

You include Diana, Princess of Wales, and Marilyn Monroe in your list of twentieth-century icons, and indeed they have much in common – blonde, beautiful, unintellectual and dead in mysterious circumstances at much the same age. Is it this last unhappy fact that makes them stand out from all the rest and will make them unforgettable?

I think they were lucky to die young. If we had seen a sixty-five-year-old Marilyn Monroe, as we saw a sixty-five-year-old Ginger Rogers, the whole glamour would have gone, and I think Diana would have been the same. If Diana had married Dodi I think she would have disappeared out of the icon league because of what people would have regarded as bad judgement on her part. Both Marilyn Monroe and Diana loved the camera, and the camera loved them. Diana was also a great actress and she recognized very early on the importance of being photographed with a starving black baby. It was a wonderful image in her fight against Charles. Her involvement with Dodi led to a kind of tarnishing of the icon image, but now that she's dead the icon will manage to survive.

Are you resigned to oblivion when you die or would you like to think that there is an afterlife?

I belong to one of the most underrated professions in the world, namely journalism. Journalists are underrated largely because we call ourselves hacks and scribblers, we denigrate ourselves all the time. We forget that Orwell, Belloc, Chesterton and Graham Greene were all journalists – even Evelyn Waugh was a journalist at one time. I'd certainly rather be remembered as a well-known, successful journalist than a critic. As far as I am concerned, however, my books are all that will remain of me after my death. All my books are bound, so that they look as if they're Balzac or Anatole France, and I don't know which of my children is going to get them. But they are my only monument.

INTERVIEW CONDUCTED NOVEMBER 1998

CLAIRE TOMALIN

CLAIRE TOMALIN

Claire Tomalin was born in 1933 and educated at Dartington Hall and Newnham College, Cambridge. After several years as a publishers' reader she began working as assistant literary editor for the *New Statesman* in 1967. She was literary editor from 1974 to 1977 and held the same post at the *Sunday Times* from 1979 to 1986. Her books include *The Life and Death of Mary Wollstonecraft*, which won the Whitbread First Book Prize for 1974; *The Invisible Woman: The Story of Nelly Ternan and Charles Dickens*, which won the Hawthornden Prize and James Tait Black Memorial Prize for Biography; and *Jane Austen: A Life* (1997). Her anthology of writing from three decades, *Several Strangers*, was published in 1999.

Your father was French and your mother English . . . what effect did this have on you and your sister?

I think it gave me an advantage in life because I was born in 1933, a time when everybody was somehow 'placed' in English society. Since I had a French name which nobody could pronounce, this meant that nobody knew where I came from. When I was at Cambridge and when I started my career, I was somehow outside the divisions of English society. I liked that; it meant being free.

Do you feel totally English, or not quite?

I think I do feel completely English, partly because the English language has meant so much to me. I started writing poetry in English when I was about seven years old, and Shakespeare was my favourite author by the time I was twelve. I've never written poetry in French and I've never married a Frenchman either. But I love French, and had I not got into Cambridge I would probably have gone to university in France, and I expect I would then have become French.

I read an article about your childhood in which you describe the happiness of your first years before you moved to Kensington, after which you say your parents were never so happy again. They eventually divorced ... how traumatic was this for you and your sister?

Very traumatic, although in fact my parents never got on. The marriage was viewed as a mistake, particularly by my father. He thought that the marriage was doomed, and this had the curious effect of making me feel for a great many years that my father didn't like me very much. One of the great blessings of my life has been that as my father has lived on we have become very close. When my first husband was killed my father and my stepmother were magnificent, and they took upon themselves a responsibility towards the children. My father, seeing that my children had lost their father, became a very good grandfather to them. The people we love most in our lives are the people who love our children; this is a very strong bond.

You describe your mother as having been 'obsessively unforgiving'. What did this entail? Did it mean you were denied contact with your father?

There was a period when we had very little contact with my father, because my mother was very bitter. But she was also a wonderful mother to me – she introduced me to the English poets, she encouraged me, she believed in me. She was also a considerable artist herself, and I do feel that in some sense she sacrificed the pursuit of her art to being a good mother. I owe her a great deal. She was the sort of mother Freud writes about – as a child you feel you are the most loved creature and you know life will never defeat you entirely.

But when you say she was 'obsessively unforgiving' ...

I don't remember saying that, though I don't doubt that I did say it. No, she never recovered. In that generation of women, if your husband left you, you always felt that it was in some way your fault, and the anger and bitterness were connected with that.

In fact, later, when your own marriage was in difficulties, your mother said that a failed marriage was always a woman's fault. Had she come to believe this or was it simply intended as a rebuke to you?

It was part of her culture, it belonged to that world of women. She had a lot of close women friends, all of whom were very sympathetic and indignant about the bad behaviour of my father. It was part of their ethos, that somehow a woman ought to be able to manage a man. They didn't see that sometimes marriages fail.

As an adult did you come to understand your mother's feelings in a way in which you were not able to as a child?

I think my sister and I both understood them at the time; we were both passionately sympathetic. As we got older I suppose we felt that sometimes things have to be put behind you, that you can't go on cherishing the quarrel or the grievance for ever. When my first marriage was in difficulties, I went through a period of thinking that perhaps I was re-enacting all those horrors of my parents' lives. But I quickly realized that I was not, that I was living my own life and that I didn't have to go through all the same things again.

At sixteen you became rebellious and didn't want to live with your mother any more, and so you were sent to Dartington Hall. Was that a success? Did you fit in well to that progressive school?

I am extremely grateful to Dartington Hall. It was in a beautiful part of Devonshire, and it was a privilege to be given very good teaching and to find oneself amidst tolerant people, both the other children and the teachers. The headmaster was a wise man, wise in more ways than I realized at the time. I was very happy there and a lot of pressures were taken off me.

The 'several strangers' in the title of your latest book refer to yourself at three different stages of your life. You quote Jane Austen's belief that 'seven years are enough to change ever pore of one's skin and every feeling of one's mind'. Of course, as we get older, our attitudes may change, but do we really look back and see a stranger? And then another stranger?

I do see different people. For example, the girl who went up to Cambridge was very brash and callow, and simultaneously very pleased with herself, not very confident, yet wanting to conquer the world. All those things get knocked out of you by life, and I suspect if the person I am now met the person I was then I might not like her very much. I still shudder when I remember some of my attitudes. Girls of my generation very easily became snobbish, and in a sense you were encouraged to look for high-achieving young men. And we were very spoilt in one sense when I was at Cambridge. There were ten men to every young woman, so we were much in demand, we were like little princesses.

When we talk about people changing, I suppose it is a question of degree. We can all look back and see our lives at different stages and know that those stages are in the past, but doesn't something about us remain essentially the same, something right at the centre of our being?

It may be so. However, one way in which one changes utterly as a woman – I can't speak for men – is when one is seized by what Bernard Shaw calls the life force. My instinct to have children became the strongest thing in me, and I was absolutely devoured by the need to have children. I sort of held it off when I was at Cambridge and took my degree. I no longer have that impulse, and I really think that I was somebody different then, and that I could not fight against it. There was that whole business of marrying young – and most of our generation did – and we all thought we were making individual choices, that we were doing something we ourselves had planned and thought about. But if one looks back at it, I think we were all simply carried along by this overwhelming urge.

And that's how you see your younger self?

Well, I am now chastened by life, so I look back at that young woman and I feel sorry for her in some ways, and in other ways she's mysterious to me. I don't entirely understand what was going on. People say to me, you must have been pretty ambitious, but I don't remember being ambitious at all.

You graduated from Cambridge in 1954 and the following year you married Nick Tomalin. Did you have it in mind at the time to have your own career or was it enough at that stage to be married and have children?

I had always assumed that I would work – my mother had worked, my French aunt had worked, my French grandmother had worked, so I had plenty of models. I thought that what you did as a woman is that you tried to have work which you could fit in with bringing up your children, and that's what I did. I was fortunate in having the job in publishing since I was literally able to breast-feed my babies while reading a manuscript. That worked pretty well but I had no real aspirations. One of the rather odd things was that women were not more encouraged when we got towards the end of our time at Cambridge to go out and conquer the world. There was the feeling that probably we were going to get married and not do very much; we might become schoolteachers, or civil servants, but I don't remember any encouragement to aim high.

You and your husband both wanted to have six children, and in fact you had five. Why so many hostages to fortune? Did that aspect of parenthood never occur to you?

No, we just had this vision of a wonderful, happy family life, children playing string quartets, a very romantic vision, not an impossible one, of course. I think it is rather sad nowadays that people on the whole, rightly, feel that they mustn't have large families. There is something a bit sad about being an only child. I do remember Nick's uncle questioning why we were having all these children and wondering how we would afford it. But we were young, and we didn't think about that. I suppose I slightly thought God would provide somehow, and that if you have the children they will make their way.

That is the Catholic idea, that God will provide...

Well, I'm not a Catholic, I'm not even a Christian. We just use the phrases of Christianity because they are woven into our language and our culture.

In 1973 your husband Nick was killed while reporting on the Golan Heights. By that stage in your marriage he had become what you call a 'bolter', and although you grieved for him, you also felt a sense of release and freedom. I wonder if you found the conflict of emotions arising from his death almost more difficult to deal with than the death itself?

I felt and still feel deep grief. It was terrible for him to die as he did. We all loved him, our children, his parents and my parents – there was a community of grief. I didn't want to claim more sympathy than I felt I should have – that was the problem. Our marriage really was on the rocks by then, and it hadn't been a good marriage. The position of widows is always one that receives a great deal of sympathy and attention. I felt grateful for that, but it was also slightly worrying given what our marriage was at that point. It was just difficult for me to sort out the various strands: here was a terrific man, an adorable man, a man of huge promise, who had been foully killed. He was also greatly loved and indeed I myself loved him, but no longer in the way I had loved him.

You say somewhere: 'To all intents and purposes he had left me already.' Had the grieving already been done in a sense?

The grieving for the loss of the dream of the young marriage had happened a very long time before, yes, but I had come to terms with that. I was very starry-eyed when I got married; I really believed that we would always be together, although I fairly quickly was made to see that that wasn't Nick's dream. I think I realized even then, and now with hindsight even more, that he had experienced an extremely difficult upbringing and a very disordered childhood, and that part of what he was playing out was the result of what had happened to him as a little boy. When you get to be old you can forgive practically anything, because if you look back far enough you can see perhaps where it comes from.

Would you consider yourself a romantic by nature?

I have a certain element of romanticism, yes, I'm afraid I have, but I try to keep it under control. I can remember quite consciously arriving at a decision at some point in my forties that, charming as it is to embark on love affairs with people you find delightful, it's better not to, because you probably will wreck a friendship, or worse. If you are a single woman in society you probably ought just to watch the way you behave.

One can only guess at the grief that you have had to endure as a mother: a baby son who died, a beloved daughter who suffered from depression and took her own life, and Tom born with spina bifida and paralysed. Did you ever feel singled out? That the gods were against you?

Yes, very much so. And of course you blame yourself if things go badly wrong. For somebody who was a passionate mother and who longed to have many children, it was very difficult when my children had such difficulties. But again, these things are arbitrary, and it is very fruitless to sit, like Niobe, and weep. You must get on with life. It helps that my son Tom, who will be thirty this year, has never repined, never complained. He has shown such extraordinary courage and willpower that he is a great lesson to me, and I have learned from him that you mustn't give up, you mustn't sit down and feel sorry for yourself. It is easier for me to say that than it is for him, since I can get up and walk out of the room, whereas he can't; and yet he *does*, as it were. He travels, he does things, everything he makes up his mind to do.

Your mother was a Christian Scientist, a religion which demands strength and self-reliance. Did your upbringing with her, even if you were not a Christian Scientist, help to breed these qualities in you?

I have to say I think Christian Science is a ridiculous religion but I am quite grateful to have been brought up by somebody who made light of physical pains and ailments. My mother, as it happened, had stalwart health and was never ill, and I have pretty good health too. The good thing, I suppose, that I have taken from my mother is that I don't fuss much about medical problems.

Do you have any religious faith? What has enabled you to remain apparently unbroken by so much tragedy, do you think?

Do I have a religious faith? No. I am a humanist like my father before me and I think his parents before him – it may be genetic. I intensely love a lot of Christian art, the King James version of the Bible, the cathedrals of Europe, the poetry of George Herbert. Indeed, there was a very brief period when I was at Cambridge when I flirted with Christianity because I was so entranced by Herbert. But then I moved on to the eighteenth century, the Enlightenment, and I abandoned it again and I have never returned to it. I just lack any sense of what is going on really in the Christian myth. I see its power as a myth, I understand the power of the stories. But I find the whole thing of God's bargain, Christ dying for us, incomprehensible, and I think the effect of religion on the world has been almost always to make people cruel, intolerant and beastly.

Have you come to believe that the human spirit somehow manages to bear whatever is asked of it?

Alas, that is obviously not true. People go mad, people find what they are asked to bear too much. I think there is a tremendous luck of the draw in what you are born with, what is chemically going on in your brain. Life is random and unfair. It is extraordinarily lucky in terms of life expectancy and education and comfort to have been born in England in the mid-twentieth century. Most human beings endure terrible lives and have done throughout most of human history

Do you believe in fate?

No, I don't believe in fate. I believe in arbitrary misfortune. I might walk out of this building and somebody on a building site might drop a brick on my head. You might want to call that fate, but I would say it was just chance; and chance is not the same as fate. I think we all try to shape our lives, and we all try to see the shape of our lives. As a biographer I am very interested in this, and I certainly believe as we get older that we wish to construct some shape out of our own lives and make some sense of it. This is one of the very interesting things that people have been doing in the last few hundred years, taking their own lives as some kind of raw material for art or making a narrative out of their lives.

Your son's life was saved at birth by an operation and you have sometimes wondered, given his years of difficulty, if you should have given consent to it. Have you asked Tom how he feels about that decision?

We have talked about it. I suppose what I felt was that I wasn't actually given the true picture. I had never heard of spina bifida at that point. As soon as he was born I was told he could have his back closed in an operation, and if there was no operation he might be worse off and get more damage to the spinal column. I naturally gave permission to operate, but a year later the neurosurgeon said to me that Tom would certainly have died if we hadn't done the operation, so I wasn't given the full information in the beginning. If I am asked a theoretical question about severely handicapped foetuses, I would quite strongly suggest it is better to avoid giving birth to such children. What I have said to Tom in the past is that if he hadn't been born and I had had another child immediately afterwards, it might have been him, as it were, without those problems. But actually, as soon as Tom was born, I loved him as passionately as you can love any child, so the whole question then really ceased to have any meaning. It is obviously not something one talks over at great length, because what he needs to do is to live his life and not brood about things, and that is indeed what he is so good at.

The suicide of a child is the worst agony that a parent can envisage or be asked to endure. I'm sure you can never get over it, but what strategies have you employed to come to terms with it?

When it happens within your own family you feel it is the worst thing that could possibly happen, not just to me, but to Susannah's sisters and brother. What you are left with is this very strange sensation that somehow the life of your child is enclosed within your life. You expect your children to outlive you, yet what strikes me now is that it is nearly as many years now since she died as the number of years she lived. Obviously I never lose the thought of her. I am sure all parents of dead children think the child who died was exceptional; but she was exceptional, exceptionally gifted and full of life, kind, sweet-natured, fiery, passionate, and those who loved her among her friends and within the family all keep her memory very much alive. Sometimes people ask me if I mind talking about her. Quite the contrary – I love to talk about her because I loved her so much, and when people die, they've gone from the world, and there isn't much occasion to talk about them.

You say that Susannah's death blew the family apart and caused her two sisters to turn their backs on the idea that the intellect is supreme and on the idea of success. Are you saying that they blamed you for valuing these ideas?

I find it slightly difficult to speak for my children; it always seems a bit impertinent. What I would say is that they both began to question the whole idea of competition, partly because it was the ethos of the age, and they both turned their backs very strongly on the idea that life was a ladder up which you climbed. I don't think I myself saw it in those terms either, but on the other hand if you looked at my life I obviously had been climbing a ladder. And so both Emily and Josephine set off in different directions, and I must say I admire them both very much and have learned a lot from them. But it was a very painful period because they did just go away. They were of an age when they would have been going away anyhow, but having had this large family, the three girls and Tom, all of us particularly close after Nick died, it felt sad when it all just went.

During your years at Grays Inn Road, you write that you became fierce in defence of words and the intellectual values which you felt were sometimes under threat. In the light of what was going on in your personal life, did you ever come to see words and intellect as being utterly inadequate? What I mean is, were you forced to reassess your own values?

In journalism I don't think you can ever turn your back on words. People say that one picture will tell you more than a hundred words, but I don't actually believe that myself. I am forever wedded to the written word, and in the context of the literary pages of the *Sunday Times* I believed it was actually worth running reviews for their intrinsic intellectual interest rather than because the books were on the bestseller list or written by a celebrity. I had to do battle with Andrew Neil on this one, and stuck to my fairly austere Cambridge ideas about the value of good book reviewing. Book reviewing isn't the most important thing in the world, but critical standards are important, and as a literary editor I regarded them as being of crucial importance, as something worth fighting for.

A lot of your writing has been about women badly treated by men, and you seem to have a fondness for them all. Virginia Woolf seems to be particularly admired and you are able to forgive her occasional cruelties and snobbery. Do you ever think you might be guilty of special pleading?

Virginia Woolf is not a woman I am supremely interested in. I have written only an introduction to *Mrs Dalloway*. It's true I have written a good deal about women, but I have also written about men. It so happened that my first book was about Mary Wollstonecraft, the great eighteenth-century feminist. She is extraordinarily interesting because she was a terrific thinker and fighter, lived an extraordinary life, went to Paris during the French Revolution and produced the first real polemic about women's rights. At the same time she lived the life of a romantic heroine. In her case I don't feel indignant at the way she was treated by individual men particularly; it's the pathos of her personal life that interests me, the conflict between her high intellectual achievement and the rest of her life.

In the case of Ellen Ternan, the woman who was probably the mistress of Dickens, again it is her story that is central. Here was a young woman whose life became entangled with that of a great man and the interaction is fascinating. When you publish a book the press very often likes to extract a simple message from it, be it a great scandal or focus of indignation. But books are usually rather more complicated and subtle than that, so while I have been concerned to point out when women were badly treated – and this might have involved a bit of re-writing of history – I have been mainly interested in the lives of those women. Their bad treatment has not been the main point of my writing.

In your biography of Ellen Ternan, you give Dickens his due as the literary giant he was, but I couldn't help thinking you were quite hard on him as a man. You say: 'He behaved with inexcusable injustice and cruelty to his wife whose only faults seem to have been that she was fat and dull.' But we all know that men fall in love with other women even if their wives are neither fat nor dull, and his liaison with Nelly seems, as you say, to have brought him neither happiness nor calm. Do you think you were a little harsh in your judgement perhaps?

No. I agree you can fall in love with other people when you are married but you don't have to behave as badly as Dickens behaved. Dickens's problem was that he felt he had to defend his reputation. He had a particular relationship with the English reading public on which he was economically dependent, and this led him to try and show everyone that he was right. He didn't just make some sort of discreet arrangement with his wife; no, he published great statements in *The Times* saying that it was all her fault. He just did behave like a madman. We probably all behave in mad ways under the impulse of great emotion at one time or another, but I think it is still allowable to criticize. I don't take back a single word I said about Dickens. I revere him as a novelist, and indeed I think if I had met him I would have found him the most delightful, perhaps slightly exhausting, man. But I still think he behaved very badly.

In her review of your biography of Katherine Mansfield, Fiona McCarthy detects what she calls 'a natural affinity for women temperamentally on the cussed side', and says she sees the lurking figures of your mother and mother-in-

law, both, like Katherine Mansfield, 'talented and gifted outsiders'. Is that
right, would you say?

I actually say in the introduction to that book that my mother-in-law,
whom I loved, was a rather wild colonial girl who came into English
society and had a good time and behaved in quite an *outré* way. I was
thinking of her and I said so, which suggests Fiona McCarthy wasn't
exactly discovering anything; she was simply reading my own introduction
to the book. When you are working on a biography, when you are living
with a subject, month after month, year after year, you are rather as an
actress taking a part. If you're playing Lady Macbeth, for example, you've
probably never murdered anybody, but you look to your own experience to
illuminate, to let you play the part. If you are working on a biography you
seek in your own experience, in your own circle, elements that could help
you to understand what you are looking at.

Many biographers have made good novelists. I am thinking of Margaret
Drabble, Victoria Glendinning and Margaret Foster. Why do you reject so
firmly the idea of novel writing?

I don't think I could do it; it's too difficult, too brave. To write a novel you
have to really believe. You have to believe for long enough that there is
some point to doing it, whereas to write a biography you always have a
thread in your hand, a piece of string you hold on to which is what you can
find out about this life. Biography is safer, and it's easier.

Victoria Glendinning described biography as 'an extremely dodgy exercise', by
which she meant that it was often a piece of self-indulgence on the part of the
author, that the authoritative tone is highly questionable, that you can never get
the whole picture, and so on. What are your own views?

Well, I would say I eschew the authoritative tone. This is a subject I have
discussed with Victoria, I may say. I see what she means, but I do think it
all boils down to the tone, to the approach you make. There are lots of very
bad biographies, bad novels, bad plays, and we might as well all give up if
we go by the fact that there are bad examples.

Doris Lessing famously said that there is no doubt that fiction makes a better job of truth than biography. Do you have any sympathy with that view?

I think there is room for different approaches. I have also noticed that a lot of people who are rude about biography make ruthless use of other people's work. Tom Stoppard and Alan Bennett, to name just two, are habitually rude about biography, yet they both write plays in which they have either drawn their material from their own biographical researches or from somebody else's. I suspect that somebody has to do the job. People are interested in other human beings' lives, and it is a perfectly legitimate interest.

You said of your first husband that he was 'constantly, irresponsibly and perpetually unfaithful'. Can one be 'responsibly' unfaithful, do you think?

That's a very good question. I suppose one could be more or less discreet. The tradition of bourgeois marriage in which discretion is observed is a more humane tradition than one in which everything is out in the open and everything goes crashing down all the time. It doesn't mean there is no pain, but then pain is part of life.

You say somewhere that you incline to the Freudian view that in the end all that matters is love and work. Is it in that order of importance, would you say – love first, then work?

I would say they are equally balanced. One is very lucky if one has work which one finds absorbing, and one is very lucky to have the love of a husband, of children, of parents. I regard them as pretty equal forces.

Would you say that work has perhaps protected you to some extent when love has let you down, or when you have experienced the painful aspects of love?

I think work is certainly an escape. What is wonderful about it is that it may start off as an escape then it becomes productive in itself, and it leads you on. I've had a lot of bad things happen, but I have also had a great deal of good fortune, good luck and happiness. My life has been very tranquil for the last twenty years, and I value that tranquillity. As writers, Michael and I both know the need to withdraw into work at times and yes, you need to be tranquil in order to be able to do that. All the same, life throws up delightful things like the birth of a new grandchild, or the marriage of a child, and you must then set aside your work and rejoice. It is important to remember that the younger generation is going through all that excitement that one went through oneself.

Your mother died as you put it 'extremely distressingly' of Alzheimer's disease and you have said you would prefer to be given a pill rather than go through that. Is that something that weighs heavily on you?

I don't think about it all the time. I did say to Michael some years ago that if I started getting confused he was to give me a pill, and he replied that I was quite confused already.

I wonder what you thought of John Bayley's account of Iris Murdoch's last years? His book has been praised as one of the great love stories of all time. Nevertheless the indignities he describes did nothing to diminish the fears about Alzheimer's and they did upset some readers. What was your view?

I don't think his book is full of indignities. It's a very curious account of the marriage altogether – it was obviously an odd but very successful relationship. For example, he says somewhere that he only really felt at home when she wasn't in the house – a rather amazing thing to say. Also, he was obviously describing her mental retreat, but he certainly wasn't facing the physical problems I had to face with my mother. However, I thought it a remarkable piece of writing.

Do you think that writers have a moral responsibility towards their readers?

I don't know about my moral responsibility. I hope to interest my readers, to take them by the hand and say, listen, I want to tell you something. Muriel Spark gave advice on how to write a novel to the effect that you should imagine you're talking to a friend, and that's what I want to happen. And if in the process I drop in a few comments which help to show why I am interested in the subject, and how my relationship with it has fluctuated and grown and developed, then I hope this will intrigue readers and that they will enjoy reading.

In Several Strangers *you talk about the impossibility of observing ourselves accurately. I think it is fair to say that when other people observe you or look in on your life they can't fail to notice the intensity with which it has been lived and the tragic elements that go with it. Are you conscious of that yourself?*

I've been uneasy about people thinking I'm a tragic figure. I find that a little unsettling, because I feel that my life has been such a mixture of good and ill fortune. I think perhaps we can give versions only of other people. I would certainly find it very difficult to give an account of myself, very difficult indeed. It's not a matter of memory, more the impossibility of summing oneself up. I'm English enough not to want to sound bogus or pretentious or pathetic, but I have quite a peasant view of life, the idea that you just go trudging on. I'm very pleased when the spring comes, when the sun shines, and I take cover and put my head down when things are bad. I can see that this doesn't say much about me, but it is the way that I think of myself getting through life.

INTERVIEW CONDUCTED FEBRUARY 2000